MURDOCH'S POLITICS

MURDOCH'S POLITICS
HOW ONE MAN'S THIRST FOR WEALTH AND POWER SHAPES OUR WORLD

DAVID McKNIGHT

Foreword by
Robert W. McChesney

PlutoPress
www.plutobooks.com

First published in Australia in 2012 as
Rupert Murdoch: An Investigation of Political Power by Allen & Unwin.
First published in the UK 2013 by Pluto Press
345 Archway Road, London N6 5AA

www.plutobooks.com

Distributed in the United States of America exclusively by
Palgrave Macmillan, a division of St. Martin's Press LLC,
175 Fifth Avenue, New York, NY 10010

British Library Cataloguing in Publication Data
A catalogue record for this book is available from the British Library

ISBN 978 0 7453 3347 2 Hardback
ISBN 978 0 7453 3346 5 Paperback
ISBN 978 1 8496 4857 8 PDF eBook
ISBN 978 1 8496 4859 2 Kindle eBook
ISBN 978 1 8496 4858 5 EPUB eBook

Library of Congress Cataloging in Publication Data applied for

This book is printed on paper suitable for recycling and made from fully managed
and sustained forest sources. Logging, pulping and manufacturing processes are
expected to conform to the environmental standards of the country of origin.

10   9   8   7   6   5   4   3   2   1

Typeset by Midland Typesetters, Australia and Stanford DTP Services, Northampton, England
Simultaneously printed digitally by CPI Antony Rowe, Chippenham, UK and
Edwards Bros in the United States of America

CONTENTS

Foreword by Robert W. McChesney   vii

Introduction   1

1. Crusading corporation   13

2. The outsider   38

3. At the barricades of the Reagan Revolution   62

4. Gatecrashing the British establishment   84

5. Orthodoxy in the blood   106

6. Outfoxing the liberals   127

7. The reign of the *Sun* King   149

8. The road to Baghdad   172

9. False dawn on climate change   194

Epilogue   212

Acknowledgements   221

Notes   223

Index   252

To my mother,
Ruth McKnight

FOREWORD

Rupert Murdoch is unquestionably the single most important media figure of our times. He is a dominant force in the journalism and politics of the United States, the United Kingdom and Australia. Whether the world would be the same with some other person playing the same role had he never been born is an academic matter. In this world, Murdoch controls a vast media empire, which pushes his political agenda and his commercial ambitions. One studies Murdoch much like one studies Rommel: in awe of the vision but petrified by the consequences of his actions.

Of course, by 2012, the House of Murdoch is trembling, at least in the UK, thanks to the phone hacking scandal. But even there the fact that Murdoch and his News Corporation still function largely unimpeded is a testament to his unrivalled power in the political system. A lesser mortal might be doing hard time.

In the United States, Murdoch has played a central role in the evolution of both journalism and politics. His Fox News Channel has become a powerful force—arguably *the* powerful force—within Republican Party politics, and therefore all of American politics. The station has a dubious record for fairness, accuracy and integrity, but it has proven to be a supremely powerful megaphone for Republican talking points. Although, as this book demonstrates, Murdoch's global empire is vast, in the balance of this foreword I would like to make a few observations about Murdoch and the Fox News Channel.

Michael Wolff characterizes Fox News as 'the ultimate Murdoch product', because it brought tabloid journalism to American television.[1] What has been missed in the equation is the business model of tabloid journalism: it means dispensing with actual reporting, which costs a lot of money to do well, and replacing it with far less expensive pontificating that will attract audiences. For a tabloid news channel, that means the value-added is by providing a colourful partisan take on the news; otherwise the channel has no reason to attract viewers. Former CNN head Rick Kaplan tells the story of how, in 1999 or 2000, he was confronted by his superiors at Time Warner who were dissatisfied with CNN's profits despite what had been record revenues and a solid return. 'But Fox News made just as much profit,' Kaplan was informed, 'and did so with just half the revenues of CNN, because it does not carry so many reporters on its staff.' The message to Kaplan was clear: close bureaus and fire reporters, lots of them.[2] In short, Fox News is the logical business product for an era where actual journalism is deemed an unprofitable undertaking by corporations.

Fox News and the conservative media sector, including the conservative blogosphere, provide a self-protective enclave in which conservatives can cocoon themselves. Research demonstrates that the more conservative media someone consumes, the more likely they are to dismiss any news or arguments that contradict the conservative position as liberal propaganda and lies.[3] Conservative media, led significantly by Fox News, march in lock-step with the same talking points, the same issues and even the same terminology deployed across the board. They apply the core principles of advertising and propaganda. This has helped to galvanise and solidify the Right and make it more powerful than it would be otherwise. Progressives could only dream about having anything remotely close to such media power.

This is the shell-game premise of the entire conservative media con: the case is premised on the presupposition that what the mainstream news media are doing has a distinct liberal bias, deeply hostile to the Right, the military and big business. In that context, what conservatives are doing is either straight unbiased news by contrast, or they are justified in bending the stick toward the conservative direction to balance the liberal propaganda.[4] In the current system, mainstream journalism works formally to not favour either major party, and prove at every turn its lack of bias toward either party. Reporters must answer for such a bias if it is exposed. Conservative media claim they do not have to play by those rules. The irony, of course, is that Fox News insists it is 'Fair and Balanced' and that 'We Report, You Decide'—it assumes the mantle and prerogatives of professional journalism, as it goes about its partisan business.

Being a semi-surreptitious partisan player in the world of professional journalism has provided considerable power to the Right to set the news agenda. Traditional journalists get their cues about what to cover from official sources, and can dismiss some as ludicrous if they fail to meet an evidentiary standard and are opposed by other official sources. Fox and the conservative media, on the other hand, can aggressively push stories, have Republican politicians echo them, and then badger the traditional media for having a 'liberal bias' if they do not cover the stories as well. Because it believes it is in an uphill battle with liberal propagandists, Fox News can have an unabashed and breathtaking double standard, where they have very different evidentiary standards for stories that serve them versus stories that damage their politics. If facts prove inconvenient for the preferred narrative, ignore them. Republican officials are treated entirely differently from Democrats, even when the facts of a story are virtually identical. It is this opportunistic and unprincipled nature of conservative 'journalism' that draws widespread consternation outside of the political Right, and from those remaining thoughtful conservatives willing to brave the wrath of Murdoch and Roger Ailes.[5]

Between the cocoon effect and the shameless disregard for consistency and intellectual honesty, it is not surprising that professional surveys tend to find regular viewers of Fox News to be more ignorant about what is actually happening in the world compared to those who watch other networks. A November 2011 examination, by Fairleigh Dickinson University's PublicMind Poll, of how New Jerseyans watch television news concluded that 'some outlets, especially Fox News, lead people to be even less informed than those who say they don't watch any news at all.'[6] In some surveys, to be accurate, Fox News does not rank at the bottom in terms of audience knowledge.[7] But on balance, it is the clown dunce of TV news. No other network even comes close to getting the sort of assessment Fox News received from World Public Opinion, a project managed by the Program on International Policy Attitudes at the University of Maryland, in 2010. As one reporter summarized, PIPA conducted a

> ... survey of American voters that shows that Fox News viewers are significantly more misinformed than consumers of news from other sources. What's more, the study shows that greater exposure to Fox News increases misinformation. So the more you watch, the less you know. Or to be precise, the more you think you know that is actually false.[8]

What may be most revealing of all is that there is not any evidence that this bothers the management of Fox News in the least.

Most striking is the handful of explicitly liberal TV programs which all spend considerable time fact-checking, debunking and ridiculing the material on Fox News, while Fox News, conversely, never seems to even notice what the liberals are saying. They do not seem to care. Why should they? They are calling the shots, and the liberals are spending their time responding to them.

Rupert Murdoch and Fox News are fiercely dedicated to a political project that will eliminate trade unions, abolish and/or commercialise public education, increase economic inequality and the power of billionaires and big business, ignore and aggravate the environmental crisis that threatens human existence, promote endless wars and militarism, governance by and for the rich, a corrupt judicial system, and elections that go to the highest (anonymous) bidders. Above all, Murdoch champions the elimination of independent journalism. All the institutions that make for a credible modern democracy are in his crosshairs.

Of course, Murdoch and his minions rarely put it this way. In the official propaganda, it is all about keeping government small, making poor people work harder, kicking the crap out of people who have the temerity to think otherwise and live in some foreign nation, and protecting free enterprise and competitive markets. But in reality it is all about marrying monopolistic power to a large and unaccountable militarised state that works hand-in-hand with its corporate masters. Murdoch himself is the poster child of crony capitalism: his empire is built on effective government-granted monopoly franchises such as broadcast licenses and copyright. His genius is as much knowing how to buy off and cow politicians for colossal privileges as it is mastering how to win in a competitive marketplace.

Murdoch, in short, is a figure of singular importance in our tumultuous times, in the United States, the United Kingdom, and worldwide. David McKnight has done us all a tremendous service by writing this illuminating and deeply researched examination of the man, his empire and his politics.

Robert W. McChesney

INTRODUCTION

In 1995, the journalist Ken Auletta spent many hours talking to Rupert Murdoch for a profile in *New Yorker* magazine. Murdoch emerged as a ruthless man, feared by politicians and envied by his business rivals. Auletta's conclusion was that Murdoch was 'a pirate', a man who 'will cunningly circumvent rules, and sometimes principles, to get his way'.[1] Auletta's description was later embraced by the editor of Murdoch's *New York Post*, Col Allan, who said that the culture of the company meant 'we like being pirates ... we don't like conforming.'[2] The image of pirates can be that of romantic rebels, but in reality most pirates are brutal bullies.

In 2011–12, this bullying was on display at an inquiry in London headed by Lord Justice Leveson. The Leveson Inquiry was charged with probing the culture and ethics of the news media and its relations with the police and politicians.[3] Its establishment followed a dramatic series of events in which a growing number of Murdoch's journalists were arrested for hacking phone voicemails. The crisis reached a climax when Murdoch closed his profitable Sunday paper, *News of the World*, and answered hostile questions from a parliamentary committee.

The Leveson Inquiry heard about an extraordinary array of criminal activities by some of Murdoch's journalists. Starting with the hacking of the phones of members of the Royal Family, Murdoch's journalists listened in on lawyers, politicians and ordinary members of the public whose lives had become newsworthy. While the hacking of celebrities such as actor Hugh Grant has grabbed the headlines, perhaps the most poignant revelation concerned the young singer, Charlotte Church. When Rupert Murdoch planned to wed Wendi Deng on his yacht in New York harbour in 1999, he wanted the 13-year-old singer, reputed to have 'the voice of an angel', to perform for him. A fee of £100,000 was negotiated but then a deal was offered by Murdoch's lieutenants. Instead of the fee, Murdoch's newspapers would give favourable coverage to the young singer at the start of her career, to which Church's manager agreed. But favourable coverage was the last thing she obtained. She told the Leveson Inquiry of the humiliation which followed. The *Sun* newspaper featured a clock counting down to her sixteenth birthday, the day on which she could legally consent to have sex. This was accompanied by a variety of remarks with sexual innuendo. The *Sun* also revealed that she was pregnant before she had told her parents. It did not stop there. *News of the World* exposed an affair conducted by her father ('a love rat hooked on cocaine'). Another story followed on her mother's attempt to kill herself. Much of this was obtained by illegal voicemail hacking. Countless other examples of bullying and blackmail have emerged under probing from the inquiries into Murdoch and his news media. Murdoch initially described the hacking allegations as hysteria. Soon after, he changed his tune.

This book will argue that the arrogance and contempt for rules which have been revealed in the phone hacking scandal arise from a wider culture within News Corporation. At every level—journalism, politics or business—Rupert Murdoch and News Corporation push the boundaries of ruthless self-interest to their limits and beyond. As one former Murdoch editor, David Montgomery, said: 'Rupert has contempt for the rules. Contempt even for governments.'[4] For three decades, Rupert Murdoch's piratical contempt for governments has been expressed as a zealous devotion to an ideology of small government and free markets. Guided by this ideology of corporate libertarianism, Murdoch has been a buccaneer bestriding the world. These beliefs are also deeply personal. As this book will show, Rupert Murdoch's self image is that he is a rebel, an outsider and an enemy of those he calls 'the elites'. His political beliefs are based on the illusion that he represents ordinary men and women while his political enemies form a powerful establishment. He holds firm to this even after three former British prime ministers and one serving prime minister gave testimony about their contact with him because of his influence on British politics. Whatever else it will do, the phone hacking scandal demonstrates that Murdoch and his editors are far from being outsiders. They are active members of a political elite and participants in a genuinely powerful establishment of media and business insiders.

Phone hacking is just the latest example of the untrammelled power of Rupert Murdoch and his media corporation. Murdoch has been the subject of many books, but their authors have often been mesmerised by his charm, his buccaneering and by his dazzling business deals. His critics have claimed that he cares about nothing except the profits of his ever-expanding media business. His politics, they say, simply serve his business interests. By damning him in this way, his critics greatly underestimate him.

Politics, power and ideas are things about which Murdoch truly cares. This book sets out to intimately explore Murdoch's political beliefs, his political influence and the financial subsidies he dispenses to advance both. These subsidies are drawn from a personal fortune which stands at $6 billion and a media corporation worth more than $30 billion. While being ruthlessly devoted to making money, Murdoch has given equal attention to shaping News Corporation as a crusading corporation, a media institution with a mission. Publicly, his newspapers and TV interests such as Fox News systematically articulate Murdoch's political values and provide a soapbox for conservative writers and intellectuals. Privately, News Corporation has a deeply political corporate culture, sponsoring think tanks and holding political seminars for editors and executives where editorial campaigns are hammered out.

A WEB OF POLITICAL INFLUENCE

Murdoch's political values and his political influence over many decades were examined by the Leveson Inquiry into the British news media over several months. But when the inquiry questioned Murdoch in April 2012, it found that Murdoch frequently had no memory of his contacts with political leaders. He had no recollection of a discreet meeting with Prime Minister Margaret Thatcher just before he bought the *Times* and *Sunday Times* in 1981.[5] He did not remember a later discussion with Lord Woodrow Wyatt (his lobbyist and a personal friend of Thatcher's) who conveyed an assurance by Thatcher that her 1990 Broadcasting Bill would not adversely affect his control of satellite television.[6] Murdoch also had no memory of telling an editor: 'We owe Thatcher a lot as a company. Don't go overboard in your attacks on her.'[7] Murdoch also told the inquiry that he never let his commercial interests affect his decision to support or oppose a party before elections.

By contrast, the former Conservative prime minister, John Major, was far more direct when he gave testimony to the Leveson Inquiry about Rupert Murdoch's approach to power. He recalled a private dinner with Rupert Murdoch and his daughter, Elisabeth Murdoch, three months before the 1997 election. Rupert Murdoch wanted Major to change his policies on the European Union. 'If we couldn't change our European policies, his papers could not and would not support the Conservative government,' Major recalled.[8] The meeting was imprinted on Major's mind because it was rare that such a demand was made and was linked to a news organisation's support. Major refused to play ball and, shortly afterwards, the *Sun* newspaper came out in support of Labour which went on to win the 1997 election under Tony Blair.

Murdoch's reasons for supporting Tony Blair were of great interest to the Leveson Inquiry. Robert Jay, the counsel assisting, asked Murdoch whether Blair had given an assurance 'that media ownership rules would not be too onerous under Labour'. Murdoch responded: 'I have no memory of that.' When Tony Blair gave evidence to the Leveson Inquiry, he acknowledged that the Murdoch press had been 'viscerally hostile to the Labour Party' when he became leader. Blair acknowledged that he spent considerable time cultivating Murdoch and his editors. He too was at pains to play down any deal done by himself and Murdoch. He was questioned about his reasons for dropping Labour's policy which favoured an inquiry into media ownership. He admitted that 'the Murdoch media group would have been worried had we decided to launch some great inquiry into … media ownership' but that wasn't the reason he dropped the policy.[9] The inquiry later reminded Tony Blair of comments to him from the Australian prime minister Paul Keating, who said that 'You can do deals with [Murdoch] without ever saying a deal is done, but the only thing he cares about is his business and the only thing which he respects is strength.' Whatever the truth of the relationship, Murdoch steadfastly supported the Blair governments for ten years. One of Blair's former advisers, Lance Price, later said that when he worked at Downing Street, Murdoch seemed 'like the 24th member of the cabinet. His voice was rarely heard … but his presence was always felt.'[10] After leaving office, Blair became the godfather to one of Murdoch's children.

MURDOCH SWITCHES SIDES

Just as Tony Blair had been aware of the power of Rupert Murdoch when he was the leader of the Opposition, so too was David Cameron when he was in a similar position. At first Murdoch was critical of Cameron. Asked what he thought of Cameron soon after he became Conservative leader in 2005, Murdoch said: 'Not much. He's bright. He's quick. He's totally inexperienced.' In spite of this, Murdoch made a point of regularly meeting David Cameron at a series of private meals and social events. In August 2008, Murdoch welcomed Cameron on board his luxury yacht moored off a Greek island. Along the way, Cameron appointed the former editor of Murdoch's *News of the World*, Andy Coulson, as adviser and spokesman.

By September 2009, Rupert Murdoch decided to dump Labour and back the Conservatives, a message conveyed personally to David Cameron over drinks by James Murdoch. Shortly afterwards the *Sun* endorsed the Conservatives with a front-page headline ('LABOUR'S LOST IT) which was timed to coincide with, and therefore badly damage, a key speech by Gordon Brown at Labour's conference. Other Murdoch executives, such as Rebekah Brooks, also became close to the Cameron family. When Cameron was about to deliver a key speech to the Conservatives in October 2009, Brooks sent him a gushing text message saying: 'I am so rooting for you tomorrow not just as a proud friend but because professionally we're definitely in this together! Speech of your life? Yes he Cam!'[11] On the day of the 2010 election, the *Sun*'s front page featured David Cameron and the headline 'OUR ONLY HOPE'.

Murdoch's executives remained close to Cameron after Cameron formed the government following the May 2010 election. One of Cameron's first visitors to Downing Street was Rupert Murdoch, who later told the parliamentary inquiry that he entered by the back door at Cameron's request. Over the next five months, Rebekah Brooks stayed three times at the Prime Minister's country residence of Chequers, and Rupert Murdoch's son James was also a guest at the residence.[12] Just before Christmas 2010, Cameron attended a dinner at Brooks's home where he met James Murdoch and his wife Kathryn. Another social occasion with Brooks (a neighbour of Cameron's in the Chilterns) followed on Boxing Day. At the very time of these intimate social contacts, Cameron's government was deciding whether to allow Murdoch's company to make a huge takeover bid for shares in the satellite TV broadcaster, BSkyB. Murdoch already owned 39 per cent of BSkyB and wanted 100 per cent. At none of his meetings, Rupert Murdoch told the Leveson Inquiry, did he lobby in favour of his plans to take over BSkyB. James Murdoch said that he too had said virtually nothing about it, as did Rebekah Brooks. The huge corporate takeover was on the point of being approved by the Cameron government when the hacking scandal broke, government support for the takeover collapsed and News Corporation ignominiously withdrew its bid after unprecedented hostility from both major parties. Over the space of two weeks in early July 2011, Murdoch's company admitted its journalists had widely hacked phone voicemail and admitted paying bribes to police, and then finally closed *News of the World*, its highly profitable newspaper and, symbolically, the first big purchase by the young Rupert Murdoch in 1969. Worse followed with the resignation, then arrest, of senior executives, among them Rebekah Brooks. Altogether, the scandal has become the first major setback for Rupert Murdoch in Britain.

MURDOCH AND THE UNITED STATES

In the United States, Rupert Murdoch's influence is exercised in quite a different way to that in Britain. These days, the main vehicle for Murdoch's influence is television rather than newspapers, and Murdoch does not meet US presidents as often he does British prime ministers. Instead, Murdoch is a powerful force through his support for the US Republican Party. This began with Rupert Murdoch's admiration of Ronald Reagan. One former editor pointed out that while Murdoch also admired Margaret Thatcher, Ronald Reagan was his 'first love'.[13] In 1980, Murdoch personally involved himself in helping to mobilise Republican support in New York where he had recently bought the *New York Post*. Under Murdoch's ownership the *Post* changed direction from a liberal newspaper towards enthusiastic support for Republican politics. In 1984, the *Post* helped destroy the Democrats' presidential campaign through their attacks on Geraldine Ferraro, the vice presidential candidate, with stories suggesting that she was linked to organised crime.[14] The most damaging was a 'scoop', later revealed to have been passed to the *Post* by Reagan's campaign team (see Chapter 3). Murdoch was so close to the Reagan administration and family that he later became one of fifteen trustees for the Ronald Reagan Presidential Foundation.

After the heady days of Reaganism, Murdoch found the Republican Party of George H.W. Bush far too tame. But in the mid-1990s, Murdoch made two key moves which were to give him great political clout in the United States in general and in the Republican Party in particular. The first was the realisation of his long-held dream of creating a conservative television news operation. Since its founding in 1996, Fox News has introduced a new kind of divisive, partisan politics in television. It helped foster some of the most extreme elements of the Republican Party, becoming, for example, the main outlet for the denial of climate change in the US news media. Murdoch regularly defends Fox News as 'fair and balanced', but this is doubly false. Fox News is not fair or balanced, nor is it primarily a news channel but rather one in which political comment and opinion are far more significant.

Murdoch's other key move in the 1990s was less spectacular. He discovered a group of activists within the Republican Party with whom he deeply identified and began financially supporting them. From the 1990s, he became the key backer of the neo-conservatives led by William Kristol. With Kristol, Murdoch created and subsidised the neo-conservative magazine, the *Weekly Standard*. It was the *Standard* which pioneered the call for a US attack on Saddam Hussein, well before September 11, 2001.

In the wake of 9/11, Murdoch swung his worldwide media organisation behind George W. Bush's disastrous invasion of Iraq, promoting the falsehoods that Iraq possessed weapons of mass destruction and had had regular contact with Al Qaeda. Murdoch's US media outlets, such as Fox News and the *New York Post*, had campaigned strongly for George W. Bush in 2000 and 2004, with the News Corp. Foundation giving $250,000 to the 2004 presidential inauguration.[15] In the final years of the Bush presidency, Murdoch complained that, apart from the *New York Post* and the *Wall Street Journal*, the US news media launches 'a monolithic attack' on George W. Bush 'every day of the year'.[16] Unsurprisingly, his news media monolithically backed the McCain/Palin team in the 2008 presidential election. After Barack Obama won that election, Fox News helped create the political climate in which the Tea Party movement flourished. (See Chapters 1 and 6). Today, Fox News is one of the most powerful political weapons available to a single individual in the US. Tim Dickenson of the *Rolling Stone* skilfully captured the role of the Fox News and its boss, Roger Ailes, in the following terms:

> Ailes has used Fox News to pioneer a new form of political campaign—one that enables the GOP to bypass sceptical reporters and wage an around-the-clock, partisan assault on public opinion. The network, at its core, is a giant soundstage created to mimic the look and feel of a news operation, cleverly camouflaging political propaganda as independent journalism.[17]

In 2011 and 2012, Fox News was central to the process of choosing the Republican Party's nomination for presidential candidate. The channel devoted an exceptional amount of air time to debates between Republican rivals and to discussion on which one would make the most powerful opponent of Obama while still remaining a strong conservative. But as the process of selecting a Republican candidate began in 2011, it became apparent that the news channel was even more deeply involved. Fox News had employed as commentators four of the Republicans then vying for nomination as the GOP presidential candidate, including former Alaskan governor Sarah Palin, former speaker of the House of Representatives Newt Gingrich, former Arkansas governor Mike Huckabee and former senator Rick Santorum. And these were just the best-known names. Later, *New York* magazine published an 'incomplete list of political figures who have received News Corp. checks at some point in their careers'. The 36 names on the list included congressmen, senators, governors and White House staffers.[18] As former Bush speechwriter David Frum said: 'Republicans originally thought that Fox worked for us, and now we're discovering we work for Fox.' The behaviour of Fox News paralleled that of its owner. As the competition for the Republican nomination quickened in 2011, Murdoch played the Republican king-maker. Along with Republican stalwarts like Henry Kissinger and Nancy Reagan, he privately urged the governor of New Jersey, Chris Christie, to run. Fox News boosted Christie with supportive coverage. Murdoch also made it his business to dine with another candidate, the Texas governor Rick Perry. They had steak at a fashionable restaurant close to Murdoch's luxurious Fifth Avenue apartment.

But the Republican who won Murdoch's support in 2012 was one of the most conservative. On the eve of the Iowa caucus in early 2012, Murdoch used his new Twitter account to urge 'all Iowans [to] think about Rick Santorum'. Santorum, he said, was the 'only candidate with a genuine big vision for country'. When Santorum did well in Iowa, Murdoch was lavish with praise. Santorum 'showed principles, consistency and humility like no other', he said. Santorum's 'big vision' includes outright opposition not only to abortion but also to contraception. During the campaign, Santorum declared 'Our rights come from God, not just any god but the god of Abraham, Isaac and Jacob'. While he was still working for Fox News (he left when he became a candidate), Santorum was paid $239,000 by Fox News to act as a commentator.[19] This sum paled by comparison to Sarah Palin, who was paid $1 million annually by Fox News.[20] When Santorum failed to win the 2012 nomination, Murdoch was displeased. He complained that the successful Republican candidate, Mitt Romney, was too weak. 'When is Romney going to look like a challenger? Seems to play everything safe', Murdoch tweeted. When members of the Romney team privately complained to Murdoch that he was damaging the campaign, he tweeted them back: 'Romney people upset with me! Of course I want him to win, save us from socialism, etc but should listen to good advice and get stuck in!'[21]

The other major Murdoch media outlet in the US is the *Wall Street Journal*, which he acquired in 2007. These days, it often carries Murdoch's personal imprimatur. When the phone hacking crisis began to engulf News Corporation in mid-2011, Murdoch gave an exclusive interview to the *Journal*. His company, he said, had handled the crisis 'extremely well' and made only 'minor mistakes'. A few days later, an editorial in the *Journal* discussed the phone hacking scandal. It sneered at the 'righteous hindsight' of critics and scorned the 'moral outrage' of those alarmed by the breaches of privacy. Rather than any wrongdoing by editors and executives, the accusations were grounded in the 'commercial and ideological motives of our competitor-critics', it insisted.[22] A few months later, the *Journal* had to confront its own ethics problems when it was accused of secretly buying copies of its own paper to artificially boost its circulation figures and therefore the amount it could charge for advertising.[23] As part of the deal, business partners were promised favourable coverage if they took part in the arrangement.

Since he bought the *Journal*, promising to maintain its high standards, Murdoch has presided over a series of disturbing changes. Long before the purchase, through its editorials and opinion pages, the paper had been a supporter of rock-ribbed conservatism. Its news pages, however, were quite different and reflected a tradition of fierce independent scrutiny of politics and business. Today, this tradition is being eroded and articles on the news pages are being skewed to reflect Murdoch's political agenda (see Chapter 1).

When Ken Auletta described Murdoch as a pirate, he was identifying a strand of Murdoch's personality in which he saw himself as free from normal rules. The freebooting corporate culture which this notion spawned blew up in Rupert Murdoch's face with the hacking scandal. But in spite of the damage to his reputation and the legal actions against his executives, Murdoch will survive one way or another. He is driven not simply by profit and business goals but by something more complex. As he told Auletta, the key to understanding him was that he is 'not just a businessman' but a man 'interested in ideas'. Murdoch is not only one of the most powerful businessmen on the planet but also one of the most politically motivated.

It would be wrong merely to denigrate and dismiss Rupert Murdoch. The ideas he expresses are among the most influential in the democratic world and have formed part of a conservative revolution in thinking over the last thirty years. They are shared by many powerful people and have already transformed the economic and social institutions of many nations. Rupert Murdoch is a man of strong opinions who arouses strong reactions. This book is one of them.

CHAPTER 1
CRUSADING CORPORATION

I think what people don't understand about me is that I'm not just a businessman working in a very interesting industry. I am someone who's interested in ideas.[1]

Rupert Murdoch, 1995

For better or worse [my company] is a reflection of my thinking, my character, my values.[2]

Rupert Murdoch, 1996

The 2004 convention of the Republican Party, held in New York's Madison Square Garden, was a triumph for President George W. Bush. Still lauded by many at the time as the hero of the Iraq war, Bush defeated John Kerry for the presidency later that year. At the end of the convention, as most delegates were leaving their seats, a revealing incident occurred. At CNN's floor set, where hosts Judy Woodruff and Wolf Blitzer were conducting interviews, some delegates began chanting, 'Watch Fox News! Watch Fox News!' They saw Fox News as their friend and CNN as the enemy in their midst.[3]

CNN once infuriated Rupert Murdoch. During his daily ride on his exercise bike, he used to frown at the successful news network and dream of building a television news operation to rival what he called the 'liberal' and 'left-leaning' CNN. Today, CNN's rival flourishes and consistently beats it in the ratings war. Murdoch's Fox News is a powerful persuader in US politics, credited not only with influencing its loyal audience but with affecting the tone of all

US television, an influence summed up by the term 'the Fox News effect'. Its shouting heads broadcast a nightly mantra of fear-filled messages to their three million viewers. Its swirling graphics and dramatic music intensify its 'Fox News Alerts' about the latest threat from terrorists, liberals, gays—and Democrats.

President Barack Obama has been a particular target. When he was running for the Democratic nomination in 2007, Fox News commentators rushed to air a false report that as a child growing up in Indonesia Obama had been educated at an Islamic school, a madrasah. In the post–September 11 United States, an association with a madrasah was likely to prompt suggestions of an association with Islamic terrorism. Later, during the presidential campaign, one Fox commentator flippantly suggested that Barack and his wife, Michelle Obama, had greeted each other with a 'terrorist fist jab'. The commentator later apologised, as did another Fox commentator who had joked about assassinating Obama and Osama bin Laden after supposedly muddling their names. Throughout the campaign, one of Fox News' belligerent hosts, Sean Hannity, nightly attacked Obama for being an 'arrogant elitist' and suggested that he had been a friend of terrorists and black radicals, echoing pro-Republican attack advertisements. Obama referred to these as 'rants from Sean Hannity' and was particularly upset by the attacks on his wife.

In the middle of the campaign, Rupert Murdoch met Obama, along with Fox News chief Roger Ailes. Obama sought common ground with Murdoch, asking about his relationship with his father (the subject of Obama's *Dreams of My Father*), but to Ailes he said that he didn't want to waste time talking if Fox was going to keep attacking him and his wife, relentlessly portraying him as 'suspicious, foreign, fearsome—just short of a terrorist'.[4] Ailes suggested he appear on the channel, and after the meeting relations between the future president's minders and Fox normalised, though the hostility of its talk show hosts was barely moderated. When

Murdoch's biographer Michael Wolff reported the meeting in *Vanity Fair*, stating that Murdoch was sometimes embarrassed by Fox News, Ailes was outraged, and Murdoch quickly denied the report and praised Ailes. While Murdoch regularly denies that Fox News is politically aligned, this seems at odds with the presentation to Ailes in 2011 of the Luce Award, a top honour from the powerful right-wing think tank the Heritage Foundation, 'for contributions to the conservative movement'.[5]

Murdoch had another, less direct, connection to the Republican campaign for the presidency that year. One of his editors 'discovered' Sarah Palin, promoted her as a rising Republican star and then supported her when she became the vice-presidential candidate beside John McCain. Bill Kristol, editor of the *Weekly Standard*, Murdoch's insiders' magazine, visited Alaska on a cruise ship along with other leading US conservatives. He met Palin, who was the Republican governor of Alaska, and later Kristol's neo-conservative *Standard* described her 'shining victory' as governor while the rest of the Republican Party was demoralised.[6]

As it turned out, Fox News' support for the McCain–Palin ticket and its relentless hostility to Obama were not enough to hold back the tidal wave of support for the Democrat candidate. But this was just the beginning. To mix a metaphor, Fox didn't change its spots. Obama's victory lifted the hopes of many Americans but deeply troubled many conservatives, who saw their chance to fight back when Obama increased government spending to cope with the worst financial crisis in 80 years. Within a few months of his in-auguration a new political phenomenon was born, the 'Tea Party', which attacked the spending and tax increases needed to deal with the global crisis. For the first time in many years, conservative politi-cal action took the form of angry street protests. Fox News leaped on this: its talk show hosts urged their audiences to support the rallies, its website gave details of the locations and times of the events. A particular devotee of the street protests was Fox News' host Glenn Beck, whose incendiary remarks accusing Obama of being a 'racist' with 'a deep-seated hatred of white people or the white culture' shocked many. In the weeks before the first major Tea Party rallies in April 2009, Fox News promoted them aggressively, urging viewers to 'vent your anger'. At the rallies, several high-profile hosts, including Sean Hannity, Neil Cavuto and Greta Van Susteren as well as Beck, gave live coverage. (Murdoch's *New York Post* also backed the anti-Obama tea parties right from the start and listed the times and locations of the rallies.)

The White House was rattled by the Tea Party rallies and described Fox News as a wing of the Republican Party. Obama's spokeswoman Anita Dunn said that when Obama appeared on Fox he understood that 'it is really not a news network at this point'. A few days later, Murdoch responded by saying that the Obama administration had a reputation for being 'anti-business'. He was smug about the attacks on Fox: 'Strong remarks have been coming out of the White House about one or two commentators on Fox News. All I can tell you is that it's greatly increased their ratings.'[7]

Fox News consciously manipulated the language of political debate once Obama was in power. When his health package was being discussed, a senior Fox executive sent a 'friendly reminder' to staff urging them to use the term 'government-run health insurance' and to avoid the term 'the public option'. If the latter phrase had to be used, it was better to refer to it as 'the so-called public option'.[8] In similar fashion, the *New York Post* and the *Wall Street Journal* routinely referred to 'government-run health care' and 'the so-called public option'. This coincided precisely with advice given by Republican strategists to their party.

In early 2010, a minor political eruption occurred close to Rupert Murdoch. His son-in-law, Matthew Freud (great-grandson of

Sigmund), husband of his daughter Elisabeth Murdoch, told the *New York Times* his views of Fox News:

> I am by no means alone within the family or the company in being ashamed and sickened by Roger Ailes' horrendous and sustained disregard of the journalistic standards that News Corporation, its founder and every other global media business aspires to.[9]

Freud, one of London's leading public relations executives, would have weighed every word of this personal attack on Ailes' standards. For his part, Ailes said of Freud that he needed 'to see a psychiatrist'. Just who else Freud's statement represented was unclear. His wife later distanced herself from it, but it strengthened rumours that Rupert Murdoch's children and heirs had been unhappy with Fox News' coverage of Barack Obama's presidential campaign. In the lead up to that campaign, Elisabeth Murdoch held a fundraising event for Obama in Britain, and her brother James was also said to have supported the Democrat. Along with their brother Lachlan, Elisabeth and James will control the global media giant when their father dies or chooses to relinquish control. So Freud's words were intensely examined by observers looking for clues about the post-Rupert political orientation of News Corporation. Freud's statement was one straw in the wind that could signal future changes to the kind of political influence exerted by News Corporation across the United States, Britain and Australia.

A UNIQUELY POLITICAL BUSINESS

News Corporation is sometimes seen as a typical creature of the new age of globalisation. Like a small number of other global corporations it has vast assets, makes fabulous profits and does business all over the world and around the clock. In the United States it operates a major television network, Fox Broadcasting, as well as the movie studio 20th Century Fox. It also has the cable channel Fox News, the *Wall Street Journal* and the *New York Post*. In Britain it controls

BSkyB as well as the *Sun,* the *Times* and *Sunday Times*; in Australia it owns the biggest newspaper chain which includes the top-selling *Herald Sun* and the national daily the *Australian*. News Corporation also controls the global book publisher HarperCollins and a string of smaller businesses. Like all public companies, the overt goal of News Corporation is to maximise returns to its shareholders. The desire for profits is the one thing on which Rupert Murdoch's critics and supporters agree: his critics denigrate him as a grasping businessman interested only in money; his supporters (and his many biographers) are dazzled by his undoubted business acumen. All agree that he has a ruthless devotion to profits at the expense of everything else. Indeed, Murdoch endorsed this view of his single-minded pursuit of profits. He told his British biographer William Shawcross:

> All newspapers are run to make profits. Full stop. I don't run anything for respectability. The moment I do, I hope someone will come and fire me and get me out of the place—because that's not what newspapers are meant to be about.[10]

But this is merely corporate chest-beating. It's also not true: Murdoch is at least as devoted to propagating his ideas and political beliefs as he is to making money. And so to imagine that News Corporation is a *typical* global media giant would be a big mistake; it is a unique business. Its singularity begins on the most fundamental measure of a corporation: the bottom line. Most global companies are bureaucracies staffed by efficient technocrats and headed by chief executives who avoid the limelight. News Corporation is different: it is an empire run by an autocrat whose personal idiosyncrasies dominate in place of the needs of shareholders who are, legally, in control. Murdoch's board of directors includes many old friends along with co-thinkers who share his political beliefs, such as Spain's former prime minister José María Aznar and the controversial former New York schools manager Joel Klein. Murdoch has a particular conservative world view that has evolved over the years and on whose evangelisation he spends many millions annually, through both corporate spending and personal (often secret) donations. Key parts of his empire are deeply enmeshed in their nation's politics and operate as megaphones for Murdoch's values and leverage. Murdoch revels in political gossip and loves to play the powerful political insider to whom politicians defer. Political leaders do this because Murdoch has used his media assets countless times to advance his political beliefs and play favourites with governments and political parties. Both Fox News and the London *Sun* make vast amounts of money, and both operate as powerful political levers to support or oppose political parties and their leaders. The treatment meted out by Fox to Barack Obama has been similar to the hate rained on the former British Labour leader Neil Kinnock by the *Sun* in the early 1990s. And just as Fox News supported George W. Bush, so the *Sun* shone on Tony Blair.

News Corporation has spent hundreds of millions of dollars propping up loss-making newspapers that advance Murdoch's personal political beliefs and influence. The prime example is the *New York Post*, purchased for $37 million in 1976, which has never made a profit and at the time of writing was costing an estimated $15–20 million a year. (All dollar amounts are given in US dollars, unless otherwise noted.) Forced to sell it in 1988, Murdoch quickly repurchased it in 1993, admitting afterwards that his previous thirteen-year period of ownership had cost him $100 million.[11] The London *Times* also runs at a vast annual loss, which a report in 2007 said amounted to $89 million in 2004, with this significant loss being subsidised, in good times, by its profitable sister paper, the *Sunday Times*.[12] In 2009, both newspapers lost £87 million.[13] The *Australian* lost money for its first twenty years and still does not always make a profit.[14] These newspapers are, in effect, political subsidies designed to give Murdoch a seat at the table of national politics in three English-speaking nations. In 2011 he launched an iPad-only newspaper, the *Daily*, which was necessarily subsidised, being a wholly new venture. It seems likely that if the *Daily* gives him political leverage in a strategic group of readers its subsidy may extend beyond the stage of experimentation. On the rare occasions that Murdoch acknowledges the losses made by his newspapers, he argues that he simply offers competition and choice for readers. But this is nothing more than code for the advocacy of his conservative beliefs and values.

In opposition to the view that he is deeply motivated by politics is the commonly quoted opinion that 'Murdoch backs winners'. For critics, this presents Murdoch as a man who believes in nothing but profits. The most frequently cited evidence is his 1997 electoral support for a Labour government in Britain under leader Tony Blair. Supporting Blair is offered as proof of Murdoch's political pragmatism and of his ruthlessness in disowning his previous support for the Conservative Party. Yet, while Murdoch is certainly ruthless, in the case of Blair, at least, the 'Murdoch backs winners' mantra is incomplete and misleading. It is equally likely that his support for the Labour Party in 1997 simply recognised that the political centre in Britain had moved towards a new Thatcherite consensus that Blair and Labour shared. Rather than Murdoch shifting to support Labour, Labour had shifted its views dramatically. Indeed, Murdoch's newspapers helped to create this shift in the nation's political consensus, which underlay the convergence of its political parties. Backing winners can have its advantages, since they can indeed affect Murdoch's business interests, but in this case the Labour winner was known to be amenable to Murdoch's desire to be left alone by regulators to conduct his business.[15] This was the message delivered by Blair when he travelled halfway around the world to address one of News Corporation's editorial conferences before the 1997 election that brought him to office.

Other evidence that might be said to suggest that Murdoch

always puts profit before politics and principle can be found in his 1990s cultivation of the Chinese communist leadership in the hope of doing business in China. To this end, Murdoch was extra–ordinarily deferential. In 1993, he praised technological advances that were 'a threat to totalitarian regimes everywhere', angering the Chinese leadership, but the following year he withdrew the British Broadcasting Corporation service from his Asian Star TV network after complaints from China that 'the BBC was driving them nuts'.[16] Later, his publishing company HarperCollins released a dull, uncritical biography of the leading economic reformer, Deng Xiaoping, written by his daughter Deng Rong, for which it paid a reported $1 million.[17] In counterpoint, HarperCollins dropped a contracted book on China by Chris Patten, the former governor of Hong Kong, who was hated by the Chinese leadership. However, while these moves once again demonstrate Murdoch's ruthless-ness, they concern a country in which he has no interest in being a political player or insider. Murdoch's elevation of politics to equal his business interests occurs only in countries in which he or his news media can affect events and governments. Moreover, China in the 1990s was not the China that anti-communists like Murdoch once feared and hated.

The primacy that Murdoch gives to politics and political influence goes well beyond support for political parties at elections, involving a more diffuse and decades-long desire to promote a set of values regardless of what party is in power. The British media scholars Steve Barnett and Ivor Gaber have recognised that Murdoch's support for formal political parties may vary. But, leaving aside party political support, they say:

> There are consistent messages within his newspapers that taken together constitute a coherent ideology . . . Those who have followed the Murdoch papers—not just in the UK but around the world—will recognise here the values that infuse his publications and which, when a particular issue of political significance arises, usually colour its coverage.[18]

For example, when Murdoch took over the *Wall Street Journal*, a key ideological appointment was Gerard Baker, a conservative British journalist, who was appointed deputy editor-in-chief in 2009. Baker had strong connections to Murdoch's most right-wing outlets, having been a Fox News contributor for several years and a contributing editor to the neo-conservative *Weekly Standard* between 2004 and 2007. He had the task of 'policing the newsroom for left-leaning ideological bias', according to an account by a former journalist at the *Journal*.[19]

Murdoch's political crusade extends to unlikely parts of his empire, including HarperCollins, which published *Going Rogue: an American life*, by the 2008 Republican vice-presidential candidate Sarah Palin. Following the book's success, HarperCollins announced that it would create a specialist imprint, Broadside Books, for books on conservative topics by conservative authors. The head of the new imprint, Adam Bellow, said he would publish 'books on the culture wars, books of ideas, books of revisionist history, biographies, anthologies, polemical paperbacks and pop-culture books from a conservative point of view'.[20]

HarperCollins was publishing conservative books long before the success of Palin's *Going Rogue*, however, including blockbuster titles about former national leaders Ronald Reagan, Margaret Thatcher and John Howard and other conservative politicians,[21] and a host of more obscure right-wing books that formed a part of the ideological war against Bill Clinton in the 1990s.[22] While some of these books made sense commercially, others resembled pet projects of an eager-to-please publisher.[23] Murdoch makes his book-publishing executives aware of his political likes and dislikes, just as he does his newspaper editors. A former publisher at HarperCollins, William Shinker, told a journalist in 1995: 'Rupert would accuse me on several occasions of not publishing enough conservative books ... He'd joke: "You're all a bunch of pinkos".'[24]

Over the years, Murdoch has donated a great deal of money to political causes, usually quietly. Two less discreet donations were the $1.25 million that he gave the Republican Governors Association and the $1 million given to the US Chamber of Commerce in the run-up to the 2010 elections for the US Senate and House of Representatives. Both groups targeted the Democrats with television attack advertisement on a scale never seen before. When discussing the Republican Governors' donation, a News Corporation spokesperson said that the association, like News Corporation, believed in 'the power of free markets'. In 1993, Murdoch made donations to the Project for a Republican Future, established by Bill Kristol, a former adviser to the US vice-president Dan Quayle; the project was widely credited with stiffening the spine of the Republicans to destroy Hillary Clinton's health care plan. Kristol went on to edit Murdoch's *Weekly Standard*, which never made a cent but pioneered the campaign to invade Iraq. In 2003, Murdoch donated $300,000 to an anti–affirmative action campaign to ban the collection of race-based data by Californian state and local governments. (He later fought furiously to prevent the release of this information by a court.) This followed a $1 million donation to Californian Republicans to defeat Bill Clinton and oppose affirmative action in 1996.[25] During the years of Margaret Thatcher's prime ministership of the United Kingdom, he arranged to pay £270,000 to an ultra-Thatcherite group that ran a campaign of anonymous smears against members of the British Labour Party. He has also funded a far-right British propagandist who worked closely with the CIA and British intelligence. Beside these donations, his financial support for conservative journals of ideas such as New York's *Commentary* and Australia's *Quadrant* seem small.[26]

Murdoch has always loved the buzz of being a political insider, even when in earlier times his political sympathies were different and he secretly funded progressive, not conservative, causes. One of these was the successful campaign by the Australian Labor Party to win office in 1972, in which he paid for advertising and ran free advertisements in his own newspapers. His British newspapers also supported Labour. Also in 1972, he funded an anonymous campaign of lurid street posters that called for a boycott of whisky and gin produced by the Distillers Company.[27] This campaign supported the *Sunday Times*' legal battle with Distillers, which made the baby-deforming drug thalidomide—and which was slow in compensating its victims. Murdoch had released an executive of the *News of the World* to organise it. One wonders how many other political subsidies made by Murdoch have never seen the light of day. After consternation in 2010 about donations to the US Republicans, News Corporation decided to reveal all further political donations.

The uniquely political nature of News Corporation is on display at its regular meetings of editorial staff and top executives. While in-house meetings of senior corporate staff are common in many businesses, no other corporation designs them around high-profile political speakers and political topics. Most businesses, including the media, avoid overt engagement in politics and being identified too closely with any political party. News Corporation's global editorial gatherings, however, revel in the themes of the US Republican Party and the British Conservative Party. Such highly politicised meetings are doubly unusual for a media organisation with a news division that reports on the same issues in politics and public life.

The global meetings of editors and other senior staff have been held since 1988, when former US president Richard Nixon was choppered in to Aspen, Colorado. Also speaking that year were the neo-conservative intellectual Norman Podhoretz, the former head of the Federal Reserve Paul Volcker, Defense officials from the White House and British political leader David Owen.[28] One editor said later: 'We were being feted like generals from some all-conquering army'.[29] At another conference at Aspen, in 1992, there was a panel discussion with the title 'The threat to democratic capitalism posed by modern culture'. The panellists included Lynne Cheney, a morals campaigner and wife of Dick Cheney (who also attended and was at the time the US Defense secretary); former Thatcher adviser John O'Sullivan; and the 'godfather of neo-conservatism', Irving Kristol. At a subsequent meeting in Australia in 1995, Labour opposition leader Tony Blair spoke, and he impressed the gathering. The next meeting, in 1998 at Sun Valley, Idaho, heard British chancellor Gordon Brown, while the one after that, in Mexico, included speeches from George W. Bush's national security adviser Condoleezza Rice and from the then leader of the British Conservative Party, Michael Howard.

Such meetings can act as a barometer signalling News Corporation's political shifts. The first sign of its change of heart on climate change appeared at a global editorial conference in July 2006, at Pebble Beach, California. One of the guests was former Democratic presidential candidate Al Gore, who screened his film *An Inconvenient Truth*. Other invited speakers who discussed climate change were the serving British prime minister Tony Blair and Californian governor Arnold Schwarzenegger.

A UNIQUELY POWERFUL BUSINESS

Rupert Murdoch, then, is a man who enjoys the power that comes from ownership of newspapers, television and publishing outlets, not to mention the power to grant political subsidies from his personal wealth. In 2007, journalist Ken Auletta spent considerable time with Murdoch for a profile in the *New Yorker*. Auletta commented:

> At least a couple of times each day, he talked on the phone with an editor in order to suggest a story based on something that he'd heard. This prompted

me to ask, 'Of all the things in your business empire, what gives you the most pleasure?'

'Being involved with the editor of a paper in a day-to-day campaign,' he answered instantly. 'Trying to influence people.'[30]

Perhaps his most significant campaign was his aggressive support for the invasion of Iraq in 2003. Like a single mighty battleship, the guns of his newspapers and television channels all pointed in the one direction. The collapse of the justification for the war and its terrible human cost have brought no apology from the editors or their leader.

Yet the nature of Murdoch's power is elusive. Few people doubt that outlets like Fox News and the *Sun* help to fashion a climate of public opinion, but it is not always easy to pin this down. Research on the influence of the news media long ago rejected theories that simplistically see them injecting false ideas and propaganda into the minds of their passive audience. More popular are theories that argue that they help to set a broad agenda for public debate. In this way, the news media validate some issues and invalidate others. They designate certain issues as key and others as peripheral. They frame the language of debate, as Fox News did in insisting that Barack Obama's health care be described as 'government-run insurance' and not 'the public option'. In formulaic terms, news media do not tell the audience *what* to think, but *what to think about*.

Interestingly, Murdoch himself seems to accept the idea that his media set an agenda. In a 1998 interview, he was asked whether the *Sun* had the power to 'make or break a political party at an election'. Murdoch responded that this was 'very exaggerated' and then added that 'between elections you can help, if you're relevant and intelligent and know how to popularise an issue, you can help set the agenda. There's some power there, there's no doubt about it at all.'[31] In 1993, the *Economist* made a similar point: 'Perhaps Mr Murdoch's biggest influence has been not so much in persuading people how to vote as in moulding a cultural and moral climate for politicians of varying hue to exploit.'

But Murdoch's power to influence public opinion is not confined solely to those who actually read and watch his news and commentary. Those outside the news media usually do not realise that journalists obsessively follow their news rivals. They watch competing newspapers and television news, primarily because they are worried about being beaten to a story, but also because they are seeking ideas for future stories of their own. Radio and television producers voraciously read newspapers for segments and topics. The world of journalism is very self-referential. This ability of parts of the news media to influence other parts has been dubbed 'inter-media agenda setting' by those who study the flow of news and ideas.[32] While derided as 'legacy media', newspapers are still the key to this process. They have the biggest staffs and specialist reporters. Newspapers lead, and the electronic media (including blogs and internet sites) follow. Most importantly, for historical reasons, politics is central to the purpose of newspapers in a way that it is not to electronic media, whose prime strength is in entertainment. Because of this, Murdoch's loss-making newspapers in the United States, Britain and Australia begin to make political, if not economic, sense. Subsidised by the more profitable parts of his empire, they help to set an agenda not only for their audiences, but also for political parties and other news organisations.

Moreover, the world of news and politics is an interdependent ecology. When a new element is inserted into that ecology—such as a right-wing newspaper or Fox News—it alters the balance and composition of the whole. An extremist newspaper or television channel extends the parameters that define debate. The high-pitched nature of Murdoch's tabloid media and their overtly conservative stance, for example, can bend the terms of the conversations that a city or nation has with itself, with the boundaries skewed much further to the Right than would otherwise be the case. For this reason, journalists talk about the 'Fox News effect', which refers to the way in which the ultra-tabloid style of news presentation on Fox News affected other news media such as CNN. This was particularly evident in the Murdoch media's campaign to invade Iraq. The top CNN journalist Christine Amanpour, in a moment of candour, said that the news media generally, including her own, were intimidated by the Bush administration 'and its foot soldiers at Fox News'. The result was self-censorship and a reluctance to ask hard questions.[33] This process of 'inter-media agenda setting' may well be part of the secret alchemy of Murdoch's influence on politics of the US, Britain and Australia.

In this way, Rupert Murdoch promotes his political views around the world. But exercising influence in three continents is not easy, even for such a hyperactive mogul. A former Murdoch editor, Eric Beecher, described his method as 'by phone and by clone'. Murdoch relies on his editors.

While researching this book, I was assured (often without having raised the question) by several senior Murdoch editors that Murdoch had never instructed them to do anything. Their comments suggest the only way that Murdoch can exert influence is by issuing commands but he is more sophisticated than this. Martin Dunn (former editor of *Today* and the *Boston Herald*) explained:

> Murdoch is *the* intellectual force within the company. His key lieutenants totally understand his positions. The option is always available to ignore those views—but as with everything in a business so heavily dominated by one man, ignoring those views can carry a heavy price.[34]

A former News Corporation executive, Bruce Dover, described his editors' behaviour as a sort of 'anticipatory compliance'.[35] Another argued that Murdoch is 'less hands-on than people assume . . . It's not done in a direct way where he issues instructions. [Rather,] it's a bunch of people running around trying to please him.'[36]

After Murdoch bought the *Sunday Times* in 1981 he appointed as editor Frank Giles, who initially resisted pressure from Murdoch. Later, he recalled:

> Though Murdoch had not up to then given me any explicit instructions about the political line of the paper—indeed he never did, throughout my editorship—I knew enough about his views through hearing him express them, to recognise that he and I were a long way apart politically.[37]

Giles heard Murdoch's views privately and publicly. The latter is often overlooked. While many leading businessmen never publicly talk politics, Murdoch frequently does. To find out what their boss thinks, his editors simply have to read newspapers or watch television. Giles was replaced by Andrew Neil, who explained that Murdoch's control is subtle.

> For a start he picks as his editors people like me who are generally on the same wavelength as him: we started from a set of common assumptions about politics and society, even if we did not see eye to eye on every issue and have very different styles. Then he largely left me to get on with it.[38]

David Yelland, an editor of the *Sun*, said that Murdoch editors ultimately end up agreeing with everything Murdoch says. 'But you don't admit it to yourself that you're being influenced. Most Murdoch editors wake up in the morning, switch on the radio, hear that something has happened . . . and think, "What would Rupert think about this?" '[39] An Australian editor, Bruce Guthrie, made an almost identical comment in 2010, adding that Murdoch was 'an all-pervasive presence, even when he's not in town'.[40]

A UNIQUELY IDEOLOGICAL BUSINESS

Rupert Murdoch's sponsorship of his senior editors' ideological talk fests shows a passion for political ideas that few businessmen share and, if they did, that fewer would admit to. On several occasions, however, Murdoch has argued that his motives for publishing cannot be reduced to making profits alone. 'I think what drives me are ideas and what you can do with ideas,' he once said.[41] In a speech to an Australian free market think tank, Murdoch quoted a statement by the economist John Maynard Keynes about the significance, at least subconsciously, of philosophical ideas to men who regard themselves as supremely practical. Murdoch added that in the media business 'we are all ruled by ideas'. But this is not true, of course. Other global media chief executives are not 'ruled by ideas' in the way Murdoch is.

When Murdoch talks about ideas, he means the philosophical and policy ideas of the kind that conservative think tanks produce. More than any other global corporate giant, Murdoch has supported and participated in conservative think tanks in the United States, Britain and Australia. In 1988–89 he took a seat on the board of the Hoover Institution, during the high tide of Reaganism, joining former Reagan official Jeane Kirkpatrick and former Defense secretary Donald Rumsfeld. At the same time, in Australia Murdoch joined the council of the Institute of Public Affairs and remained on it until 2000, regularly giving generous donations to the influential think tank[42] (while his journalists continued to regularly report on the institute and its political campaigns). In 1997, he joined the board of the Cato Institute, a Washington-based libertarian think tank set up by the owner of one of the largest private companies in the US oil industry. At that time, the institute was running an active campaign of climate change denial, as were oil companies such as ExxonMobil.[43] In Britain, News Corporation was deeply involved in the country's oldest free market think tank, the Institute of Economic Affairs, which played a vital role in laying the intellectual foundations on which Thatcherism was built, especially its policies on free markets, deregulation and privatisation. Murdoch's *Sunday Times* and the institute co-published a series of pamphlets attacking the welfare state for producing an intractable 'underclass'.[44] From 1988 to 2001, the founder and director of the institute, Lord

Harris of High Cross (Ralph Harris), was a director of Times Newspapers Holdings, Murdoch's holding company for both the *Times* and the *Sunday Times*.[45] In New York, a similar link exists between the *New York Post* and the free market Manhattan Institute, whose 'fellows' regularly write opinion pieces for the paper. In 2003, a *Post* editorial praised the institute on its 25th birthday. Headed 'Ideas matter', the article said that the institute had 'changed the terms of the American debate on a host of social issues, challenging the prevailing orthodoxies'.[46] The *Australian* regularly publishes feature articles and columns by writers from the Institute for Public Affairs and the Centre for Independent Studies, other free market think tanks. Editorials cite policy from these think tanks, and at one point the Centre for Independent Studies' analyst on education was appointed as the 'schools editor' on the *Australian*.[47]

It is impossible to name any other major media corporation with such sustained and intricate connections with the ideological currents represented by these organisations. On this score alone, News Corporation is unique.

The puzzle of what deeply motivates Rupert Murdoch has occupied many minds. What is the purpose of his power? Does it aim for ultimate ends? Murdoch's ideological beliefs are not a neat package. To begin to understand them, it is easier to see what he is against.

For someone who has a genuine love of newspapers and a deep interest in television, Murdoch has very odd views on journalism and the media. He is contemptuous of most journalistic ideals. While the rest of the world hailed the investigative journalism of the Watergate scandal in the 1970s, Murdoch scorned it as 'the new cult of adversarial journalism'. He reserves a special contempt for what he calls the 'liberal media', which encompasses the vast majority of big newspapers and major television networks in Britain, the United States and Australia.

The claim that large parts of the mainstream media are liberal or left-wing emerged in the 'Reagan Revolution' of the early 1980s. Conservatives began to see themselves as victims of a powerful force in spite of their own high profile within the mainstream media.[48] Murdoch was one of the most outspoken proponents of this perceived victimisation. In 1984, he formally debated the editor of the *Washington Post* Ben Bradlee about the existence of a liberal media elite.[49] He complained about the critical media coverage of Ronald Reagan's policies, and he particularly attacked the *New York Times*. The press was trying to change the country's political agenda and its traditional values, he claimed. In the years since Murdoch's attacks on the mainstream media have been regular, yet they are like reflections in a distorted mirror, or what psychologists call 'projections' of one's own flaws onto another. They decry exactly what Murdoch's critics say *he* has done for 40 years.

The need to battle against the liberal media is not merely Murdoch's opinion; it is fundamental to his media strategy. It is both a passionate cause and a business model. In the early days of Fox News, it operated as a form of product differentiation in a crowded market for news and television. In Australia and Britain, Murdoch's war on the liberal media takes the form of attacks on the public broadcasters, the British Broadcasting Corporation and the Australian Broadcasting Corporation. Columnists on the *Sun* and the *Times* attack the BBC for left-wing bias and elitism. This was particularly evident during the Iraq invasion but has been a consistent theme from the early 1980s. Similarly, the *Australian* rails against the news programs of the ABC, which it says are 'guilty of a consistent left-liberal slant'.[50] Murdoch's main newspaper rival in Australia is Fairfax Media, which publishes competing broadsheets such as the *Sydney Morning Herald* and the *Age*. These too are subject to attacks for liberal bias.[51]

After Murdoch's takeover of the *Wall Street Journal* in 2007, his new editors scorned its journalists, who, they said, were 'too liberal', while Murdoch aimed his artillery at his long-time bête noire, the *New York Times*, and at the Sulzberger family, which owns it:

> I think that Arthur Sulzberger, over the years, has made it very clear that he wants a very liberal paper, and that he wants a staff that reflects that community. For five years, he didn't want any white heterosexual men hired.[52]

Murdoch has since made moves to change the *Wall Street Journal* into a more general newspaper, taking it away from its specialist niche. In a world in which the future of newspapers lies in specialised content, this makes business sense only if the *Journal* aims to compete with and ultimately defeat the *New York Times*.

Murdoch's battle cry against the liberal media is sometimes heard. His remarks resonate with the latent and widespread public scepticism towards the media in general and thus give News Corporation a characteristic that sets it apart from its commercial competitors: it is the member of the media that is anti-media. In the long run, having one major news organisation regularly denouncing its rivals for political bias encourages the rest of the news media to become more partisan.

If Murdoch and his editors were opposed merely to left-wing ideas and liberalism, this would hardly distinguish them from a long list of press barons and media oligarchs over the last 150 years. Almost every media corporation has supported conservatism since the emergence of the popular press in the last half of the nineteenth century. What is unique about the political view that distinguishes Murdoch and News Corporation is the idea that left-wing opinions and liberalism are promoted by a powerful elite. Most commonly, this is expressed in the phrase 'the liberal elite', and sometimes in references to an 'intellectual establishment' or, in British terms, the 'chattering classes'.

Born of his early years in Australia, Murdoch's distaste for elites and establishments is quite sincere. He has refused knighthoods offered by the British government and, for a long while, travelled in commercial airliners rather than his own corporate jet. Tony Blair has rightly argued that Murdoch's self-image as an 'outsider' is 'crucial to understanding him'.[53] His lack of pretence and his attacks on snobs gave him a refreshingly honest personal charm for many years, but they were transmuted into the bizarre view that conservatives are oppressed by liberal elites who have captured government, the mass media, science and the universities, and whose ideas on culture and politics dominate by virtue of the orthodoxy of 'political correctness'. In part, this anti-elitism is a product of the tabloid mindset, which routinely poses as the protector of the interests of ordinary men and women. Historically, anti-elitism originated with poor farmers and the working class, which railed against the power of money and privilege. In political theory, the name for this resistance to elites is 'populism'.[54] Populism can be associated with the Left or the Right, but since the 1980s a rhetorical populism has become a weapon used by conservatives such as Richard Nixon and Ronald Reagan to garner support from working-class voters.[55] Seeing the world as divided between the oppressive liberal elites and conservative rebels is a familiar tune that has been played ever since by the right wing of the US Republican Party. It is a right-wing reverse version of what Marxists once called the 'class struggle'.

Murdoch's fight against elitist political correctness led to two of the most outlandish ideas ever promoted by News Corporation. The first is that climate science and the consequent threat of global warming are nothing more than 'orthodoxies' propagated by an elite of politically motivated scientists. (Orthodoxies are beliefs that are accepted because they are supported by the powerful voices of authority, not by any intrinsic merit.) According to this view climate change deniers, regardless of their lack of evidence and (in most cases) scientific qualifications, are brave dissidents against an orthodox doctrine. Murdoch's media have provided a platform for this since the 1990s, except for the short interlude during which Murdoch relented. The second idea surfaced when health authorities were battling the stigma and prejudice attached to people suffering from the disease AIDS. Parts of the Murdoch media, led by the *Sunday Times*, began a campaign against the 'medical establishment', which had proposed that the HIV virus causes AIDS. Based on strong medical research, this perfectly accurate deduction was treated as the 'orthodoxy' of an oppressive, politically correct elite. One or two contrarian medical researchers were lionised as heroic dissidents against the orthodoxy, and the *Sunday Times* undermined all public health warnings about the condition. When reputable scientists strongly criticised the *Sunday Times* for its AIDS denialism, the newspaper loudly accused them of censorship.

All of this suggests a pattern: when the Murdoch media oppose certain ideas, they describe them as 'orthodoxies'. Yet to regard well-founded scientific research as an orthodoxy demonstrates the kind of postmodern relativism that Murdoch newspapers also attack. Extreme relativists believe that history depends on the teller, and they deny the possibility of objective facts. They believe that physics is merely a human construct and that scientific knowledge is just another discourse to be accepted or rejected depending on circumstances or political belief. In this rhetorical populist battle against political correctness, reality is topsy-turvy and black becomes white. It suggests the immensely flattering idea that Murdoch and his editors, far from being smug journalists with conventional ideas, become rebels and outsiders who defy establishments and elites. Glamour appears where none exists. Attacks on the elite by Murdoch's editors and commentators become the legitimate protests of an oppressed group struggling against unjust domination. Naturally, such an image is convenient to very wealthy and powerful men like Murdoch, who has an extremely good claim to being part of a genuine social elite.

Rupert Murdoch's populist crusade against the orthodoxy of the liberal elite conceals an orthodoxy in which he himself passionately believes. His preferred form of political correctness prescribes small government, low tax, free trade, privatisation and the extensive use of market mechanisms in all parts of society. Murdoch's embrace of this was symbolised by his celebration of the *Wall Street Journal* takeover, when News Corporation bought worldwide advertisements for a new corporate brand under the slogan 'free markets, free people, free thinking'.[56]

Free market economic orthodoxy has long been the accepted wisdom in the business elite in which Murdoch moves. Always the crusader, he has been involved with free market experiments far beyond the economy. One of these is the attempt to transform public education so that schools form a competitive marketplace. Murdoch has become personally involved in this, giving $500,000 to one initiative and $5 million to another.[57] His preferred model is the New York school system under its controversial former chancellor Joel Klein. As with Murdoch's other crusades, there is a business angle. In November 2010, Murdoch appointed Klein to the board of News Corporation and also made him a senior executive with a brief to advise Murdoch on how the company could profit from education. As part of this move, Murdoch bought an educational software company, Wireless Generation. Explaining the purchase, he said that the schools market represented a $500 billion sector in the United States 'waiting desperately to be transformed by big break-throughs that extend the reach of great teaching'.[58] The software and other tools developed by his new company were used to implement a national regime of standardised testing of students. The test scores, along with parent choice, helped to create a competitive marketplace. Not everyone was happy with a highly political corporation moving into education. After Murdoch announced his company's new asset, one stockbroking analyst commented: 'We want our kids educated in as impartial a manner as possible.' Both Fox News and Murdoch have a 'very strong political bent', he added.[59]

Like many ideologically based theories, Murdoch's version of school reform can seem seductive until it is actually applied. In New York, after the Klein regime of standardised testing, sacking teachers and closing schools had been applied for several years, the test scores of students showed little or no improvement—a deeply embarrassing turn of events.[60] On top of this, some of the original conservative supporters of this free market theory became its most powerful critics, including Professor Diane Ravitch, a Republican-appointed assistant secretary of Education.[61]

Since the turn of this century, many of Murdoch's political and economic beliefs have come increasingly under siege. His support for the invasion of Iraq proved to be founded on falsehoods about weapons of mass destruction; his erratic stance on climate change looked ill-judged, and the scepticism to which he finally reverted is simply wrong; and his confident belief in free market orthodoxy was shaken by the 2008 global crisis in the deregulated financial system. But in order to exert influence a powerful man like Rupert Murdoch does not need always to be right; he simply needs the ability to exercise advocacy, and he can do this through his ownership of a global news empire.

CHAPTER 2
THE OUTSIDER

A long time ago, the British always thought in terms of their empire and were pretty patronizing toward us Australians, pat you on your head and say, 'You'll do well,' and when you do well they kick you to death.[1]

Rupert Murdoch, 2005

Working with [Murdoch] for seven years I saw what drove him. It was not making money, as useful as that was, but gaining acceptance by and then influence with people in positions of power.[2]

John Menadue, former News Limited executive, 1999

Rupert Murdoch grew up in a country that has largely vanished.[3] Australians of the late 1930s and 1940s looked to Britain for cultural guidance and military protection. In ordinary conversations of the time, it was referred to as 'home' or 'the old country', and Australians were legally 'British subjects'. The Australian government, in the name of British monarch, bestowed imperial honours on its most worthy citizens. Rupert Murdoch's father, Keith Murdoch, was knighted in 1933, two years after Rupert's birth. Rupert attended Australia's most elite private school, Geelong Grammar, and studied at Oxford University. Despite leading a rebellion against the liberal elites in the current century, Rupert Murdoch himself was born into a social elite.

FAMILY VALUES

The Murdoch family lived in Melbourne, a city distinguished by its boom town origins thanks to the gold rushes of the nineteenth century, which gave it a raffish side. Sir Keith Murdoch's family was part of a quite different side, a stuffy establishment of church men, businessmen and professionals. Keith was a man of high social status, and at the time of Rupert's birth he was in charge of the growing Herald group of newspapers and magazines. Through the 1920s and 1930s, the group bought up newspapers in other Australian cities such as Adelaide, Perth and Brisbane. Keith Murdoch's taste was opulent. Before his marriage to Rupert's mother, his bachelor home was the subject of a story in a Herald magazine that described 'Sung pottery, a William and Mary table from the collection of Sir James Horlick, a walnut tallboy from Lord Swaythling's collection, a Tang dynasty horse, pieces by Chippendale, Georgian silver candlesticks, and a Charles II mirror'.[4] In these surroundings, Keith was looked after by servants who prepared his meals and laid out his clothes.

In 1928, Keith married Elisabeth Greene. Rupert was born in 1931, and by the end of the 1930s he had three sisters. It was a happy, wealthy family, which owned a large farm on the outskirts of Melbourne as well as a lavish city mansion. For Rupert and his sisters a nanny was employed, and when Sir Keith and Lady Elisabeth visited Britain for a holiday in 1936 they brought back an English governess. Rupert's biographer William Shawcross described the family at play:

> Out for a ride in the country lanes, [Keith Murdoch] was always impeccably dressed in a well-cut tweed jacket, jodhpurs and polished riding boots . . . Lady Murdoch would be on a half-wild racehorse, liable to bolt at any moment, and the guests and children on a diverse collection of ponies and old police horses and whatever else was in the stables or fields at the time . . . After the ride . . . everyone would have a shower and change clothes before a traditional English lunch—perhaps roast beef and a good claret. That too was all part of Sir Keith's style.[5]

To see Rupert Murdoch's upbringing solely in these privileged terms would be unfair. After all, he did not choose to be born into a social elite. Moreover, it would miss a vital dimension of his emotional and political makeup that is central to his motives today. Australia was modelled on Britain and run by an Anglophile elite, but it also had a very different side, first explored in an influential book by historian Russel Ward. *The Australian Legend* identified what Ward called Australia's 'national mystique' and the Australian people's 'idea of itself'. In its national myth, said Ward,

> the 'typical Australian' is a practical man, rough and ready in his manners and quick to decry any appearance of affectation in others . . . [He is] sceptical about the value of religion and of intellectual and cultural pursuits generally. He believes that Jack is not only as good as his master but, at least in principle, probably a good deal better . . . He is a fiercely independent person who hates officiousness and authority . . . Above all, [he] will stick by his mates through thick and thin.[6]

Ward saw this rebellion against authority, this egalitarianism and dislike of pretence, originating in the convict ethos and refined by trade union conflicts between pastoral workers and land-owning squatters in the late nineteenth century. By the twentieth century Australia had an official culture of Britishness, but underneath was an unofficial culture imbued with scepticism towards the pretentious British values and hostility towards the country's class society and snobbery. Above all, Australian culture was populist: it celebrated the ordinary citizen, opposing the elite and seeing social conflict in terms of a sensational morality tale of right versus wrong.

The journalist Phillip Knightley caught a glimpse of the Murdoch's populism when he was a young Herald journalist. Assigned to help Sir Keith for a few days, he found himself standing outside his employer's hotel, waiting to see him for the first time.

> I watched a procession of government limousines and the occasional Bentley come up the driveway. Would Murdoch have a Bentley or a Rolls? Finally, a

battered, dirty, utility truck pulled up with Murdoch in the passenger seat and a young man about my age driving. Murdoch got out to let me in, and I squeezed my knees around the gear shift. 'This is my son Rupert,' Murdoch said.[7]

Such a scene, between a very junior cadet journalist and a knight of the realm and managing director with his son, would have been unthinkable in Britain.

As well as hostility to elites and class-based pretence, there was another powerful force. Murdoch was raised in a family of strong evangelical Protestants. Both his great-grandfather and his grandfather were clergymen. Keith Murdoch too was deeply religious. In a letter sent from London he described the city's depravity: 'A shocking feature of London is the immorality stalking the streets,' he said, a reference to prostitution.[8] The result of this for Rupert was not a deep religiosity but a profound sense of right and wrong combined with the zealot's beliefs that in the middle ground lies cowardice and that complexity can be brushed aside by a decisive move. Murdoch's religious upbringing explains his love of campaigning journalism, his ferocious work ethic and his early puritanism about moral issues, which survived his newspapers' images of voluptuous women with bare breasts and re-emerged as political support for the religious right, including its choice for US president in 1988, evangelist Pat Robertson. Rupert Murdoch is as much a preacher and a moralist as he is a businessman.

The military disaster at Gallipoli in World War One is a founding myth of Australia. Gallipoli, a rocky peninsular in Turkey, was the battleground that saw the young Australian nation, a loyal part of the British Empire, given a baptism of blood. For the Murdochs, this national myth was also a part of the family history.

As a young journalist, Keith Murdoch had the fortune to be assigned as a parliamentary reporter in the early days of the national Australian parliament. He became close to two giants of Australia's

Labor Party: Andrew Fisher, who became prime minister, and his attorney-general Billy Hughes. In 1915, Murdoch asked Fisher for permission to visit Gallipoli, where a large number of Australian, New Zealand and British troops were fighting Turkish forces.

Armed with letters of introduction, Murdoch travelled to the area, interviewed generals and others, including an official British war correspondent, Ellis Ashmead-Bartlett, who told Murdoch that a military disaster was unfolding, thanks in part to incompetent British military leadership. Murdoch had already come to a similar conclusion and agreed to evade strict military censorship by carrying a letter from Ashmead-Bartlett to the British prime minister, but the plan collapsed when Murdoch was searched by British officers, who confiscated it.

Enraged by this, Murdoch composed his own letter to his friend Andrew Fisher, confirming the military disaster at Gallipoli. He described the poor physical quality of the British troops in comparison to the 'magnificent manhood' of the Australians. The British forces were full of 'countless high officers and conceited young cubs who are only playing at war. What can you expect of men who have never worked seriously, who've lived for their appearance or social distinction?' The letter had a remarkable effect. Within a few months, the commander of the Gallipoli forces whom Keith Murdoch had attacked, Sir Ian Hamilton, was replaced, and the Australian troops were withdrawn.

Years later, Rupert Murdoch was enormously proud of his father's Gallipoli letter. He told an interviewer that 'it depicted a very idealised sense of the Australian soldier being sent to slaughter by the gin-and-tonic-swilling Brits', adding that 'it may not have been fair but it changed history, that letter'.[9]

The Murdoch family valued the qualities of daring, defiance of authority and standing up for noble causes, backed by conservative political and religious principles. Not surprisingly, when the young

Rupert Murdoch was packed off to boarding school, he rebelled against its strictures.

Geelong Grammar is a private school for the sons of Australia's rich farmers and industry chiefs, sometimes styled 'the Eton of Australia'. At Geelong, Rupert was something of a loner. Football, cricket and rowing were popular, but Rupert hated organised sport. Popular prejudice against the media and his father's top role in them made him a target for bullies. His rebelliousness showed itself early in school debates, including one about elite private schools. The sixteen-year-old Rupert argued that he did not see why birth into a rich family should enable some people to enjoy an education they did not deserve. He once defended trade unions, causing such an uproar that he finally had to protest he was 'not a Commo'.[10] At a later debate, the topic was the American way of life. Rupert accused Americans of racial intolerance and argued that that country had fallen into the hands of capitalists.

By the time Rupert arrived at Oxford, in October 1950, he was cocky, confident and opinionated. Always the Australian nationalist, he was unimpressed by fellow Australians in Britain: 'There were a lot of Australians who embraced everything that was English and rejected everything that was Australian.'[11] At the time a socialist and a supporter of the British Labour Party, he had a bust of the Russian revolutionary Lenin in his Oxford room, though this was one of his classic provocative acts. At elections he took part in Labour's grassroots campaigning, knocking on doors in cities and towns, seeking to convince voters to support the party. He stood for the secretaryship of the Oxford Labour Club but was ruled ineligible because he openly campaigned for votes, banned under club rules. Forty years later, Murdoch was still livid about the ruling. His father had earlier introduced him to the legendary Australian Labor prime minister Ben Chifley, and the nineteen year old wrote to him from Oxford about the 'dishonest and downright despicable'

Tory hypocrisy while also expressing a liking for the Labour MP Richard Crossman, who had 'a brilliant mind thoroughly clear and yet totally convinced in the rightness of socialism'.[12]

COVERING YOUR POLITICAL BASES

The sudden death of Keith Murdoch in 1952 was a turning point for Rupert. Keith had arranged journalistic cadetships for him in the United Kingdom and Australia, and these were vital in his next venture: running his first newspaper. Keith's will said that he desired his son to have 'the great opportunity of spending a useful, altruistic and full life in newspaper and broadcasting activities'. But things began badly. Although Keith had managed the influential Herald group of newspapers, he had not owned a large enough shareholding to guarantee his son a high position within the group. And although Keith had been a member of the Melbourne establishment, Rupert was excluded from it. He wanted recognition and acceptance, and when he didn't receive them he felt deeply slighted. Nevertheless, Rupert Murdoch's 'altruistic and full life' in newspapers began with the one thing his father had been able to bequeath him: a provincial newspaper, the *News*, published in Adelaide, which later gave its name to News Corporation.

The *News* taught Murdoch a ruthlessness that became central to his power in the years to come.[13] A clash with the establishment of Adelaide taught him that idealistic newspaper crusades are exhilarating but dangerous: you had to cover your political bases, he later said. Murdoch's teacher and mentor was the distinguished journalist Rohan Rivett, editor of the *News*. Knowing he could die suddenly, Keith Murdoch had deliberately placed Rivett as the editor of the asset he had bequeathed to Rupert. The plan seemed good. While Rupert had been at Geelong Grammar, Rivett had been in captivity in a Japanese prisoner of war camp and spent three years 'behind bamboo', the title of a popular book he later wrote about the experience. Like Rupert, Rivett had studied at Oxford and was London correspondent for the Melbourne *Herald* while Rupert was there; he played the role of older brother to the tearaway rebel. When 22-year-old Rupert arrived in Adelaide to claim his inheritance Rivett was fourteen years older, though his life experience was far greater. Rivett was a nationally known author and distinguished journalist, while Rupert sported the nickname 'the boy publisher' for his chubby, youthful looks and excitable manner.

Adelaide was known as the 'city of churches', and a conservative religiosity closed pubs at 6 o'clock each night and all day on Sunday. The capital of the state of South Australia, Adelaide quietly prided itself on never having accepted convicts, unlike other parts of the colony. The smug establishment was happy with the premier of the state, Sir Thomas Playford, whose political power was based on a classic gerrymander in which sparsely populated rural seats outnumbered the fewer but bigger urban seats. For quite some time, Rupert Murdoch's anti-establishment outlook synchronised with Rivett's. In 1959 the *News* campaigned on the 'Stuart case', in which an Aboriginal Australian man was sentenced to death for murdering a child. The newspaper forced Playford to appoint a royal commission into the conviction, but the commission's judges deeply resented the campaigning and coverage of their inquiry by the *News* and, in January 1960, Rivett and the company were charged with criminal libel against them. The charges ultimately failed but created national attention that began to interfere with Murdoch's business plans. He said later that after the controversy and the courtroom battle he had wanted to 'cool it'; the *News* issued an editorial that retracted some of its earlier claims and climbed down from its crusading stance. A few weeks later Murdoch sent an abrupt letter sacking Rivett, who was devastated. In his first clash with a genuine establishment, Murdoch had run up the white flag.

From the 1960s, Murdoch's business assets were in the ascendant. In 1960, he broke into the Sydney newspaper market by buying the *Daily Mirror*, a poorly performing downmarket tabloid, which he brightened up with the sensational formula that became his trademark. He has repeated his success many times in buying failing newspapers and re-energising them. In 1964 Murdoch founded the *Australian*, which became his flagship national daily. He also bought magazines and tried to acquire television licences. All of this set a pattern for decades to come.

Meanwhile, Murdoch's political direction was something of a zigzag. In Adelaide, while running the *News*, he had met with the aspiring Labor leader Don Dunstan and spoken at a meeting of the socialist Fabian Society. But shortly after his clash with Rivett, Murdoch published an editorial supporting the White Australia policy, which restricted non-white immigration to Australia. Then, in 1960, he visited Cuba and returned singing Fidel Castro's praises; soon after, he began to cultivate an acquaintance with the crusty leader of the Australian Labor Party, Arthur Calwell, giving him lunch several times at his office and praising him to his top journalists. At the federal election of 1963 Murdoch backed Labor, but it lost badly. It was a short-lived alliance, but it gave Murdoch the taste of mixing personally with a national political leader. By 1966 Murdoch had flipped again, and his new daily, the *Australian*, backed the conservative government in an election fought over Labor's pledge to withdraw troops from Vietnam.

The founding of the *Australian*, a national broadsheet, in 1964 was Murdoch's attempt to win the respect and influence that his tabloid newspapers could never deliver. In one move, the 33-year-old newspaper owner catapulted himself to the centre of Australian politics. Embodying his own outlook, the paper was proudly nationalistic at a time when many Australians automatically looked to

Britain or the United States rather than to themselves for ideas, innovations and values. With an idealistic staff and a visionary owner, the *Australian* sought a niche for itself as the newspaper of an open-minded and liberal reader. In an editorial on its first day, the *Australian* said it would promote 'independent thinking' and a 'new approach to national journalism'. It welcomed its new readers, which it described as 'the thinking men and women of Australia' who were 'welcome to this company of progress'.

During this period, Murdoch become personally close to a giant in Australian politics, the deputy prime minister and leader of the Country Party, John 'Black Jack' McEwen. Murdoch's economic beliefs were at that stage almost diametrically opposite to his current beliefs. Like McEwen, Murdoch was a patriot and an economic nationalist. He supported protective tariffs to keep out cheap foreign imports and protect local manufacturing. He favoured 'nation-building' projects like railways, ports and roads, all paid by government. As he was spending a lot of time in Canberra, where the *Australian* was based, Murdoch decided to buy a farm just outside the city, as his father had done in Melbourne 30 years earlier. He enrolled McEwen to help him choose a suitable farm. They chose Cavan, an old stone house with sweeping views to a river on several thousand hectares. Caught up in his rural fantasy, Murdoch even toyed with the idea of becoming the local MP.

Murdoch's first years as a publisher revealed his unusual personality, capable of enormous charm. An early executive, Rod Lever, recalled being invited to Murdoch's farm, where he was astounded one morning when Murdoch cooked breakfast for him and his wife and took it to their room on a tray. Lever also remembered conferences with editors at which Murdoch would go through the pages of a newspaper uttering 'Bullshit' and 'Crap', or 'I've told you over and over and over again not to run this sort of rubbish but you never listen to me. No one ever listens to me.' These conferences, said

Lever, 'were generally a theatrical performance which a psychologist would say demonstrated a desire to dominate. He wanted to rattle people, keep them off balance.' Within politics, Murdoch's fundamental motivation was a desire for acceptance and respect. Lever observed:

> Nothing made Rupert more hurt and angry than to be ignored or seen as insignificant ... As a schoolboy, his father had introduced him to [former prime minister] Robert Menzies. Menzies, who had a supercilious manner anyway, and thereafter always treated him as a schoolboy.[14]

By the mid 1960s, Murdoch's deep fascination with politics and his desire to be a player, not just an observer, were clear. Just before Christmas 1967, he had his first opportunity of political king-making.[15] It began with a national tragedy at a lonely beach near Melbourne. The Australian prime minister, Harold Holt, was an outdoors man who loved diving and spear-fishing. On this occasion he didn't resurface, and his body was never found. Holt's death left a vacant prime ministership, which would normally have been filled by a member of the Liberal Party, the senior party in the Coalition government. However, Murdoch urged the editor of his *Australian*, Adrian Deamer, to run a campaign to elect 'Black Jack' McEwen, the leader of the junior Country Party, as prime minister. It was the first occasion on which Murdoch was deeply enthusiastic about an idea whose absurdity was obvious to everyone else.

Deamer recalled: 'I told him you just can't do that, he's a Country Party bloke and the Liberal Party would never accept it.'

Murdoch shot back: 'He's the best man for Australia!'

'He may be,' Deamer retorted, 'but no one else wants him!'[16]

Murdoch did not give up. The likely winner was the Liberal Party's William McMahon, a free trader bitterly opposed by McEwen. But just before the vote, the *Australian* dropped a bombshell. McEwen had tipped off Murdoch that he would refuse to serve in a coalition under McMahon because of his 'associations'. This was a reference to one of McMahon's friends, the journalist Max Newton (also a free trader), who was retained by the Japanese government to alert it to changes in Australian economic policy. This damned Newton as an 'agent of a foreign government'. Newton had also been (briefly) the first editor of the *Australian*, and his departure had led to bad blood with Murdoch. The *Australian's* story prevented McMahon from becoming prime minister. The man who was chosen instead, John Gorton, developed a warm relationship with Murdoch. Gorton was a nationalist with big, if erratic, visions for Australia. Like Murdoch, he was something of a maverick within politics. Murdoch supported Gorton at the 1969 federal election, but the result was a strengthened vote for Labor.

Despite his increasing entanglement in conservative politics, Murdoch always made sure that he kept channels of communication open to the other side. In 1967, he appointed John Menadue as a Sydney-based executive. Menadue was one of the bright young men in the Labor Party, and for the previous seven years he had been private secretary to Labor's deputy and later leader Gough Whitlam. Menadue immediately saw how political his new employer was.

> He was and still is, a frustrated politician. He can't leave politics alone . . . Working with him for seven years I saw what drove him. It was not making money, as useful as that was, but gaining acceptance by and then influence with people in positions of power.[17]

In 1969, Rupert Murdoch took his first step towards global expansion with the purchase of the *News of the World*, Britain's biggest selling Sunday newspaper at the time. It was a sensationalist tabloid whose standard stories were of ministers of religion accused of adultery or scoutmasters charged with interfering with small boys. It was universally known among journalists by its nickname 'News of the Screws'. Nevertheless, Murdoch's capture of the newspaper showed that a determined 'colonial' could outsmart the Brits and seize a British institution from under their noses.

Shortly after taking control of the paper, Murdoch decided to spice it up by recycling the memoirs of Christine Keeler, an attractive callgirl whose liaison with a Tory minister and a Russian official had created a sensation some years earlier. This time, the newspaper promised, it would tell 'the full story' and add new revelations. It didn't do this, but its publishing of the memoirs brought about events through which Murdoch first articulated his nascent view that life was mostly about the struggle against elites and establishments. In the eyes of the establishment, the Tory minister at the centre of the sex scandal, John Profumo, was expiating his guilt by working for a charity assisting the London poor. One of those who felt sorry that Profumo's private life was being exhumed for a cheap newspaper sensation was the television journalist David Frost, who invited Murdoch onto his chat show. This proved a disaster for Murdoch: rather than chat, Frost grilled him relentlessly with questions about his shameless ethics and cheap sensationalism. To a sweating, fidgeting Murdoch, this was a show of moral superiority that evoked his Australian contempt for British snobs and their patronising attitude to colonials like himself.[18] The satirical weekly *Private Eye* dubbed Murdoch the 'Dirty Digger', a nickname he hated. He later told an interviewer: 'The British always thought in terms of their empire and were pretty patronizing toward us Australians, pat you on your head and say, "You'll do well," and when you do well they kick you to death'.[19] When the Press Council criticised the *News of the World* for publishing the salacious memoirs, Murdoch's response was blunt: 'If the Press Council is going to behave like an arm of the establishment, I'm not going to take any notice of it.'

In the same year, Murdoch bought the most important newspaper of his life: it turned into a money machine, funding his purchases of US film studios and television channels and, more importantly, it gave him an unrivalled position at the heart of British politics. The *Sun* was originally owned by the Trade Union Congress and then sold to the Mirror group, which wanted to offload the sickly broadsheet. Murdoch believed he could boost its circulation into the millions and told other journalists the *Sun* would become a 'radical' newspaper.

The new *Sun* began by serialising the spicy novel *The Love Machine*, giving inside gossip on soccer and offering competitions to win cars and television sets. In late 1970, it published its first bare-breasted model and relished the ensuing scandal. The *Sun*'s political stance for Labour was clear: the tabloid carried a long interview with Harold Wilson, the Labour prime minister, as well as the slogan 'forward with the people'. When the newspaper was accused of being unprincipled, Murdoch retorted that it did have principles, and in a two-page editorial he explained them. He produced, in fact, a checklist of the politics of the 1960s, which he later came to despise. The *Sun* opposed capital punishment, apartheid in South Africa, racism in Britain, the Vietnam war, entry to the European Common Market and the hydrogen bomb. It endorsed, above all, the permissive society. 'Anyone—from the Archbishop of Canterbury to Mick Jagger—is entitled to put forward his own moral code,' Murdoch said.[20] Evoking the newspaper's anti-establishment views, an early editorial called for the abolition of the honours system that had bestowed a knighthood on Murdoch's father.

In the *Sun*'s first few months, Harold Wilson made a point of cultivating an alliance with Murdoch. He lunched several times at Murdoch's offices and later invited Murdoch and other newspaper editors to Chequers, the prime minister's country residence. For a 39-year-old Australian junior press baron, this was enormously flattering.

For the 1970 British election the *Sun*'s headline was 'Why it must be Labour', and an editorial explained that Labour cared more about ordinary people and social justice, and it opposed the Conservative Party's scare campaign on immigration and law and order.

But at the election, Labour lost to the Conservative Party's Ted Heath. Murdoch's reaction was not to dump Labour and cosy up to the new prime minister, however. When Heath declared a state of emergency to deal with the 1972 miners' strike, the *Sun* supported the miners and opposed restrictions on trade union laws. Murdoch later commented: 'We certainly pushed public opinion very hard behind the miners.'[21] For the man who ten years later destroyed the unions' grip on the newspaper industry, this was a remarkable statement.

The 1970s were a time of political upheaval for Britain. In 1974, as an economic crisis engulfed the country, an editorial in the *Sun* described Murdoch's own views of the election choices at the time:

> The *Sun* is a radical newspaper. All our instincts are Left rather than Right. We would vote for any candidate who could properly describe himself as a social democrat. This much is sure. Neither Heath nor Wilson will do. They are tired and discredited. They do not inspire.[22]

Murdoch's views were beginning to change, and he gave unenthusiastic editorial support to the Conservatives in early 1974.

Meanwhile, in Australia, Rupert Murdoch's editor of the *Australian*, Adrian Deamer, presented Murdoch with a problem. The *Australian* had had a shaky start, but Deamer's appointment had stabilised it, boosted its circulation and pioneered a style of journalism not found in its hidebound rivals, the *Age* and the *Sydney Morning Herald*. The *Australian* covered a strike by Aboriginal Australian stockmen at Wave Hill, a remote cattle station in the outback. The strike proved to be the catalyst in a long struggle for land rights by Australia's Indigenous people. Stories about Aboriginal people did not impress Murdoch, however: Deamer's liberal politics irritated people in positions of power. His waspish tongue and refusal to defer to Murdoch did not help. In 1971, a protest movement was swelling against the tour of all-white South African footballers in Australia. The *Australian* chimed in with a front-page editorial condemning the tour and the government's generous support for it. A month later, Murdoch was in town and bitterly complained to Deamer about the editorial and the *Australian*'s overall stance, which had gradually made it the most liberal newspaper in the country. Deamer recalled that Murdoch complained about 'long haired stuff in the paper . . . bleeding heart stuff, all this Aboriginal stuff', saying, 'Aboriginals don't read our papers, you're wasting space on it.'[23] Deamer's sacking was part Murdochian politics, part Murdochian impulse. The paper remained reasonably liberal for a few years then swung sharply to the Right and stayed there. But before this, it played a role in the drama in which Murdoch, for the first and last time, helped to overthrow a conservative government.

A week after sacking his editor, Murdoch met the leader of the Labor Party, then in opposition. Gough Whitlam, a lawyer, was the new, smooth face of a party traditionally led by men from the trade unions. Whitlam was imperious and aloof. He had carved out new policies for Labor, reformed the party structure and, while identifying with the progressive mood of the nation, had been careful to distance himself from the growing Labor Left. Murdoch was keen to cultivate an alliance with Whitlam, whose prospects for the 1972 federal election were bright. At a lunch with Murdoch in 1971, Whitlam was surprised to hear Murdoch ask, 'How do we get rid of this government at the next elections?'[24] Murdoch did not immediately change his newspaper's policies, but his comments reflected a sea change in the mood of the Australian nation. Vietnam was the catalyst for frustration with the conservative government, which had been in office for 23 years when it faced electors in 1972. That year, in a speech on Australia Day, Murdoch captured the mood for political change in the country: 'What we are witnessing is the rebirth of a vigorous Australian nationalism, something that has lain dormant for most of this century—to the heavy detriment of Australia's progress and enlightenment.' Australia had to be more than 'a metal quarry for Japan, a pastoral lease for distant investors, a province of Madison Avenue', he argued. Australians were imbued with a new spirit. They are no longer content to be a pale echo of great and powerful friends, to be a second-hand society, a reflection of another hemisphere and sometimes another age. They are seeking a fresh, vigorous Australian identity of their own.[25]

Murdoch's idealism was as sincere as he was eloquent.

It was Labor's luck that, six months before the crucial 1972 election, Murdoch bought another Sydney tabloid, the *Daily Telegraph*, and its companion, the *Sunday Telegraph*. This magnified his political clout. Slowly but distinctly, through the year his newspapers became increasingly positive about the Labor Party and Whitlam. But, never a man of half measures, Murdoch did much more than slant his newspapers towards Labor. Throughout the campaign, he was in almost daily touch with the Labor campaign team and Whitlam's office. He wrote drafts of speeches for Whitlam, gave public relations advice and played a major role in planning the last week of Labor's television advertising blitz. On one occasion, he helped to write a Labor press release that announced that military conscription would end within a week of the election of a Labor government. A Labor staffer rang the editor of Murdoch's *Daily Mirror* to promote the press release. When the editor, Mark Day, asked 'What's new about that?' he was told, 'As far as you're concerned, mate, what's new is that it's Rupert's idea.'[26]

Murdoch also published, free of charge, advertisements from the front group Businessmen for a Change in Government. The group was spurious, having been devised by one of Murdoch's journalists and the Labor advertising agency. Murdoch loved the intrigue around the group and paid for its advertisements to be published in papers other than his own. It was the start of his habit of making political donations, sometimes secretly.

On the night of Whitlam's final campaign speech, Murdoch dined with him. Murdoch later believed that his newspaper group had put Whitlam's government into office, but this was a fantasy. The biggest swing to Labor was in the state of Victoria, where Murdoch owned no newspapers. Years later, he recalled: 'We did some dreadful things to the other side ... A lot more happened than even they have managed to find out.' With his new tabloid the *Daily Telegraph*, 'we all really threw ourselves into the fight, to get a change. It did break twenty years of conservative government. Not a bad thing to do.'[27]

After such a long period in opposition, Labor's ministers were filled with visions of change. But they were inexperienced and often inept, and their new policies stirred intense anger from business. Despite this, the momentum of popular support carried the government on a wave of hope through a second election in 1974, but by the following year Whitlam was in deep trouble. Having supported Labor in 1974, Rupert Murdoch's newspapers began to hunt in a pack, eager for the government's blood. Murdoch later explained that he had come to vehemently oppose Whitlam because he was introducing 'a European type of socialism which caused ruin and misery in other countries'.[28]

In the final months of 1975, a political crisis broke out that tore apart the fabric of Australian politics for at least a decade. The conservative opposition decided to block the passage of Labor's budget in the Senate, crippling the government because it would be unable to pay its bills. The country drifted into uncharted waters. Murdoch's newspapers joined the opposition in demanding that the governor-general dismiss the government to solve the problem. As the Queen's representative, the governor-general technically had the constitutional power to do this, but the idea seemed so bizarre that it was widely dismissed.

Meanwhile, Murdoch's journalists were in revolt against the *Australian*'s slanting of the news. Seventy-five signed a letter to Murdoch stating: 'We can be loyal to the *Australian*, no matter how much its style, thrust and readership changes, as long as it retains the traditions, principles and integrity of a responsible newspaper. We cannot be loyal to a propaganda sheet.'[29] Murdoch ignored the letter.

Two weeks later, the political crisis deepened when the governor-general did the unthinkable and dismissed the Labor government, installed the opposition leader as temporary prime minister and ordered an election. This action, dubbed a 'constitutional coup' by Whitlam, split the country and led to violent political protests. The *Australian* endorsed the sacking of the government whose praises it had once sung and continued its slanted headlines and stories. The crusade cost Murdoch a great deal of money, as Whitlam supporters organised a boycott of the *Australian*, which resulted in a sharp drop in sales. Soon, wharf labourers refused to handle its newsprint supplies. In the week before the 1975 election, Murdoch's journalists in Sydney walked out in the first strike over newspaper bias in their history. In talks with the journalists' union, Murdoch made furious accusations of disloyalty. It was a period of heady confrontation which ended in the election of a conservative government led by Malcolm Fraser.

Years later, Murdoch acknowledged his newspaper's highly partisan role in the 1975 crisis and subsequent election of the Fraser government. As usual, he saw himself at the centre of the events.

> My concern at the time was that Malcolm Fraser, having taken the country to the brink, might lose courage and back off. Maybe if the *Australian* hadn't been so firm on the constitutional issue then Fraser might have lost courage.[30]

Throughout this political crisis, Murdoch had been not only utterly hostile to Whitlam's government but also intimately aware of the opposition's moves to force a 'constitutional coup' dismissing the government. A few days before the governor-general sacked the government, Murdoch had lunched with John Menadue, his former executive, who was at that time the head of the Prime Minister's Department. Murdoch told Menadue that Whitlam would be sacked, but predicted that he, Menadue, would remain as head of the Prime Minister's Department to help with the transition and then would be appointed as ambassador to Japan.[31] This is exactly what occurred.

THE GREAT TRANSFORMATION

Rupert Murdoch's single-minded campaign to destroy Australia's Labor government, combined with his disillusion with both British Labour and Conservative parties, marked a deep political transformation in his values and beliefs whose causes are little understood but have been central to his political ideology ever since. What emerged was played out in British, US and Australian politics for the next 35 years, both because Murdoch became a media giant and because he rode the surging wave of a new kind of conservatism in Anglo-American politics. Through his newspapers, Murdoch became the populariser, the advocate and ultimately the beneficiary of a philosophy of the free market, deregulation and globalisation.

Murdoch's transformation into a free market conservative began just after the Australian Labor government took office in 1972. His first inkling that he had helped to install a government he would come to despise occurred in its first weeks. Just before Christmas 1972, US president Richard Nixon ordered a ferocious aerial bombardment of the North Vietnamese capital, Hanoi. Swedish leader Olaf Palme compared the bombing to the Nazi massacres, and other European governments also condemned the action. In Australia, the new prime minister, Gough Whitlam, privately joined the criticism, but several Labor ministers went much further: one asked whether 'maniacs' were in control of US policy; another described the bombing as 'mass murder'. Trade unions began to ban US shipping. A crisis had developed in the relationship between the United States and Australia. This touched Murdoch personally: he liked the United States and had visited Nixon the year before and been impressed.[32]

So when State Department officials asked him to quietly approach the Labor leader of the government he supported, he obliged. Murdoch's overtures to Whitlam were rejected, but Whitlam soon reined back his government's criticism, and Murdoch was thanked by the US officials, although he continued to be embarrassed by the government's initial stance and was later contemptuous of its inept economic policies. The writer Thomas Kiernan, to whom Murdoch related this account, concluded that it had 'thrust him firmly in the direction of the hard-nosed American political conservatism symbolised by Nixon'.[33]

In 1974, Nixon resigned in disgrace from the US presidency, an event that left Murdoch shocked. It followed the Watergate inquiry, which discovered that Nixon had authorised criminal behaviour, including a burglary of the offices of the national body of the Democrats. The connection between the break-in and the White House was explored by several journalists, most notably Bob Woodward and Carl Bernstein of the *Washington Post*. Their investigations became the stuff of legend and were transformed into the movie *All the President's Men*. But to Murdoch such journalism seemed an abuse of power. He admitted later that he had differed from most people on this.

> I believe the new cult of adversarial journalism has sometimes been taken to the point of subversion . . . It's a disgrace that we can and do read thousands upon thousands of words about our national defence and our foreign policy every day without so much as a nod of recognition to the enormous risks to our freedom that exist today.[34]

The role of journalists in particular disturbed him. He told a friend at the time: 'The American press might get their pleasure in successfully crucifying Nixon, but the last laugh could be on them. See how they like it when the Commies take over the West.'[35] Such bizarre statements placed Murdoch outside the political mainstream, but that is something that has never worried him. Years later Nixon became

Murdoch's informal foreign relations adviser.[36] What Murdoch had first called 'adversarial journalism' he later termed the 'liberal media', something that has been an enemy ever since.

Another influence in Murdoch's political transformation occurred in London. Murdoch's purchase of the *News of the World* and the *Sun* was a brilliantly successful gamble for a young and very minor newspaper baron from Australia. He jazzed up the papers, and this soon began to pay off and set the stage for more newspaper conquests. But there was a problem: around the world a technological revolution was sweeping through the printing industry. The new computer terminals allowed journalists to type their stories, subedit them and then produce a photographic image of the text that could be pasted down on mock pages, the whole thing photographed and a printing plate produced. The process replaced the traditional method, in which journalists' stories were typeset in hot lead using linotype machines, a job done by the 'inkies', blue-collar printers who worked in the grimy bowels of newspaper offices. Printers and their trade unions had to either accept that technological change was inevitable and cut a deal (meaning big job losses) or to resist the change and fight to the death.

Britain's printers were in a strong position: they controlled the production process and could use this to advance their pay and conditions. They chose to resist the change, thereby continuing the history of conflict between themselves and the newspaper owners. From the moment they started to strike, press owners such as Murdoch were losing money. In one dispute, the *Times* simply did not appear for almost a year. Strikes became frequent, and production was often a nightly confrontation. Unsurprisingly, this enraged Murdoch. As a young Fabian socialist and Labor supporter, he had not previously despised trade unions, but his encounter with the printers in London changed his opinion. He later told one interviewer: 'I was pretty much turned into a pretty strong free market type conservative by . .

. the most searing experience of my life [which was] having 17 years of dealing with the Fleet Street chapels.'[37]

By the end of the 1970s, Murdoch had lost all connections and sympathy with the left side of politics, though he wasn't particularly enamoured of traditional conservatism either, since he considered himself a radical and an innovator. But on the horizon was a political leader to whom Murdoch ultimately showed the most sincere admiration. His *Sun* editor Larry Lamb, also a former Labour sympathiser, identified her attraction first. His editorials and stories began to favour the leader of the Conservative opposition, Margaret Thatcher. Murdoch was initially unenthusiastic, worrying that this would alienate the paper's working-class readership. He would telephone Lamb, asking with exasperation: 'Are you still pushing that bloody woman?'[38] But his prejudice soon gave way to enthusiastic support, which lasted for the next ten years. At the 1979 British election, the *Sun*'s huge front-page editorial was headlined: 'Vote Tory this time, it's the only way to stop the rot.' An accompanying headline explained that this was 'a message to Labour supporters'. By this time, the *Sun* had overtaken the Labour-oriented *Daily Mirror* in circulation.

The 1979 election was a watershed in Britain, and its influence extended further afield. Margaret Thatcher delivered radical change, rather than stability, after she took office. Her militant brand of politics was a break from traditional conservatism. She began to emphasise the free market and meritocracy rather than respect for the class system and established authority. A new conservative politics was emerging, based on a backlash against the cultural revolution of the 1960s. It appealed to people who were disturbed by attacks on authority, the rejection of religion and the rise of feminism, anti-racism and gay liberation. Thatcher was able to appeal to working-class voters and claimed to better represent the interests of ordinary people. Later, Ronald Reagan's presidential campaign in the United States made the same appeal, courting traditional working-class voters, who became known as 'Reagan Democrats'. At the same time, this conservatism picked up on the new spirit of freedom of the 1960s and channelled it into support for small government, low taxes and the free market, bringing about the birth of a new populism, which claimed to represent the little people against big government, big unions and political correctness fostered by the new social movements.

Murdoch found this militant conservatism with its opposition to elites inspiring. Happily, it also fitted his formula for tabloid newspapers, which claimed to protect the interests of ordinary people. Finally, Murdoch had discovered a way to blend the exaltation of the ordinary man and resentment against government into a political ideology. The rebel child of the Melbourne establishment was becoming the dragon slayer of the liberal elites world wide.

CHAPTER 3
AT THE BARRICADES OF THE REAGAN REVOLUTION

Mr. Murdoch . . . says he was hardly the most powerful figure in the English-language media. 'That is flattering but it is just not true . . . maybe it would be if I tried to impose my views but I just don't do it.'

New York Times, 7 April 2003

Rupert Murdoch used the editorial page, the front page and every other page necessary to elect Ronald Reagan President.[1]

Jack Kemp, Republican member of Congress, 1981

On 21 March 1983, Rupert Murdoch and a group of eight other businessmen met US President Ronald Reagan in the White House to discuss a mutual problem. The meeting was jointly called by the Reagan's national security adviser and by the US Information Agency, the propaganda arm of the US government. The problem was the widespread and growing opposition to the Reagan administration in Europe and Britain. The resistance had arisen from the stationing of nuclear missiles in Europe, which many feared was a sign of a dangerous escalation of the cold war, accompanied as it was by an increase in warlike rhetoric from the United States. Two weeks before the meeting, in a speech to evangelicals, Reagan had described the Soviet Union as 'an evil empire', a phrase that suggested a religious crusade fought with nuclear weapons. Two days after the meeting, Reagan announced the Strategic Defense Initiative, 'Star Wars', whereby satellite-stationed weapons would be targeted to destroy Soviet missiles. All of this underlined Reagan's break with détente, the previous Western policy that had up until then helped the world avoid nuclear conflict.

Reagan's plans to deploy Cruise and Pershing missiles had sparked massive demonstrations in Britain, Germany and France. Not only students and radicals were alarmed; leaders of mainstream labour and social democratic parties supported the spread of 'nuclear-free zones' within Europe and saw Reagan as a cowboy and extremist. Within the United States, the 'nuclear freeze' movement was also mobilising opposition to the president.

Murdoch's meeting with Reagan had been initiated by Charles Wick, a former Hollywood producer appointed by the president to be impresario and chief of the US Information Agency. 'Charlie' Wick was also a friend of Murdoch's, who later appointed him to the board of News Corporation. In a 1983 memo to Reagan's national security adviser, Wick argued that Reagan needed a plan 'to counter the *avalanche* of public criticism of deployment' of nuclear weapons in Europe.[2] Several of the participants at the meeting were ideally placed to counter the opposition. Along with Murdoch, who owned four newspapers in Britain including the influential *Times*, those present included John Kluge, who chaired Metromedia, a large television broadcaster in the United States; Joachim Maitre, representing the huge Springer publishing group in West Germany, which included the national broadsheet *Die Welt* and the popular tabloid *Bild*; Sir James Goldsmith, owner of the French weekly *L'Express*; and several wealthy right-wing US businessmen as well as a former CIA officer who was attached to the National Security Council. The main reason for the meeting was to raise money that would be 'allocated to private US organisations which could conduct certain programs overseas more easily than the [US government]'.[3]

Among these 'private US organisations' were the Scaife group, the Olin Foundation and Freedom House, bodies which funded right-wing causes, some continuing to this day. Crudely, Charles Wick was hoping to raise slush funds outside Congress to promote propaganda for the Reagan administration.

At the meeting Reagan urged Murdoch and the businessmen to join Wick in what he called 'Project Democracy', a campaign against Soviet 'disinformation and propaganda' in Europe.[4] The Soviets, he said, 'are fighting on the ideological battlefields of Europe. We must counter our adversaries both in the near and longer term ... That is why I asked Charlie to pull this group together, to form a nucleus of support in the private sector for programs critical of our effort overseas.' Project Democracy, the name Reagan gave to his new policy, aimed to confront communism and export democracy. Great hopes were held for private diplomacy funded by wealthy individuals such as Murdoch, Kluge and the others. Documents revealed later suggested that participants at the meeting donated a total of $400,000, which went to fund European groups that supported the US missiles program as well as, surprisingly, Accuracy In Media, a US-based group whose main targets were US news media.[5]

The initiative soon fizzled and knowledge of the White House meeting became public ten months later. Quizzed at that time, Murdoch denied giving any money to this 'private sector public diplomacy' initiative.[6] Later, a covert, separate side of Reagan's diplomacy, also sometimes called 'Project Democracy', asserted itself. This involved defiance of a Congressional ban on funding to Nicaraguan Contras (because of their gruesome human rights record) by way of arms sales to Iran. Much of what we know about Murdoch's involvement in Charlie Wick's move to popularise Reagan's nuclear policies in Europe comes from White House documents released because of the Iran-Contra inquiry. Accepting Murdoch's word that he donated no money to the project, his presence at the meeting—

an exercise in government propaganda—raises questions about his motives as a news media chief.

Murdoch met Reagan in the White House on two other occasions in 1983, surely a record for a private citizen. At one in January, Murdoch had been accompanied by Charles Wick and a friend of Murdoch's, Roy Cohn, whose law firm was retained by Murdoch at the time. Notorious as the aggressive chief counsel to Senator Joe McCarthy in the 1950s, Cohn was later three times indicted and three times acquitted of fraud, blackmail and perjury. Three years after the meeting with Reagan and Murdoch, Cohn's legal career ended in disbarment. Cohn was a sleazy character but had good access to Reagan's White House, demonstrated a few days after the January meeting. Reagan had visited Boston, and Murdoch had offered to do a major spread on the visit in his *Boston Herald* but was ignored by White House officials. Murdoch felt rather insulted, so Cohn wrote a letter on his behalf, which was hand-delivered to members of Reagan's key staff. Murdoch received an instant apology.[7]

Cohn was only one of Murdoch's fortuitous links with Reagan. Mary Jane Wick, the wife of Charles Wick, was Nancy Reagan's best friend, and a columnist on the *New York Post*, Joey Adams, was an old acting pal of Reagan's from his Hollywood days.

THE *NEW YORK POST*

While Rupert Murdoch's love affair with the Republican Party began with his support for Richard Nixon, it was his purchase of the *New York Post*, in late 1976, that gave him access to US politics at a high level. By February 1980 he was lunching with President Jimmy Carter, discussing whether the *Post* would endorse him in the Democratic primary in New York. A few days after the lunch, Carter received the *Post*'s endorsement as the Democratic candidate. However, when asked by a friend how the Carter lunch had gone, Murdoch is said to have replied: 'Very good, but he is going to get a hell of a shock when I support Reagan.'[8] The *Post*'s subsequent endorsement of the Californian governor in the presidential race deeply irritated Carter, who complained that Murdoch, after all, was an Australian citizen, not an American.[9]

When Reagan first visited Murdoch and his *Post* staff, in November 1979, he was a contender for the Republican nomination. Murdoch became deeply involved in his campaign for the presidency, meeting his aides to discuss maximising the Republican vote in traditionally Democratic New York. An important part of this was Reagan's alliance with New York Democrat mayor Ed Koch. Murdoch, who had backed Koch for mayor, suggested he formally receive Reagan at the mayor's official residence; this helped to dispel hostility towards Reagan. Later, the *Post* tried to launch Koch as state governor, obtaining an endorsement from Reagan, but the bid failed.[10]

The *Post* did more than endorse Reagan in editorials: news stories slanted in favour of the former film star were also frequent. After his November 1980 victory, Reagan invited Murdoch to the first White House state dinner in honour of the British prime minister Margaret Thatcher and also sent him a presidential plaque. A New York Republican representative, Jack Kemp, said: 'Rupert Murdoch used the editorial page, the front page and every other page necessary to elect Ronald Reagan President.'[11]

MURDOCH'S 'FIRST LOVE'

Ronald Reagan and Reaganism were the most important influences on Rupert Murdoch's political world view. Murdoch was later remarkable for his enthusiastic support of George W. Bush and the Iraq invasion, and for the notorious Fox News and his media's hostility to US president Barack Obama. All these attitudes were formed in the late 1970s and early 1980s under the influence of Republican politics in the United States rather than through the politics of the British Conservative Party and Margaret Thatcher, but this fact is often obscured because so many of Murdoch's biographers and critics regard his defining moments as occurring in Britain: above all, his smashing of the print unions and his outspoken support for Thatcher at the British elections in 1979, 1983 and 1987. Andrew Neil recalled, however, that his *Sunday Times* was regularly able to find fault with Thatcher, in spite of Murdoch's adoration of her, whereas 'criticizing Ronald Reagan was a more risky business: Reagan was Rupert's first love'.[12] This became apparent to the editors and staff of the *Times* and *Sunday Times* when Murdoch first descended on the papers after he bought them. He complained about the *Sunday Times* reporters' coverage of Central America, jabbing his finger at articles that reported Reaganite policy, saying of the writer: 'That man's a Commie.' Editor Frank Giles recalled Murdoch's opinion that 'anyone who deviated from Ronald Reagan was left-wing'.[13] Deputy editor Hugo Young said that

> reports from El Salvador which allowed for any possibility that US foreign policy was in error were clearly potent evidence that the Commies had the *Sunday Times* in their grip . . . a term of abuse I personally heard more than once.[14]

In defence of Reagan, Murdoch was prepared to dump Thatcher. This became evident in the days following the US invasion of the Caribbean island of Grenada, on 25 October 1983. The ostensible justification for the invasion was fear for the safety of 1000 US citizens on the island, whose government had been deposed by 'a brutal group of leftist thugs', according to Reagan. White House officials were alarmed by the presence of Cuban and Soviet advisers and spoke of 'Soviet imperial expansion'. Murdoch was deeply impressed by the attack, which to him symbolised the United States' farewell to its post-Vietnam torpor. The *New York Post* vociferously supported the invasion, claiming that what was going on in Grenada posed 'a clear threat to peace in the entire Caribbean area—and by extension, in all of Central America'. Grenada, it said, was 'a

Soviet forward base'. Editorials attacked the *New York Times* and the Washington press corps because they questioned the administration.[15] The invasion caused a crisis in British–US relations. Grenada was a member of the Commonwealth, like many English-speaking former colonies: its governor-general had been appointed by the Queen. When Reagan gave perfunctory notice of his invasion plans to Prime Minister Thatcher she urged him to reconsider, but the plan was already underway. In parliament, Thatcher and her foreign minister Sir Geoffrey Howe came under sustained attack for refusing to criticise the Americans publicly, though it was obvious that they had been privately angered by the humiliatingly short notice of the attack. A rift opened between the Reagan administration and the Thatcher government. Murdoch bitterly attacked Thatcher: she had 'run out of puff', 'gone out of her mind' and was not 'listening to her friends'.[16] He told his biographer Thomas Kiernan:

> I supported her when she went 10,000 miles to invade the Falklands [in 1982]. How dare she criticize Reagan for going a few hundred miles to enforce an American policy that's infinitely more valid! She waged a war over property rights, and she bloody well botched it up, if you ask me. Reagan's Grenada action has to do with the freedom of the Western world, including England's.[17]

Later, he told Kiernan that he had given Thatcher a dressing down for her criticism of the invasion.

After Ronald Reagan's first term, there was no doubt that the *New York Post* would endorse him for a second. But what was the *Post*'s support really worth? After all, it was the third out of three newspapers in New York, a Republican paper in a Democratic city. The answer was that, politically, the *Post* was worth a lot. In 1984, it boomed that Reagan had 'unleashed the boundless energy, innovation and enthusiasm of America'. Far more important, however, was the fatal wound that the newspaper inflicted on the Democratic candidate for vice-president, Geraldine Ferraro. Shortly after Ferraro's nomination beside Walter

Mondale, a revealing memo was written by Steve Dunleavy, Rupert Murdoch's metropolitan editor at the *Post*, planning how the paper would damage Ferraro's reputation. It was 'time we took the gloves off', said Dunleavy, adding that Ferraro's voting showed she was a 'big L liberal. She has to be nailed on abortion.'[18] Her stance on a woman's right to choose whether or not to have an abortion had infuriated Murdoch, according to one of his editors.[19]

The *Post*'s campaign synchronised nicely with plans for Reagan's re-election. The president's national campaign director Ed Rollins revealed later that, on Nancy Reagan's initiative, a 'dirt unit' combed through Ferraro's life and, to cover its tracks, used non-Washington media to disseminate its findings. It struck a deal with Murdoch's *Post* and the *Philadelphia Inquirer* to make it appear that the dirt had been unearthed by the newspapers themselves. In October 1984, ten issues of the *Post* featured negative front-page headlines about Ferraro, most of them insinuating that she was linked to organised crime.[20] The most damaging was the 'scoop', secretly passed to the *Post* by Reagan's campaign, that in the 1940s her parents had been arrested (but never convicted) for illegal gambling. The revelation devastated Ferraro, who cancelled several appearances and threw the Democratic presidential campaign into turmoil.

On the night the *Post* published the Ferraro 'scoop', Murdoch was being honoured by the Catholic Archdiocese of New York. Afterwards, he invited his executives and editors back to his luxurious apartment for a drink. While there, he was told of Ferraro's response to the *Post* story at a late-night press conference. Angry and distraught, she had spoken of her mother's pain at the *Post*'s smear: 'Rupert Murdoch is an individual with all his money, with all his power, with all his connections to the White House, who does not have the worth to wipe the dirt under her shoes.' When this was read out, the assembled editors whooped and laughed, and Murdoch poured more champagne, according to one eyewitness.[21] Commenting on the affair, the *Post*'s executive editor Roger Wood declined to apologise. 'His papers are right wing newspapers. He believes he can influence people with them,' he said. 'We don't crusade but when we endorse someone, we're pretty wholehearted about it.'[22]

The Ferraro story is also an example of the way Murdoch manages to exert influence, even when he owns the weak and unprofitable third newspaper in a three newspaper town. During the election, the *Post*'s direct influence via its readers was small. But influence works on many levels. News reporting is a competitive business and the news media watch each other's coverage very closely, especially during election campaigns. The *Post* was able to exert influence not simply by swaying its New York readers, but by influencing other news organisations in a process called 'inter-media agenda setting'. The intensity and duration of the *Post*'s Ferraro-bashing, while not wholly accepted at face value by other news media, nevertheless focused attention on her background and suggested there was something sinister there. Today, Fox News plays a similar role in influencing the political agenda of other TV news organisations in the United States. The high pitched nature of Murdoch's tabloid media, and its overtly conservative stance, has skewed the country's terms of debate much further to the Right than would otherwise be the case. This process of setting an agenda for competing news media is one of the secrets behind Murdoch's ability to influence politics in the US, Britain and Australia. It arises in part from a kind of political war that Murdoch's newspapers and TV stations regularly conduct against rival media. The enemies in this war can be summed up in a single phrase, recognisable and repeated in many of Murdoch's outlets: the 'liberal media'.

THE LIBERAL MEDIA AND THE WAR OF IDEAS

Journalists, editors and media owners generally share the view that a central role of the news media is to hold authorities, especially governments, to account. They see themselves as part of a democratic process, revealing to the public facts that those in authority would prefer to keep quiet. During the Reagan years, however, Rupert Murdoch denounced the idea that the national press should act as a watchdog on his beloved president's administration. 'The press is sitting around here doing its usual thing, sneering at Reagan and waiting to pounce on him the moment he stumbles . . . The whole Reagan package needs much more support by the press,' he told one biographer.[23]

Murdoch didn't explain on what grounds the press should support the 'Reagan package', but he used this same argument in a celebrated debate at a Washington think tank in 1984 titled 'Is there a liberal media elite in America?' Murdoch's opponent was Ben Bradlee, the editor of the *Washington Post*, under whose auspices the Watergate revelations had occurred. The debate proved to be a dialogue of the deaf. Bradlee answered the question by rattling off the social and family backgrounds of his reporters which, he said, placed them among ordinary Americans, not among the elite. Murdoch responded with a contradictory ramble that argued that the news media had a right to scrutinise power but that their scrutiny of Reagan's economic policy was biased. The press generally he accused of 'attempting to change the political agenda' and of ignoring 'the traditional values of the great masses of this country'.[24]

That the news media are dominated by a left-wing elite is a belief that Murdoch has been repeating since 1984. It is central to his political beliefs as well as being one of his motives for creating new media outlets such as Fox News and buying old ones like the *New York Post*. But it is not original to Murdoch. It was a distinctive theme of the Right under Nixon, whose vice-president, Spiro Agnew, denounced the news media as 'the nattering nabobs of negativism'. The belief also inspired the creation of conservative media watchdogs such as Accuracy in Media and the Media Research Center. In the

Reagan era, however, the notion of systematic liberal bias on network TV and in big newspapers took on a life of its own. Reagan himself argued that television networks should focus on 'some of the truly admirable things being done by the American people' rather than on 'bad news'. The best answer to this came from television host Dan Rather, who said that Reagan was trying 'to convince the public that problems are not problems [but] that the people who call attention to them are the problem'.[25]

Attacks on the so-called 'liberal media' in the United States from 1980 onwards formed part of a larger war of ideas. This was in some measure a conservative reaction to the loss of Vietnam and the cultural revolution of the 1960s, but it was also a radical rethinking of the Right's foreign policy and its economic and social ideas. Reagan confronted the Soviet Union, discarded détente (the policy that had helped the world to avoid nuclear conflict) and popularised supply-side economics and free market economists like Milton Friedman. On the social front, the Christian-based Right attacked movements such as feminism and gay liberation. It was because Reagan symbolised this renewal and radicalisation of the Right's ideas that Murdoch was particularly attracted to him. Reagan was not simply a conservative; he was a rebel pitted against the old Republican leadership and the lazy ideological consensus of the American Right. The same was true of Margaret Thatcher. In Murdoch's book, they were both 'anti-establishment'. Murdoch's support for Reagan was much more than mere endorsement at election time; his news media were foot soldiers in the war of ideas throughout the 1980s.

By the time Murdoch confronted Ben Bradlee in the 1984 debate, he had been practising what he preached for at least a year. In 1983, the *New York Post* had begun a column by an intelligent and waspish neo-conservative columnist, Dorothy Rabinowitz, whose brief was to criticise the liberal 'media elite'. Rabinowitz had been a long-time contributor to *Commentary*, the neo-conservative magazine edited by Norman Podhoretz. She was on the same wavelength as her employer. Her first column had attacked a television interviewer who hadn't asked tough questions of a doctor who had called for health support rather than military support for the El Salvador regime.[26] She went on to criticise network television for stories revealing children's fears of a nuclear war. A particular target was the CBS network. In one logic-chopping column, she noted that Soviet television was grotesquely critical of the United States, and that US network television was critical of poverty in the United States. Therefore, she asked:

> How has it come about that the press of the most democratic nation known to history has come to see eye to eye on these matters with the press reporting for the most rigidly controlled system of totalitarianism known to man?[27]

Shortly after Rabinowitz started her regular assaults on the 'liberal media', the *Post* began publishing a column by a former CIA officer, Cord Meyer, whose speciality with the agency had been media disinformation and propaganda.[28] The *Post*'s editorials also regularly attacked the *New York Times* as a bastion of journalism critical of Reaganism. In the wake of the Grenada invasion the *Post* went into overdrive, with one editorial asking: 'Whose voices does the *Times* represent?' Another castigated 'a newspaper besieged by its own delusions'.

The *Post* particularly disliked celebrities who used their fame to publicly oppose Reagan's policies or to criticise their beloved president. These celebrities joined the paper's political shit list. Editor Steve Cuozzo said later: 'The *Post* did not give you a sixty-forty break if you were on its shit list ... Celebrity coverage did not mean celebrity worship.'[29] Actor Paul Newman, who supported a range of progressive causes and opposed the Vietnam war, was, according to Cuozzo, Public Enemy Number One.

He topped our permanent, ineradicable hate list. Newman, a box-office superstar, was one of those movieland liberals who could do no wrong in the eyes of an adoring press. He was in need of a reality check—and only the *Post* was willing to provide it.

Cuozzo's tough guy talk was no bluff: the *Post* so hated Newman that it simply banned him from its pages. Cuozzo cheerfully admitted: 'The exception was bad news. Otherwise no Newman. We banned him from the TV listings.' Far worse than that, in April 1982 the *Post* ran a long book excerpt on the accidental death of Newman's son from drugs and alcohol at age twenty-eight.[30]

The political targeting of liberal celebrities contradicts the common assumption that the Murdoch formula for tabloid newspapers was sleaze, scandal and crime stories with some tub-thumping right-wing politics. While this is largely true of the *Sun* in Britain and his tabloids in Australia, Murdoch's US newspapers in the 1980s were more than raucous tabloids. The *Boston Herald*, *Chicago Sun-Times* and *New York Post* included commentary and opinion pages written by some of the leading figures of the intellectual Right, a matter of some significance, since they were the distinctive and crucial heart of the Murdoch package but have been almost entirely ignored by his critics. For Murdoch, the opinion pages of the *Post* were every bit as important as its sensational populism, epitomised by headlines such as the famous 'Headless body in topless bar'. It was on the opinion pages that Dorothy Rabinowitz's columns appeared. Other contributors included Patrick Buchanan, a former Nixon speechwriter whose first column in the *Post* attacked a protest by university students ('the children of affluence') against cuts to the loan scheme for higher education (an act that demonstrated 'the manifest selfishness of the elite').[31] Another columnist was Maxwell Newton, an old friend of Murdoch's from Australia. Eccentric yet intelligent, Newton was a publicist for deregulation, small government and other mantras of Reagan's supply-side economics. His views became the unofficial Party

Line in News Corporation's global media, appearing in the *Boston Herald*, the London *Times* and the *Australian*, as well as in several other minor News Corporation papers. His work at the *Post* attracted the attention of one of the most influential US economists, Milton Friedman, who wrote to Newton, praising him as 'an extraordinary person who is expressing so well and so effectively the ideas that [my friends] and I believe in'.[32]

One of Murdoch's generals in this ideological war was Bruce Rothwell, an Australian who worked at the *New York Post*. He had earlier been editor-in-chief of the *Australian* when it had campaigned so bitterly against the Labor government that its own journalists had walked out on strike. In the middle of the 1984 presidential campaign, Rothwell died suddenly. Reagan sent a personal message of condolence to his widow, Anna, while Murdoch was left without an editor of the *Post*'s opinion pages. Finding a replacement was not easy, but eventually Murdoch's choice was another deeply ideological figure, John O'Sullivan, a British journalist who had worked for the right-wing Heritage Foundation and later became an adviser to Margaret Thatcher.

One of O'Sullivan's first acts as editorial page director was to introduce a new columnist, Norman Podhoretz. Podhoretz was one of the most sophisticated articulators of Reaganism, who exerted an intellectual influence on a range of Reagan ministers and advisers. Years later, the ideas of Podhoretz and his neo-conservative co-thinkers influenced the policies of George W. Bush's administration. Murdoch had previously given not only political but financial support to Podhoretz and his magazine *Commentary*, according to Henry Kissinger.[33] The welcome that Podhoretz received on his arrival at the *New York Post* was unprecedented for a newspaper columnist: in a newspaper sceptical of intellectuals and elitists, he was treated like royalty. In the week before his column began the *Post* published a series of interviews with him by *Post* editors, over three consecutive days, in which he scorned the arms talks that Reagan had begun with the Soviet Union. Such talks probably increased the risk of nuclear war, he said.[34] Gay rights was another problem: toleration was fine, but gay rights meant 'preferential treatment', he said. 'I do not believe that this kind of society can or should give its official blessing to certain kinds of values and behaviour.'[35] In subsequent columns, he spelled out the neo-conservative world view, which was frequently echoed in *Post* editorials. This included the opinion that peace in the Middle East would come only through a closer support for Israel and that critics of Reagan's Central American policies were actually 'appeasers' of communism.

The need for US support for the blood thirsty anti-communist Contras in Nicaragua became a regular theme in Podhoretz columns. In March 1986, he referred to the distinction drawn by fellow neo-conservative Jeane Kirkpatrick between authoritarian and totalitarian governments. The US could support the former in order to prevent the latter. The Sandinista government, he claimed, clearly fell into the latter category, thus justifying a CIA-supported onslaught. According to Podhoretz, the Sandinistas might cunningly agree to elections if they thought this would end US support for the Contras. 'But it is naïve to the point of dementia to believe that they would ever really follow through. To do so they would have to renounce their Leninist commitment to one-party rule,' opined Podhoretz.[36] Yet this is exactly what occurred in 1990 when the Sandinistas held elections, lost and then accepted defeat.

Podhoretz was unshakeably anti-communist, a mindset shared by the *Post* and its proprietor. In the name of anti-communism, the newspaper opposed democratic social change in countries like South Africa and the Philippines. For instance, the *Post*, along with the Right generally in the United States, urged Reagan to tone down his resistance to apartheid in South Africa because apartheid's opposition was said to be communist. In 1986, an editorial attacked Archbishop

Desmond Tutu, who had criticised Reagan for opposing sanctions. '[Tutu's] oratory echoes the views of the Soviet-backed African National Congress which openly advocates Marxist revolution', it claimed.[37] The following year, the *Post* criticised the US Congress' imposition of limited economic sanctions on South Africa, which, it said, reduced US 'leverage' and could 'only benefit the extremists'.[38]

In the Philippines, when the 'people power' movement began to oppose the dictatorship of Ferdinand Marcos, Murdoch's first instinct was to support the pro-American dictator. At a private dinner, he told his *Times* editor Charles Wilson and the UK foreign minister Sir Geoffrey Howe that Britain should support the Reagan administration's defence of Marcos in the name of anti-communism.[39] In the *Post* and the *Chicago Sun-Times*, Podhoretz defended Marcos on the basis that the United States had abandoned Cambodia and a genocide had followed; he said that something similar could happen in the Philippines.[40] Backed by Murdoch's growing global reach, Podhoretz's columns supporting Marcos also appeared in the London *Times*.

Murdoch's position on the Philippines and South Africa relied on the neo-conservative distinction between authoritarian and totalitarian dictatorships. On this basis, all kinds of brutal regimes were supported by the United States, rationalising as it did any form of abuse or torture as long as it was perpetrated in the struggle against 'communists', the definition of which was loose and broad.

The Reagan Revolution became famous for its assertion of family values, which were defined so as to exclude and punish homosexuals. The *Post*, like other Murdoch newspapers, resolutely opposed the movement to accept homosexuality and to end the vicious social stigma attached to it. In early 1986, this became an issue in the paper's home town, where the New York City Council began to discuss a law forbidding discrimination against homosexuals. The

Post immediately began a campaign against this, confident that it could bully the council into retreating. The case that discrimination existed against homosexuals has 'simply not been made', it said. Homosexuality is 'an internal disposition against which other people cannot discriminate unless the homosexual insists on informing them of it'.[41] The *Post*'s crusade then took on a hysterical edge. Over ten days, it carried seven editorials. 'Gay Lifestyle Bill will mean Gay Pride courses!' said one, warning that the new law was actually intended to endorse homosexuality as 'a morally valid lifestyle'.[42] When the law had first been mooted, an editorial had published the names and phone numbers of city councillors. When the law was passed, another editorial listed the names of councillors who had been in favour of it and urged readers to vote against them at the next election. It amounted to crude, homophobic bullying. Throughout the campaign, Rupert Murdoch's name appeared above the editorials as 'publisher and editor-in-chief'.

The 1980s saw the emergence of AIDS. On this subject, the *Post* consistently favoured policies such as compulsory testing, which could actually hinder the fight against the spread of the disease. Along the way, it also reinforced anti-gay prejudice. In 1987, the newspaper backed the 'compelling case' made by Reagan for mandatory AIDS testing of prison inmates, marriage licence applicants, would-be immigrants and hospital patients. Mandatory testing would 'give researchers a far better understanding of this dread disease'.[43] Ultimately, Reagan's proposal was dropped, because wiser heads realised that mandatory testing would fuel social stigma about the disease and drive likely carriers away from medical help. The *Post* supported other questionable strategies to combat the disease. It praised a move by New York mayor Ed Koch to produce TV advertisements 'stressing the virtues of sexual abstinence—particularly for teenagers' and criticised earlier advertisements that had promoted safe sex and the use of condoms, because they suggested that casual sex was 'basically OK'.[44] It also contributed to the AIDS crisis through its own unethical brand of journalism. In his celebratory account of the newspaper, Steve Cuozzo noted that on one occasion reporter Joe Nicholson was told to do a story on the likelihood that AIDS was spread by kissing. 'When Nicholson protested that the supposition had yet to be proven, he was taken aback by city editor Steve Dunleavy's scoffing retort, "Let's not be too technical mate— it's a good yarn".'[45]

REAGAN: NOT CONSERVATIVE ENOUGH?

The Reagan era saw a momentous improvement in US–Soviet relations. This was largely initiated by the Soviet president Mikhail Gorbachev, who began peace moves immediately after his accession to power, in 1985. After initial hesitation, and to his everlasting credit, Ronald Reagan acknowledged that the moves were genuine. Alas, Rupert Murdoch and his writers at the *New York Post* did not.

Since the 1970s, it had been a neo-conservative article of faith that the Soviet Union was becoming stronger and its nuclear arsenal more threatening. This view was initially influential in the Reagan admin-istration and fuelled a major US arms build-up. As events ultimately showed, the neo-conservatives' claims were exactly opposite to the truth: the Soviet Union was weakening through the 1970s and 1980s, and its economy (on which its military might depended) was unable to function with even a modicum of dynamism. Partly because of this, reform-minded Gorbachev emerged at the top of the Soviet hierarchy.

Neo-conservatives seemed utterly unable to understand events in the Soviet Union. They stuck rigidly to a script in which totalitarian-ism was unreformable and could be forced to change only by military might. Indeed, Murdoch was personally affronted by the public enthusiasm aroused by Gorbachev's reforms. When he heard that the book publisher Collins intended to release Gorbachev's memoirs, he tried to stop it. At that stage, he had a substantial but not yet controlling stake in Collins. He told the company's chairperson Ian Chapman: 'He's still a communist, you know.' Chapman demurred, and Murdoch later added: 'Well, Ian, if you're content to be an arm of Soviet propaganda, go ahead and publish.'[46]

A crucial point in improving US–Soviet relations was a series of arms talks in Iceland in 1986 between the countries' leaders. In the build-up to the talks, as world hopes increased, the *Post* sneered at reforms made under Gorbachev and the talks he had initiated. An editorial proclaimed Gorbachev as 'a worthy heir to Stalin', scorned those who spoke of a 'new openness' and argued that there was 'nothing new at all going on' in the Soviet Union.[47] It urged Reagan to take this insight with him to the talks. The *Post*'s editorial page editor Eric Breindel was not taken in by the Soviet trickery. Gorbachev's spokesmen, who eagerly spoke of the 'new realities' in the Soviet Union, he reported, were as 'smooth as silk and cold as ice'.

The arms talks were a success, and the world breathed a sigh of relief. Hopes for peace rose. But such talks inevitably meant that the United States had to restrain its own nuclear ambitions. The *Post*'s columnists seized on this and denounced in the sharpest terms both Reagan and the arms talks. Dorothy Rabinowitz accused Reagan of 'the most craven, the most open capitulation yet' because of his willingness to negotiate with Gorbachev over arms. Her thoughts were echoed by Norman Podhoretz: Reagan had a 'craven eagerness for a summit meeting with Mikhail Gorbachev' and had 'an inordinate greed for popularity', he charged.[48] The *Post* continued with this style of analysis throughout 1987. Its editorials claimed that Gorbachev would set the terms of debate in the 1988 US presidential election. As the two countries edged closer to an agreement for limiting nuclear arms, the *Post* reacted with alarm. One editorial bizarrely described glasnost (Russian for openness) as 'a West-oriented public relations campaign', which was being promoted by 'the KGB's disinformation specialists'.[49] Another article, headlined, in classic cold war style, 'US licks red boots', spoke of the Reagan administration's 'willingness to grovel for a summit' with the Soviets. The article also attacked the secretary of state George Schultz, whose crime was 'moral equivalence syndrome', a damning neo-conservative accusation of holding the view that the West and communist nations were morally equivalent.[50] The piece predicted that Gorbachev would emerge as 'the leading personality in American political life, setting the agenda for political debate for months to come'. As a letter from a reader vainly protested, this ignored the release of dissidents and the thawing of artistic freedoms under Gorbachev.

The *Post* editor responsible for the article, Eric Breindel, was a key figure at the paper for ten years and later became a senior executive of News Corporation. In spite of a background that included a 1983 bust for buying heroin from an undercover cop while working for a US senator, Breindel was something of a favourite of Murdoch's. When he joined the *Post* as editorial page director three years after the bust, *Post* journalist Steve Cuozzo noted that he 'belonged to a local elite that included Norman Podhoretz and his wife, Midge Decter, Irving Kristol, Hilton Kramer, William F. Buckley, Jr., and Father Richard Neuhaus'. Pondering Breindel's impact, Cuozzo said that 'the city's intellectual life was no longer monopolized by leftist thought. The neo-conservative movement had come of age in Manhattan and it was on the *Post*'s editorial page, under Eric Breindel, where that ideology was given daily voice.'[51] After Breindel's death in 1998, Murdoch's firm HarperCollins published Breindel's 'selected writings' and established an Eric Breindel Journalism Prize, which was subsequently won by a string of neo-conservative writers.[52]

DRACULA SELLS HIS COFFIN

Throughout the early 1980s, Rupert Murdoch had increasingly praised the virtues of the free market, competition and diversity, values that were at the heart of a US law that banned cross- ownership of a television station and a newspaper in the same town. The law became a problem for Murdoch in 1985, when he purchased Channel 5 in New York: he was legally obliged to sell the *New York Post*. Such a prospect was unthinkable, 'like Dracula selling his coffin', said one critic. It appeared that the problem might be solved when the Federal Communications Commission granted a temporary waiver to the law; Murdoch hoped this could be made permanent. But in December 1987, two Democrat senators, Ernest Hollings and Ted Kennedy, managed to insert a requirement into a bill forbidding the granting of a permanent waiver. The move was clearly payback, not just for Murdoch's frequent attacks on Kennedy and for the sleaze and sensation of the *Post*, but also for the political presence of another Murdoch newspaper, the *Boston Herald*, in a Democrat town. Murdoch saw it as 'liberal totalitarianism' and he fought like a tiger, calling in political debts to stop the inexorable enforcement of the law. An attempt by sympathetic senators to repeal the Kennedy-Hollings amendment failed, with one opposition senator referring to Murdoch as 'the number-one dirtbag' in the media. In the twilight of his presidency, Ronald Reagan uttered sympathetic noises but could not change the law.

On the night in February 1988 when the sale of the *Post* was finally completed, Murdoch wept real tears, according to his publicist.[53] The importance of the paper to Murdoch's standing in the United States was underlined when he repurchased it as soon as he legally could, in 1993. Such was the momentum that his neo-conservative writers had attained during the period of high Reaganism that many remained with the newspaper until it was repurchased.

The year 1988 saw the end of the Reagan era but not of Murdoch's enthusiasm for it. So close had Murdoch been to Reagan's admin-istration that he became one of fifteen trustees for the Ronald Reagan Presidential Foundation. In 2004, at the time of Reagan's state funeral, he attended a reunion at Capitol Hill of top Reagan officials.[54] Murdoch's enthusiasm for the ideological red meat of the Reagan Revolution was demonstrated in the conflict over who would be the Republican candidate in the 1988 election: mainstream republicans favoured the moderate George H. W. Bush, but moderation was not in Murdoch's vocabulary; he instead favoured the more extreme candidate of the religious Right, the television evangelist Pat Robertson.

CHAPTER 4
GATECRASHING THE BRITISH ESTABLISHMENT

All Murdoch editors, what they do is this: they go on a journey where they end up agreeing with everything Rupert says. But you don't admit it to yourself that you're being influenced. Most Murdoch editors wake up in the morning, switch on the radio . . . and think, 'What would Rupert think about this?'[1]

David Yelland, former *Sun* editor, 2010

I give instructions to my editors all around the world; why shouldn't I in London?[2]

Rupert Murdoch, 1982

On a Sunday night in June 1987, Rupert Murdoch and his son Lachlan arrived for dinner at a comfortable house in St Johns Wood in London. Also at dinner was Richard Searby, Murdoch's friend from his school days and now the chairman of News Corporation. It was a jolly evening, spent gossiping and celebrating the landslide victory of Margaret Thatcher's Conservative government three days before. The dinner was hosted by Murdoch's old friend Woodrow Wyatt, member of the House of Lords, who had been heavily involved in the Conservative campaign. From the early 1980s Woodrow Wyatt had been a paid lobbyist and go-between for Murdoch with Thatcher. He was part of a network of Britain's powerful political and business elite. His observations of, and private opinions on, that hidden world became known when his diaries were published years later.[3] They give a revealing insight into the exercise of political and corporate power in Thatcher's Britain. They are particularly revealing over the personal and informal contact between Murdoch and Thatcher—for whom Wyatt acted as an intermediary—and they explain why Cabinet Office papers made public through freedom of information requests reveal nothing about this acquaintance.

MURDOCH AND THATCHER

In 1986, the *Times* editor Charles Douglas-Home was reported to have said that 'Rupert and Mrs Thatcher consult regularly on every important matter of policy, especially as they relate to his economic and political interests.'[4] While seized on by Rupert Murdoch's critics, the statement seemed perhaps to exaggerate his ability to acquire favours and exercise influence, yet the depth of Murdoch's involvement in Thatcher's government and its crises is remarkable.

In 1981, Murdoch was on the verge of buying the *Times* and the *Sunday Times*, a move that would make him one of the most powerful media owners in Britain, as his share of the British newspaper market would rise to 27 per cent. But his bid was threatened by the possibility of an inquiry by the Monopolies and Mergers Commission. The proposed purchase was exactly the kind of corporate takeover that the commission had been designed to investigate, but then no inquiry took place. The reasons given for this were that the newspapers were both losing money and that if an investigation were set up it would cause a delay, which the current owners said would mean they would have to close the *Times* rather than sell it.

Woodrow Wyatt had been instrumental in the abandonment of the inquiry, as he reminded Murdoch that Sunday night in St Johns Wood. In his diary he wrote: 'At [Murdoch's] request and at my instigation [Margaret Thatcher] had stopped the *Times* acquisition being referred to the Monopolies Commission though the *Sunday Times* was not really losing money and the pair together were not'.[5]

On the day of the dinner hosted by Wyatt in 1987, he urged Thatcher to prevent another inquiry by the commission, this time into Murdoch's purchase of the *Today* newspaper. And two years later, Wyatt again spoke to Thatcher and helped Murdoch to avoid further inquiry, into his media dominance. When Wyatt told him this, Murdoch said several times, 'I am very grateful to you.' Wyatt proved crucial after Murdoch moved into Sky TV, in 1989, arousing hostility from rival BSB, which lobbied to force him to become a minority shareholder in Sky, given his powerful newspaper interests. Discussing this with Murdoch in March 1990, Wyatt told him not to worry. 'Margaret is very keen on preserving your position. She knows how much she depends on your support. Likewise you depend on hers in this matter.'[6]

In 1986, Margaret Thatcher's Defence minister Michael Heseltine resigned over his opposition to a bid by the US firm Sikorsky for a big share in the British helicopter company Westland; Heseltine supported an alternative European bid. His move was widely seen as staking a claim to the prime ministership. Underlying the issue was a split over whether Britain's long-term defence links would be with the United States or with Europe. In the middle of the crisis, Rupert Murdoch offered to arrange a deal between US and British companies. His preparedness to risk considerable funds was purely politically motivated; he said to Woodrow Wyatt: 'We've got to get her out of this jam somehow. It's looking very bad'.[7] His intervention failed, but along the way his newspaper the *Times* chided Heseltine for not being sufficiently pro-American.

Shortly after these events, Murdoch and Wyatt were invited to an intimate lunch with Thatcher and her husband, Denis, at the prime minister's country residence, Chequers. Little is known of what occurred on that day but, on the way back into London, Murdoch proudly gave Wyatt a tour of his new printing works at Wapping, soon to be the scene of a violent conflict between his printers and the police. Ostensibly, Murdoch was negotiating with the trade unions, but to Wyatt he explained that he wanted his existing printers to go on strike so he could 'sack the lot'.[8] A few days later the printers voted to strike, and that's exactly what Murdoch did.

Thatcher's support for Murdoch's new plant at Wapping was crucial, and not only through the restrictive trade union laws that her government had introduced. More important was the nightly presence of British police at the gates of the Wapping printing works to fight back thousands of protesting picketers trying to stop the newspapers from being driven from the plant. The protests continued for months, but in June 1986 support for Murdoch within the Conservative cabinet seemed to wobble, with a minister privately complaining to him that six months of police support had cost £5 million. Murdoch shortly afterwards asked for and received a personal assurance from Thatcher that she would 'squash' any weakening by her ministers.[9]

Thatcher and Murdoch had a deep mutual regard, more sincere on her part than his. 'I like talking to him,' she told Wyatt when he invited them both to dinner.[10] In the political controversy over the use of British airfields by US bombers to attack Libya in April 1986, Thatcher told friends that the *Times* and the *Sun* were giving 'wonderful support', while Murdoch said he 'admired what she had done' in backing the US action.[11] We now know that their mutual regard reached bizarre heights. So highly did Thatcher regard Murdoch that she took his advice and appointed Marmaduke Hussey, a director of Murdoch's Times Newspapers, as chairperson of the BBC. When the appointment was announced, Murdoch claimed that it was 'a disastrous appointment' because Hussey was weak and the 'BBC Mafia' would run rings around him.[12] Tackled about his earlier advice to Thatcher, which she had taken so seriously,

Murdoch denied he had given it and when pressed 'seemed evasive and giggled a bit', said Wyatt.[13]

But it was Murdoch's unstinting support at election time that held the key to the relationship. In the months leading up to the 1987 election, Thatcher said privately: 'We depend on him to fight for us. The *Sun* is marvellous.'[14] That year, Murdoch decided to travel to Britain and personally oversee his newspapers for the month before the election. According to Wyatt, Thatcher 'was delighted that Rupert had promised to come over especially for the election to keep in touch with me and to have an input of advice'.[15] Murdoch's advice was that the Tories should tell the public that they stood for low tax. 'Appeal to their greed,' he said.[16] A week before the election, Murdoch sent a message to Thatcher: the *Sun* was going to do 'two shock issues ... about what it would be like under Labour'. On being informed, Thatcher said: 'Rupert is marvellous.'[17]

Many commentators and critics see the relationship between Thatcher and Murdoch simply as one of mutual convenience, a crude exchange of newspaper influence for government favours. But this reduces them to one-dimensional figures with simple motives; in fact, while both had a clear sense of their own interests, they also shared a distinct ideological world view, and this was the reason that Murdoch backed Thatcher so strongly for more than a decade. Thatcher represented a sea change in conservative political philosophy, and Murdoch's own political evolution had brought him to a similar position, with the added ingredient of Republicanism from the United States.

When he first supported Thatcher in 1979, Murdoch could still see himself as the rebel conservative outside the establishment. After his purchase of the *Times* and *Sunday Times* in 1981, however, he began to be taken seriously by a broader part of the British elite. One reason is obvious: his broadsheets, unlike the *Sun* and the *News of the World*, routinely dealt with matters of high policy in the nation—debates about foreign affairs, government spending and public policy on health and education and a large number of other matters. As well, these newspapers were places for debates on long-term ideas and philosophies. The opinion page of the *Times* reaffirmed and celebrated the cultural idiosyncrasies of the British middle classes. The *Sunday Times* advocated the idea of a free market as the liberator of ordinary people, an opinion derived from the United States; indeed, the *Times* argued that British interests were identical to US interests as conceived by neo-conservatives in the Reagan administration. And what became known as 'Thatcherism' was elaborated and debated, and its enemies scorned, in the *Times*' articles, columns and editorials.

INTERFERENCE AND IDEOLOGY

The dramatic events at the *Times* and the *Sunday Times* that followed Rupert Murdoch's takeover were more than simply a clash between the editors and the domineering owner. They resulted from Murdoch's breaking his promises to allow his editors independence. In the drama, the leading characters were Murdoch's appointee editor of the *Times*, Harry Evans, and the editor of the *Sunday Times*, Frank Giles. Both Evans and Giles later wrote books about the occurrences that caused the newspapers to sharply change course, describing Murdoch's ever-present demands over news stories, headlines, editorials and columnists. Interference was the key.

Murdoch did not obsessively micro-manage his newspapers; in fact, once he felt that he had editors whom he could trust politically, he did not regularly interfere or issue ultimatums. The problem for Evans and Giles was that, in Murdoch's opinion, their newspapers lacked direction and conviction. They 'had to stand for something', he said. Murdoch wanted an ideological commitment—solidarity with Ronald Reagan and Margaret Thatcher, the two leaders who represented the new conservatism and were transforming the West.

But neither editor was capable of such a commitment. Evans and Giles were by instinct politically cautious and pragmatic. Evans had voted for Thatcher in 1979, and their editorials supported the Tories, but they displayed the journalist's inclination of scepticism towards governments in general. Murdoch bitterly complained about *Sunday Times* stories by 'Commie' journalists who reported on Reagan's policies in Central America.[18] Observing this, the *Sunday Times* veteran Hugo Young argued that

> [Murdoch] did not believe in neutrality. Indeed, rather like politicians themselves, he had difficulty in comprehending it. As far as he was concerned, journalistic detachment was a mask for anti-Thatcherism. If we were not for the Government, we were quite plainly against it.[19]

Significantly, one of the earliest clashes at the *Sunday Times* concerned the protests against plans by Reagan and Thatcher to expand nuclear weapons in Britain and Europe. As stated in the previous chapter, Murdoch personally spoke to Reagan about countering such protests and using his newspapers to attack 'anti-Americanism'. In August 1981, Murdoch's managing director Gerald Long singled out a *Sunday Times* editorial that had criticised the BBC for cancelling the appointment of historian E. P. Thompson, who was to give the prestigious Dimbleby Lecture. Thompson's crime was to be active in the Campaign for Nuclear Disarmament (CND). On the basis of the editorial, Long made it clear he wanted to have 'discussions on the general lines of editorial policy' and on Giles' views on 'the political tendency of the newspaper'.[20] But such direct exchanges were not really necessary to exert pressure. Giles admits that Murdoch had never given him instructions on the political tendency of the paper. He didn't have to. 'I knew enough about his views through hearing him express them,' he said. Murdoch regularly turned up at night, spread the paper out before him, and jabbed with his fingers at articles, snarling, 'What do you want to print rubbish like that for?'

What Murdoch required from his editors became clear late in 1982, during the Falklands crisis. Giles penned several editorials about the impending Argentine invasion of the islands, which were owned by Britain. Carefully crafted, the pieces debated the alternatives for Britain, arguing that negotiation should be tried but that, if it failed, force had to be used. When it became clear that the negotiations had indeed failed, Giles wrote an editorial headed 'The war that had to be'. Murdoch's reaction to the editorials revealed that it was not sufficient for his editors to agree with his view—in this case to support Thatcher's case for war. What mattered was that his newspapers' stance should arise from an ideological position. When Murdoch was disparaging about the *Sunday Times* editorials on the Falklands, Giles protested to him:

> 'But Rupert, our line—that force should only be used as a last resort but when it was used we supported its use—was entirely consistent and unchallengeably patriotic.'
> 'Yeah,' he replied, grinning sardonically, 'but ya didn't mean it, did ya?'[21]

This was the voice of an authentic Aussie ideologue: 'meaning it' was all important.

Harold Evans spent only thirteen months as editor of the *Times*. During that period he transformed the newspaper, bringing in new staff and modernising its design. Later, however, his editorship was punctated by growing clashes with Murdoch that revealed the newspaper owner's deep commitment to the Reagan Revolution, with its blend of aggressive foreign policy and radical economics. The reason Murdoch gave for the disagreement with and the ultimate forced resignation of Evans was his overspending. Evans countered that he had never been given an editorial budget. Instead, Evans listed in his book *Good Times, Bad Times* a number of political criticisms that he received from Murdoch and recalled his boss sending him 'newspaper clippings across the Atlantic, mainly from the American new right'.[22] One was an article from the *Wall Street*

Journal that compared Margaret Thatcher's early difficulties with those of Winston Churchill. One had to remember, the piece said, that 'in the end Churchill did win'. The writer was an economics professor from the American Enterprise Institute, a key think tank of the new intellectual wave being ridden by Reagan.

In the early months of Evans' tenure, Murdoch took pot shots at 'Commie' reporters and scored copies of the *Times* with ticks, crosses and slashes. Evans' description of the pressure exerted by Murdoch is evocative:

> Murdoch's technique was not to criticise particular leaders or, after the first week, to suggest topics, but to make what would please him unmistakeably clear . . . He is not a miniaturist. He creates an aura. The aura he created in 1981–82 was one of bleak hostility to Edward Heath and the Tory rebels, and contempt for the Social Democrats. He did this by persistent derision of them at our meetings and on the telephone, by sending me articles marked 'worth reading!' which espoused right wing views, by jabbing a finger at headlines which he thought could have been more supportive of Mrs Thatcher—'You're always getting at her'.[23]

Before it discovered privatisation, the first Thatcher government was deep in the grip of monetarism, centred on controlling the money supply as an answer to inflation and declining economic output. For its devotees, monetarism was an expression of philo-sophical liberalism, an argument that government should be small, symbolised by a self-denying restriction to using the one policy lever of money supply. A great advocate of monetarism was the US economist Milton Friedman. To criticise Thatcher's monetarism was to criticise the new direction in radical conservatism to which she adhered. Into this situation Evans blundered, assuming that a reasonable debate on the subject was possible. In an editorial in June 1981 headed 'Mr Reagan's monetarism', the *Times* criticised high US interest rates and urged Ronald Reagan to delay or abandon his promised tax cuts.[24] A little later, another editorial attacked 'the ideology of do-nothing monetarism'.[25]

The debate continued when the *Times* published two articles by economist Harold Lever that criticised the liberalisation of markets and the floating of currencies, which would lead to 'a monstrous casino of currency disorder' and which Lever proposed should be re-regulated.[26] The newspaper followed up with an editorial arguing that 'monetarism alone is not enough' and warning that this direction would see 'the doles queues grow, the corrosion of political co-operation and a very serious threat to the stability of our societies'.[27] Shortly afterwards, another editorial referred to the 'British experiment in the use of radical monetarism'.[28]

Three months later, Evans committed a further faux pas. Professor James Tobin of Yale University had just won the Nobel prize for economics, and Evans sought out an article by him. Tobin repeated the 'risky experiment' characterisation and added: 'The idea that you leave money supply to determine employment and everything we want is burying your head in the sand.'[29] Not long afterwards, Murdoch was invited to dinner at Evans' home. Evans recalled:

> The tirade began in the car as we drew up to the front door:
> 'Why d'ya run that stuff?'
> 'Well, it's timely.'
> 'And it's wrong! Wrong! What does he know anyway?'
> 'Come on,' I retorted. 'He won the Nobel prize.'
> 'Intellectual bullshit.'

Evans' wife, Tina Brown, said later that she had never seen anyone 'so hunched up with resentment as Murdoch'.[30]

In the early 1980s, the cold war had become an overriding concern for Murdoch. He and Evans agreed on the need for a tough line against the Soviet Union. But at this time, Murdoch was being influenced by the emerging neo-conservative approach from Reagan's administration that prescribed a more aggressive confrontation. In particular, in the wake of the Soviet invasion of Afghanistan and military takeover in Poland, Reagan was urging an economic blockade of the Soviet

Union. Unknown to Evans, Murdoch approached a *Times* leader writer and argued the hard-line US case. Murdoch, Evans said, 'accused the *Times* of being soft. We should end detente and co-existence which amounted to appeasement. The Soviet Union was a rotten apple and if we cut off all trade and diplomatic relations, it would fall.' Rather than challenging Murdoch directly, Evans responded with an editorial of his own that supported 'precise, well planned' sanctions but described confrontation Reagan-style as an 'apocalyptic strategy'.[31] Instead of accepting the neo-conservative hype about a Soviet threat, the *Times* also criticised the Reagan administration for the way in which it

> tended to see [the Soviet Union] as a single-minded expansionist power whose spreading influence must be checked at every point around the globe. Europeans see it as a fumbling giant struggling with internal and external problems which it can neither understand nor control.[32]

By this stage, Murdoch was seeking out senior staff and complaining about the paper's insufficiently militant attitude towards the Soviet Union. One of the editorial writers, Richard Davy, recalled: 'That was always Murdoch's complaint about the *Times*: that it didn't stand for anything, whereas we always thought it stood for reasoned argument and liberal values.'[33] Yet the *Times* was hardly soft on the issues that Murdoch raised. It had supported Britain's acquisition of new nuclear submarines, a pay freeze for public servants, reform of trade union laws and support for free trade. But in the end Murdoch wanted an ideologue as editor, someone genuinely—which is to say ideologically—in tune with the new conservative Anglo-American vision. In mid March 1982 Murdoch demanded Evans' resignation, which he eventually obtained.[34]

A LIKE-MINDED EDITOR

Rupert Murdoch's new editor was Charles Douglas-Home, an ex-soldier, military historian and long-term *Times* reporter. A man of aristocratic connections, he was also the nephew of a former Conservative prime minister. As a defence correspondent in 1968, he had been arrested by Soviet forces for reporting the presence of 25,000 troops massed on the Czech border. A few weeks later, they had helped to crush the 'Prague spring'. Douglas-Home's editorship reflected the Murdochian world view, going beyond mere support for Margaret Thatcher, since nearly all newspapers supported the Conservatives at election time.

The most distinctive stance of Murdoch's two broadsheets at the time was their support of a reflexive pro-Reagan position in foreign policy. Apart from encouraging British dependence on the United States, this position dismissed the alternative, represented by Europe. Effectively a rejection of societies with regulated economies that competed with the United States for global influence, this repudiation of Europe became a theme of Murdoch's political beliefs for the next 25 years. In Murdoch's eyes, Europe's lack of enthusiasm for the free market and its refusal to fall in line with US proposals for militant confrontation with the Soviet Union constituted the worst sin of all: anti-Americanism. The new editor of the *Times* was a Reagan enthusiast and, accompanied by Murdoch, he met the president at the White House in July 1983.

The evolution in the *Times*' position towards pro-Americanism was demonstrated in its reaction to the US invasion of Grenada three months later. Just before it occurred, Reagan phoned Thatcher to tell her his plan. Instead of support, she expressed 'very considerable doubts' and asked him to 'weigh carefully' her views before acting.[35] But Reagan invaded, deeply humiliating Thatcher both privately and publicly, and forcing her to back his action. Thatcher's initial alarm was reflected in the first *Times* editorial after the invasion, which stated bluntly that the United States had 'committed an act of aggression against Grenada'. None of the United States' reasons 'provided legal justification for an attack on an independent state'.[36] Then the paper began to vacillate. A few days later, it pleaded that US interests 'have to be more fully understood in Western Europe' and warned against 'the portrayal of President Reagan as some kind of cowboy'. Nine days after its first condemnatory editorial, the *Times* had completely reversed its stance: the Soviet Union's covert methods presented the West 'with a challenge which it has hitherto had neither the clarity of mind nor the will to tackle'; Grenada was 'the first small defenceless country to be rescued from that prison [of totalitarianism]. Its rescue should be welcomed and fully consolidated.'[37]

Murdoch and his editors framed their call for militant opposition to the Soviet Union as the only choice for conservatives, but this was deceptive. There were other perfectly reputable conservatives, some in Thatcher's cabinet, who disagreed with this binary choice of one side or the other. It was easily possible to disagree with Reagan's actions and still be a determined enemy of the Soviet Union.

On several issues in the 1980s, the *Times* showed itself to be closer to US neo-conservatism than to elements of the British conservative tradition. One of these was the difficult question of how the nuclear-armed superpowers might continue to disagree without resorting to the mutual devastation of nuclear war. The solution, invented by Richard Nixon and Henry Kissinger, was détente. This came under vigorous attack within the Reagan administration; at his first press conference in January 1981, Reagan had said that détente had been 'a one-way street that the Soviet Union has used to pursue its own aims'. Under Harold Evans, the *Times* had argued that détente 'was not the appeasement that the extreme right wing in President Reagan's party says it was'.[38] But with Douglas-Home as editor, the *Times'* attitude changed radically. The newspaper now claimed that 'we want dialogue but not *détente*'[39] and argued that the Soviet Union and the threat that it posed was immutable, unending and subtly corrosive; to believe otherwise was an illusion. Some NATO allies had lowered their guard, it said, and even disagreed 'about the severity of the threat'. Such differences were Soviet-inspired: the *Times* suggested conspiratorially. 'Soviet strategy is indirect. It attempts to foment internal divisions and to encourage doubts within Europe about American leadership.'[40] Reagan had to resist 'the dangerous illusions of the period of détente in the 1970s', and US freedom of action should not be constrained by a web of agreements with a system that was 'an evil empire indeed', said one editorial in 1984.[41] One of Douglas-Home's colleagues recalled that 'to the Reagan people and to Charlie, *détente* itself amounted to appeasement'. Like Murdoch, 'Charlie divided people into false categories. They were either soft left appeasers or tough-minded anti-communists.'[42]

During this period of heightened cold war confrontation, Reagan announced the development of the space-based anti-missile system, the Strategic Defence Initiative or 'Stars Wars'. Its critics argued that the initiative would destabilise détente, which relied on a balance between the United States and the Soviet Union guaranteed by 'mutually assured destruction' in the event of a nuclear war. Star Wars gave the United States a potential defence against Soviet missiles and hence a marked superiority. This would mean the end of détente and of arms agreements and would guarantee a new arms race. On this issue, the *Times'* stance was clear: it backed Star Wars and Reagan against any other approach, including those suggested by Thatcher's cabinet. This became strikingly clear in March 1985, when Thatcher's foreign secretary Sir Geoffrey Howe distanced himself from the Star Wars strategy. There were 'no easy answers', he said, and 'the risks might outweigh the benefits'. He urged caution.[43] The *Times* exploded with anger at Howe's moderation: he had done 'untold damage' to the alliance with the United States and had caused 'astonishment and pained reaction in the inner circle of the American administration'. The speech in which Howe had aired his views had been 'mealy mouthed, muddled in conception, negative, Luddite, ill-informed' and threatened to wreck the initiative.[44] Two days later, Reagan's neo-conservative assistant Defense secretary Richard Perle was in London for a conference of cold war warriors (a number of whom wrote regularly for the *Times*). Perle made a blistering attack on Howe, who he claimed had ignored a massive build-up of Soviet arms and was misrepresenting the initiative. For good measure, Perle added that détente was 'an experiment that failed'.[45] Afterwards, the *Times* prominently published an article by Perle based on his conference speech, in which he repeated the neo-conservatives' claim that the United States had been unilaterally reducing its arms and that the Soviets now had the 'advantage'.[46]

Perle's red-blooded approach went down well with Murdoch, who sent articles from the *Wall Street Journal*'s opinion page to his British newspaper editors. 'I used to get them on Star Wars, on Reagan, on the Cold War,' recalled Andrew Neil.[47] But, as we have seen, not all conservatives favoured the road of Reaganite confrontation. *Times* editorial writer Richard Davy attempted to reason with Douglas-Home:

> I tried to persuade him that talking to the Russians did not amount to appeasement but was simple common sense when we were engaged in a perilous nuclear confrontation. Whether you appeased them depended on what you talked about and whether you gave way on vital interests. In particular I was concerned about Eastern Europe, where *détente* clearly helped to subvert the systems. He could not see that. He was somewhat obsessed with the notion that the West was going soft on communism and being taken in by Soviet propaganda, so the main point of the leaders [editorials] in the *Times* was to stiffen the back bones of the British public by constantly exposing the evils of communism. That of course, and pleasing Murdoch who was quite frank about instructing his editors.[48]

This neo-conservative mindset made it difficult to recognise real change when it came. Like Murdoch himself, the *Times* was deeply sceptical about the new Soviet leader Mikhail Gorbachev. How could a totalitarian system produce someone with whom you could bargain—and who could even offer hope? In June 1985, the *Times* said that the Soviet leadership looked different under Gorbachev, 'but it is a difference more apparent than real'. The paper scorned 'the Western media' for reproducing stories of 'Gorbachev bonhomie' and claimed that when Gorbachev didn't get his way he tended 'to behave with all the crudeness of the bully'.[49] This was the knee-jerk reaction of ideologues who found it difficult to accept facts that didn't fit their dogma. A long time after the rest of the world, the *Times* was nevertheless forced, eventually, to abandon its belief that Gorbachev's frankness represented a cunning Soviet conspiracy.

SPONSORING COVERT POLITICS

During the 1980s, Rupert Murdoch's love of politics and intrigue led him to give financial support to extreme right-wing groups. As the 1987 election loomed and Labour mounted a reasonable campaign, a hitherto unknown group, the Committee for a Free Britain, published a series of scare advertisements in Murdoch's *Sun* and other newspapers. Worth more than £200,000, the advertisements featured photos of ordinary people, each of whom said they were 'scared' of a Labour victory. 'If you vote LABOUR they'll go on teaching my kids about GAYS & LESBIANS instead of giving them proper lessons', said one. In another, a retired British army sergeant said: 'If you vote Labour, they'll get rid of our nuclear deterrent. Then our soldiers won't have a *chance* against the Russians'.[50] The advertisements were modelled on US negative campaigning and were condemned by the Advertising Standards Authority. After the election, the Committee for a Free Britain presented a signed manifesto for Margaret Thatcher's third term and only then revealed its membership. Its chairperson was a rich conservative activist, David Hart, and one member was Lord Ralph Harris of High Cross, whom Murdoch shortly afterwards appointed to the board of Times Newspapers Holdings.

David Hart wrote articles for Murdoch's *Times* between 1983 and 1989 and was a friend of Thatcher's. He had made his reputation for activism during the 1984–85 miners' strike,[51] during which he had used his credentials as a *Times* correspondent to gain access to mining districts, politically organising dissident miners and reporting personally to Thatcher. Travelling in a chauffeur-driven Mercedes, he overcame the non-striking miners' initial suspicions 'with cash and force of personality'.[52] On this basis, he launched a legal challenge to the miners' union, which wounded it fatally. As the strike dragged on and forces within the Thatcher government began to think of a settlement, Hart's *Times* columns had urged that the miners' union be crushed ruthlessly. 'Nothing short of victory', said one column.[53]

After Thatcher's 1987 landslide victory, the Committee for a Free Britain tried to radicalise Thatcherism. It urged the replacement of the National Health Service with health insurance and called for higher defence spending.[54] Hart's *Times* column urged the Conservatives to 'transform Britain', meaning a fundamental reduction in the 'role, scope and size' of the state, including the privatisation of all state schools and the introduction of an education voucher system.[55]

Many of these ideas appealed to Murdoch, who also sponsored Hart's involvement in a more covert side of politics. Late in 1989, Labour's shadow minister for the Environment, Bryan Gould, demanded an explanation from Margaret Thatcher over her relationship with Hart, who was one of her advisers. Gould had been smeared as a communist sympathiser by a newsletter supported by Hart called *British Briefing*, which was edited by a retired MI5 officer. The existence of *British Briefing* had been kept secret until December 1989, when a copy was leaked to the *Guardian* newspaper, which showed it to Gould.[56] Its title page darkly stated that it 'will not necessarily be available on request and is not available by subscription . . . [Recipients] are asked to refrain from mentioning it, or its existence, and from direct quotation'. In an earlier edition, it was then revealed, *British Briefing* had contained a four-page attack on the Labour leader Neil Kinnock for alleged communist sympathies;

the *Guardian* said that the article was an 'exercise of tenuous logic and guilt by association'.[57]

Hart was also involved with a similar publication, *World Briefing*, which retailed classic communist conspiracies. It dismissed the changes in the Soviet Union under Mikhail Gorbachev and said they were simply strategic moves to cover for 'an increasingly comprehensive multipurpose intelligence effort in the West'.[58] Like *British Briefing*, it was published using the skills of a retired intelligence officer, in this case Herbert Meyer, a former senior CIA official.

In the same year as it revealed the existence of *British Briefing*, the *Guardian* also obtained a letter from David Hart to a major company asking for £250,000 for the 'International Freedom Research Foundation'.[59] The letter outlined the foundation's activities, which focused on training young people, holding seminars and distributing propaganda to universities and colleges. It also mentioned *British Briefing* and *World Briefing*, which was oriented to world political leaders, foreign policy and intelligence officers, academics and journalists. The combined cost was £90,000. As well as this, Hart explained, money was needed to gather information from dissidents in the Soviet Union for publication in the West, including through a press agency he intended to establish. The letter concluded that '£50,000 a year for the next five years' was needed.

The appeal had already received a warm welcome from Rupert Murdoch. In July 1988, as part of his fundraising, Hart had sent Murdoch a copy of *World Briefing*. Murdoch replied in August: 'Thank you very much for your *World Briefing* analysis, which I read with great interest. Are you sending it to any of our other editors—or should I circulate it?'[60] Shortly afterwards Murdoch began funding Hart, and in February 1989 he wrote to him: 'I have today authorised Peter Stehrenberger, our group finance director of the new arrangement—£40,000 per year for three years, in addition to the £150,000 previously agreed'.

When this funding was revealed by the *Observer* and the television program *World in Action*, Murdoch acknowledged it and said he was aware of Hart's relationship with *British Briefing* and had received copies of the newsletter. But he tried to minimise his own contribution, stating that 'any payments that were made were for consultation and research, primarily in connection with Mr Hart's activities in eastern Europe'.[61]

Murdoch's relationship with Hart was more than that of a distant patron, however, to judge from other leaked letters. Murdoch took seriously Hart's opinions on his own newspapers. In January 1989, Hart wrote to Murdoch urging him to sack Charles Wilson, the editor of the *Times*, and replace him with journalist Peter Stothard. He complained that 'under Charlie Wilson the authority of the *Times* is gravely declining and, without it, its political usefulness to the free world and so, ultimately to you'.[62] The *Times*, he said, 'should provide an up-market thoroughly argued version of the *Sun*'s bold political stand'. A month later, in a scribbled note attached to a letter, Murdoch assured Hart that 'I haven't been ignoring your other correspondence and suggestions'.[63]

Hart's activities and Murdoch's secret financial support of them suggest that Murdoch's role in British politics has been far more extensive than his biographers and even his critics have acknowledged. In a 1989 letter to Hart he spoke of beginning a '*new* arrangement', suggesting that Hart's earlier activities were funded by Murdoch. The year before Murdoch's donation, Hart had organised the visit to Britain of the Nicaraguan Contra leader Adolfo Calero. Then there were the hysterical anti-Labour advertisements published in the *Sun* before the 1987 election. Hart's support of free market causes such as privatising schools and introducing vouchers was shared by Murdoch; indeed, the *Times* gave Hart a platform for his views from 1983 to 1989.

But Murdoch's connection with David Hart is not the only suggestion that Murdoch enjoyed playing a covert role in British politics. Prior to Hart's involvement with the newsletter *British Briefing* was run by Brian Crozier, a fanatical anti-communist who has admitted he worked with the British security service and the CIA. In the 1970s and 1980s, he networked between intelligence agencies and front organisations in Washington and London. Until its exposure in 1975, he ran the CIA-funded Forum World Features, which syndicated right-wing articles to newspapers. In the late 1970s, he headed the Institute for the Study of Conflict, supported by $100,000 a year from US millionaire Dick Scaife, whom he had met through the CIA.[64] This was where *British Briefing* began its life, under the name *Background Briefing on Subversion*.

Crozier was appointed as a columnist on the *Times* and contributed for several years. His articles fitted the *Times*' outlook, supporting Ronald Reagan's nuclear plans and damning détente. Others smacked of fantasy, such as one claiming that the Soviet Union was planning to build a gas pipeline to Europe using the slave labour of 500,000 members of 'the former political elite of South Vietnam'.[65] While writing for the *Times*, Crozier was a conduit for money from the right-wing US Heritage Foundation to British groups that supported Reagan's plans for nuclear confrontation with the Soviets.[66]

Crozier's group Coalition for Peace through Security staged counter-protests to large peace demonstrations, infiltrated organising committees and hired aircraft to trail anti-peace slogans over peace events. When the leader of the Campaign for Nuclear Disarmament, Bruce Kent, visited the United States, a Coalition member went to the towns where he would speak ahead of him, telling newspapers and radio stations that Kent was a communist and that the Campaign for Nuclear Disarmament was a Soviet front. In the 1980s, Crozier built up a clandestine anti-communist organisation that had an annual budget of $1 million a year, with at least part of this coming from the CIA. Its offshoots included campaign groups in Belgium, France and Germany aimed at anti-bomb and peace groups. Money for these activities was raised from the private sector but organised by CIA director William Casey, according to Crozier.[67]

In his autobiography, Crozier strongly suggested that his clandestine activities were partly funded by Rupert Murdoch. The book is titled *Free Agent*, flaunting his work with British and US intelligence, and was published by Murdoch's firm HarperCollins. It is dedicated to Crozier's financial backers in the following terms: 'Dick (the marathon supporter), Frans, Jimmy, Rupert, Elmar, and not forgetting Alphons and Jack'. Although Crozier did not fully name his backers, a friend of his, Arnold Beichman, did.[68] Apart from Rupert Murdoch, they were right-wing financier Sir James Goldsmith (Jimmy), and the American millionaire Richard (Dick) Scaife, who has since funded many right-wing US foundations. Crozier's company Sherwood Press, a publisher of extreme right-wing books, was also connected to Murdoch. In 1987, it faced losses and an accumulated deficit of £67,000. Crozier's fellow company directors asked Murdoch to seek support, and News International, Murdoch's British holding company, took a half-stake in the firm and agreed to meet all losses and debts, which by 1990 totalled £90,000.[69]

Given Murdoch's ability to exert influence in Britain via his newspapers, his secret financing of ultra-Thatcherite activists may seem puzzling, but only if one assumes Murdoch is a normal businessman for whom politics is secondary to corporate goals. For Murdoch, politics is equally as important as business. Being a political insider and an activist is supremely important to his personality and his outlook. His financial support for Hart and Crozier is an extension rather than a negation of the ideological commitment that he insisted his newspapers have.

TO THE BITTER END

By 1990, Thatcher's revolution was at ebb tide and its leader becalmed. Margaret Thatcher had made many enemies, and her plans for new taxes had sparked riots. In November, her fellow Conservatives believed her leadership was fatally wounded and that she should resign. At that stage, Rupert Murdoch was embroiled in a profound financial crisis that nearly destroyed his media empire. In spite of this, he kept in almost daily contact with Woodrow Wyatt, giving advice and exchanging views on the 'disaster' if Thatcher lost the prime ministership. But a leadership vote was called, and in the weeks before the vote Murdoch intensely pressured *Sunday Times* editor Andrew Neil to support Thatcher editorially.[70] Neil refused, and Murdoch was furious. He asked Wyatt to explain to Thatcher that he didn't agree with the paper's stance. Thatcher forgave him and told Wyatt: '[Rupert] is wonderful. He is also a very sweet person. I am very fond of him.'[71] On the eve of the Conservatives' leadership vote, Murdoch finally whipped his editors into line. Wyatt recorded: 'Talked to Rupert who said Simon [at the *Times*] would be fine in the morning. Even *Today*, David Montgomery, would be much better and Kelvin MacKenzie [at the *Sun*] would be fine as well.'[72] It was all to no avail. After Thatcher resigned, Murdoch again rallied the *Times*, the *Sun* and *Today* to support her favoured successor, John Major, while the *Sunday Times*, though under pressure, supported Michael Heseltine.

After her forced retirement, Margaret Thatcher began to prepare her memoirs. Murdoch was deeply involved in the negotiations to buy the book and recommended right-wing intellectual John O'Sullivan to work with Thatcher on the text. Murdoch offered a substantial advance, and ultimately his company HarperCollins won the contract. When the memoirs appeared, in 1993, they contained not a single reference to Rupert Murdoch.

CHAPTER 5
ORTHODOXY IN THE BLOOD

The greatest compliment that was ever paid to me was by Ian McGregor, the Chairman of British Steel, who said: 'There are only two radicals in this country—Margaret Thatcher and Rupert Murdoch'.[1]

Rupert Murdoch, 1990

It is a sorry fact that the media as a whole ... unquestioningly embrace a welfare state which divides and embitters our society without helping the truly poor and needy.[2]

Rupert Murdoch, 1992

In 1992, the *Sunday Times* began an extraordinary series of articles that shocked Britain over the three years during which they were published. It wasn't the first time that the newspaper had carried out pioneering investigative journalism: it had already built an enviable reputation for exposing the negligence of a drug company that produced thalidomide, a drug taken by pregnant mothers that produced birth deformities. When the drug company later resisted paying compensation to the victims, the newspaper campaigned on their behalf. It had exposed a cover up of Russian spy Kim Philby's infiltration of the highest levels of the British establishment. Under the newspaper's legendary editor, Harold Evans, it had produced hundreds of campaigning stories that questioned, criticised and exposed injustice and stood up for the rights of ordinary Britons. On a more prosaic note, the *Sunday Times* was a profitable newspaper bulging with ads. That's why Rupert Murdoch had bought it in 1981.

At first glance, the revelations published between 1992 and 1994 seemed to continue this awesome tradition. For some time, the newspaper had been interested in the health response to the then fatal condition of Acquired Immune Deficiency Syndrome (AIDS). In March 1990, it had serialised the book *The Myth of Heterosexual AIDS* by American conservative Michael Fumento, which argued that AIDS was not spreading into the heterosexual community and that homosexual lobby groups had shifted public attention away from high-risk groups and had spread a myth that all people were equally vulnerable. The newspaper later argued that Fumento had been a victim of 'political correctness', because no British publisher would bring out his book. Fumento was a victim of the 'AIDS establishment'.[3]

The *Sunday Times* then decided to challenge what it saw as an 'orthodoxy' about the disease. Its campaign cast doubt on the widely accepted scientific research that was key to understanding and controlling the disease, beginning with a long, in-depth article in early 1992 claiming that, after billions of dollars had been spent on research and years of 'safe sex' campaigns, 'a growing number of senior scientists are challenging the idea that the human immunodeficiency virus (HIV) causes AIDS'.[4] Moreover, it said, some sceptics argued 'that the virus is not new, that it is not normally sexually transmitted, and that it is almost certainly harmless'. It noted that 'few British voices have *dared question* the HIV hypothesis' [emphasis added]. It was strong stuff written in the best tradition of the shattering exposé. But there were not many genuinely 'senior scientists' involved although it mentioned one dissident, the molecular biologist Professor Peter Duesberg. If the critics were right, the article said, 'the HIV-AIDS link would be seen as the biggest medical and scientific blunder this century'. There proved to be a blunder indeed but of a different type.

While the *Sunday Times* was Rupert Murdoch's leading platform for AIDS scepticism, his other papers also contributed. The *Sun* suggested that only junkies, gays, bisexuals and victims of tainted blood transfusions could contract AIDS. 'Anything else is homosexual propaganda', it claimed in 1989.[5] Later, it said that the 'most important message we should be teaching our kids is that sodomy kills'.[6] The *Times* was more lofty and less brutal: one editorial questioned the amount of funding going to AIDS research and repeated the *Sunday Times'* suggestion that the HIV–AIDS link might be the 'biggest blunder' in modern medical history.[7] It also described the reaction to Duesberg as 'hysterical' and compared him to Galileo facing the Inquisition. After a few more stories reporting sceptics' claims, the *Times* dropped the issue. The *Sunday Times*, however, did not.

As with another major issue of science later taken up by News Corporation—climate change—AIDS scepticism demanded that the science completely and immediately explain all aspects of the phenomenon. It seized on acknowledged anomalies in the data, citing them as proof that the overall hypothesis was wrong. The sceptics insisted that the mechanism by which HIV precipitated AIDS be exactly known but, while scientists were sure of the HIV–AIDS link, they were not certain how precisely HIV led to AIDS. Dissenting claims were denied by researchers, who pointed to the overwhelming scientific consensus that HIV was invariably associated with AIDS. But, again, as with climate change, this simply reinforced the sceptics' belief that an establishment was at work, defending itself and its elitist orthodoxy.

During 1992 and 1993, many articles appeared in the *Sunday Times* highlighting claims that the rapid spread of AIDS in Africa was not in fact occurring, that the widely used drug AZT was damaging and that tests for HIV were 'scientifically invalid'.[8] Reports mentioning the World Health Organization, which was leading the effort to combat the disease, often noted that the organisation was seeking funding, suggesting a self-serving motive. 'Empire-building AIDS organisations' were another problem because they too wanted government funding. Global pharmaceutical companies supported the HIV theory because they made vast profits from it. 'Medical ignorance and uncertainty' surrounded the whole issue, claimed the newspaper.[9] In October 1993, the newspaper's science correspondent Neville Hodgkinson, responsible for much of the coverage, wrote a long feature titled 'The plague that never was'. It cited a French couple in Africa who had once believed that AIDS was devastating parts of the continent but later concluded that 'there is no AIDS. It is something that has been invented.'[10] Towards the end of the year, the newspaper accused the BBC and 'almost all medical and scientific journals' of applying 'a kind of self-imposed censorship on the issue'. It modestly compared its coverage of AIDS to its own exposure in the late 1960s of thalidomide as a dangerous drug.[11]

The *Sunday Times*' stance alarmed many in the scientific and medical community. The eminent science journal *Nature* was deeply concerned at suggestions that the threat to the hetero-sexual community was minimal. 'The subliminal message of these newspapers is that "normal" people (*Sunday Times* readers?) don't get AIDS', said one *Nature* article.[12] Indeed, by the end of 1993, the *Sunday Times*' campaign had so alarmed *Nature* that it undertook to monitor the newspaper each week and to publish letters that were refused publication in it. *Nature* explained its own refusal to publish a letter signed by many AIDS 'sceptics' in terms of the theory of scientific knowledge: 'The error is essentially epistemological. At its lowest, it is based on the supposition that the "true" hypothesis can be decided by some kind of democratic process in which people vote their beliefs.'[13] The *Sunday Times* reacted to being monitored by *Nature* by publishing an outraged 3000-word article, 'AIDS—why we won't be silenced', which portrayed the paper as the heroic victim of 'extraordinary attacks' and accused the journal of 'sinister intent' and censorship and the science establishment of not being concerned with the truth.[14] The campaign continued for the first half of 1994, with the *Sunday Times* attacking what it called a 'conspiracy of silence' and claiming to have made the 'discovery' that the AIDS test was 'scientifically invalid'.[15]

In his autobiography, *Sunday Times* editor Andrew Neil pleaded that the newspaper simply wanted to publish all views and 'to encourage debate'. But this understates the paper's enthusiasm for the issue and the way in which it campaigned against AIDS 'orthodoxy' and the 'medical establishment' as well as how all this fitted a wider world view, both within the newspaper and within News Corporation. The approach mimicked some versions of postmodern theory, assuming that scientific knowledge is simply a discourse that can be accepted or rejected without regard to the facts and that the dismissal of views not based on fact amounts to 'censorship' and 'suppression'. Again, the parallels with the contemporary issue of climate change are many.

TRANSFORMING THE *SUNDAY TIMES*

Rupert Murdoch bought the influential *Sunday Times* in 1981 and initially left it alone while he focused on reinvigorating the *Times*. By 1983, however, he was looking for a new editor for the Sunday paper. Andrew Neil was recommended to Murdoch by his political adviser Irwin Stelzer. Neil was the UK editor of the *Economist* and had recently finished a stint in the United States, where he 'revelled in its dynamic, can-do culture, the ease with which new technology was introduced and exploited and the free and fast social mobility between classes'.[16] Neil was an unorthodox appointment, since he had no experience in newspapers. Clearly, the personal and political simpatico between him and Murdoch was his main qualification. When Murdoch asked Neil what he thought of the *Sunday Times*, Neil said that 'intellectually, it was stuck in a sixties time-warp' and that it needed to 'shake off its collectivist mind-set to become the champion of a market-led revolution that would shake the British establishment to its bones and transform the economy and society'.[17] Even allowing for the gloss of hindsight in a memoir, this is the role Neil chose and largely fulfilled during his editorship.

Neil was very close to Murdoch through most of his eleven years in the corporation—a corporation in which one editor lasted only 24 hours—spending several Christmases with the Murdoch family at Aspen. In Neil's estimation, Murdoch 'is much more right-wing than is generally thought but will curb his ideology for commercial reasons'. Murdoch's actual political beliefs, Neil said, are 'a combination of right-wing Republicanism from America mixed with undiluted Thatcherism from Britain and stirred with some anti-British Establishment sentiments as befits his colonial heritage'.[18]

During his editorship Neil was subjected to regular sniping, sometimes because he was a Scot and not an Englishman. At first his critics came from the political Left, which believed he had betrayed the ideals of the *Sunday Times*. Several articles in the national press pointedly mentioned his early work for the Conservative Party Research Office. To the *Guardian* Neil said 'he was not a Conservative but a radical'.[19] Interviewed by the *Sunday Times* itself, Neil said the paper was 'the most important forum for political ideas in Britain'. His focus on renewal, radicalism and political ideas (rather than news or investigations) signalled a self-consciously ideological editor. When he arrived, he said, he found 'no ideological soulmates' among the senior staff; the newspaper 'was in a state of ideological decay' because of a 'liberal-left collectivist consensus'. The paper's journalists he regarded as 'the Lost Tribe of the sixties, wandering aimlessly in the alien environment of the eighties'.[20] Later in his tenure, and more significantly, Neil's critics came from the Right, which disliked his sexual libertarianism, his populism and his lack of respect for the monarchy. In 1989, the conservative columnist Peregrine Worsthorne told his readers at the *Sunday Telegraph* that Neil was unfit to be the editor of a major newspaper, after it was revealed that Neil's girlfriend was (unknown to him) a callgirl. In 1992, after the *Sunday Times* serialised a book on the marital problems of the Prince and Princess of Wales, Worsthorne called Neil and Murdoch 'moral dwarves'.[21]

Neil's vision was to re-create the *Sunday Times* as a campaigning newspaper, with a wholly new ideological direction. In this, Neil's friend Irwin Stelzer was crucial. Stelzer not only produced a column in economic commentary; he was occasionally invited to sit in on editorial conferences of the senior staff. A journalist recalled that on one occasion, as the conference discussed a list of story ideas,

> [Stelzer] asked four or five times 'What's our line on this?' After the fourth or fifth time, I responded that we did not have a 'line'—and that the item was a potential news story or topic for a feature.[22]

Under Neil, the paper did have a political line. It supported the Conservative government during the bitter conflicts with the coal miners between 1984 and 1985 and the lockout of the Fleet Street print unions from Wapping in 1985 and 1986 and strongly backed the re-election of that government in elections in 1983, 1987 and 1992. Yet its relationship with Margaret Thatcher and her successor, John Major, was not untroubled. In 1984, the newspaper deeply angered Thatcher by exposing her son's business dealings. Later, it revealed that the Queen was distressed at the Thatcher government's social policies. Other conflicts followed when Thatcher's popularity waned, and finally the newspaper called for her to resign. Other Tory newspapers supported the Thatcher government, but the *Sunday Times* was distinguished by its deeper commitment to the ideological beliefs that underpinned Thatcherism.

INSIGHT AND IDEOLOGY

Andrew Neil's ideological views were apparent in his handling of the group that, on his arrival, epitomised the *Sunday Times'* particular brand of journalism, the Insight team: a key part of the paper's investigative reputation built on the thalidomide and Philby stories. Neil disbanded the team on political grounds.

> There was a group [of staff] who thought they owned the paper. They were bitter when they realized cosy collectivism was out. They were responsible, in my personal view, for a hard-left newspaper which they hid under the *Sunday Times* label, particularly within Insight.[23]

When the Insight team was later reconstituted, its articles were often inflected with Neil's preoccupation with economic liberalism. One of the earliest stories of the new team was the London Economic Summit in 1984, which Margaret Thatcher, Ronald Reagan and other world leaders attended. The resulting article explored in painful detail how the final communiqué of this soon-to-be-forgotten summit was drafted, discussed and decided.[24]

Neil's notion of investigative journalism was odd. In his autobiography, *Full Disclosure*, a chapter on the *Sunday Times'* achievements in this area begins with a lively recounting of a significant scoop: publication of extracts of the book *Spycatcher*, the memoirs of former security officer Peter Wright. But this was not investigative journalism; it was book serialisation.

Insight continued to publish valuable stories, including exposure of British arms dealing with Iraq, the French bombing of Greenpeace's ship the *Rainbow Warrior*, Israel's secret nuclear bomb plant, and shady political donations, especially to the Tories. But frequently, a different agenda was at work. Many investigative campaigns simply reflected Neil's ideological views and his free market populism. Anticompetitive business practices became key targets for Insight. One story concerned industrial espionage by a big car-parking firm against an upstart rival. Insight also exposed anti-competitive practices by British Airways against the smaller Virgin Airlines.[25] Other stories involved bank oligopolies refusing to pass on interest rate cuts to home borrowers and similar practices by supermarket monopolies.[26]

In many Insight articles, the free market values of choice and competition were assumed to be the solution to all problems. A major investigation in January 1988 described the National Health Service as 'a massive state-funded monopoly unaffected by the disciplines of the marketplace'.[27] Fixing the service's problems required 'more competition between parts of the health service to ensure the most efficient allocation of resources'. Government subsidies also became targets. In late 1991, Insight highlighted farm subsidies being paid to wealthy and aristocratic British land owners for leaving land fallow, part of European Economic Community (EEC) incentives to take land out of production.[28] A year later, Insight 'exposed' subsidies by the EEC for regional industrial development in Spain, Crete and Portugal, a scheme denounced by a former Thatcher adviser as 'daylight robbery'.[29] A further investigation probed the European Commission's subsidies to Greek farmers to grow tobacco that was then dumped in the Third World. While the story criticised cigarette companies—a typical target of the old Insight—its main complaint was against 'fat payments from Brussels' to the farmers. At an editorial conference at which this story was discussed, Neil urged the reporters to find out how much the European Commission spent on anti-smoking propaganda, thus highlighting their hypocrisy.[30] Such stories therefore hit two ideological marks: Europe and protectionism.

Insight's path in these years fulfilled an early pledge by Neil to create a new and distinctive discourse.

> Our paper is radical and anti-establishment. What that means in practice is that on microeconomic policy—we're in favour of competition, trust-busting, deregulation, privatization—we're on the radical right. On macroeconomic policy . . . we take a view that is much closer to [Social Democrats leader] David Owen's.[31]

Conservative politics was defined as advocacy for change rather than support for tradition, and 'radical' became a word of praise. Neil conceived of himself as an iconoclast, a rebel and a contrarian, a self-image shared by his boss. Later, Neil said: 'I was urging a market revolution more complete than even Margaret Thatcher was contemplating.'[32]

Neil was aware of the reputation of Insight and the enormous credit it gave the *Sunday Times*. But, despite his efforts, people continued to cite the old Insight, not the new version. In 1991, he expressed his bitterness about this. 'It is a pity that the old guard cannot bring themselves to credit that achievement. Why we have not been forgiven is that *we turned a lot of the techniques they used against their establishment.*'[33] [emphasis added]

OVERTHROWING THE ESTABLISHMENT

'Establishment' was a key term in the new political vocabulary that the *Sunday Times* promoted in the 1980s and 1990s. In his memoir, Andrew Neil pictured himself 'locked in hand-to-hand combat with various parts of the Establishment'.[34] Normally, the term 'establishment' loosely referred to the British ruling classes. But the establishment portrayed by Andrew Neil and Rupert Murdoch in the *Sunday Times* referred to two ideological foes. The first opposed neo-liberal economic policies: revolutions overthrew establishments, and thus any group which opposed the formula of free markets, deregulation and privatisation thereby defined itself as an 'establishment'. For example, in an editorial on television policy, Neil attacked 'the broadcasting establishment' that defended the regulation of Britain's television. In 1989, when the Tory Health minister was criticised by the British Medical Association, Neil denounced 'the medical establishment for whose benefit the NHS was run'.[35]

The second foe was the intellectual 'elite'. In Neil's writing, this elite was signalled by terms such as 'the intelligentsia' and 'the chattering classes' and was often described as 'politically correct'. An editorial in 1988 argued that, although the British economy was prospering, the 'British establishment' had 'scorned and dismissed' this news.

By contrast, the editorial exalted 'the plain folk of the country' who had bought council houses or shares in privatised companies and who knew the economy was no longer in decline. Such people were wiser than 'the fashionable opinion-formers and influence-peddlers who make up Establishment opinion'.[36] This portrayal of sensible ordinary people struggling under the weight of oppressive elites was enticing. Like all caricatures, it contained an element of truth. As former deputy editor of the *Sunday Times* Hugo Young argued, the old *Sunday Times* 'saw the citizen as a victim of fraud, poverty, secrecy, business ruthlessness, inferior schooling, racial prejudice or straight-forward political power'. Murdoch's *Sunday Times* replaced this with the citizen as a consumer 'bedevilled by antiquated suppliers, fuddy duddy civil servants and restrictive government practices, all conspiring to run away from the future'.[37]

Left-liberal intellectuals and artists particularly infuriated the *Sunday Times*, which attacked recent British films and novels that had portrayed Thatcherite Britain in negative terms. Neil argued:

> [Britain's intelligentsia] has become increasingly divorced from the land it lives on. It hates everything the Thatcher government stands for; but it realizes that the nation is not listening. So it has retreated to its own left wing laager, where erudite moaning is taken for wise critique. There was a time when the intellectual left was concerned with devising practical policies to improve the lot of the Common Man. But today's intelligentsia cares not a jot that more and more ordinary people are able to own the houses they live in . . .[38]

On the subject of foreign investment, the *Sunday Times* argued that 'ordinary consumers have never shown the distrust for "evil" multinationals that has been prevalent among the chattering classes. And in that plain folk are right and the intellectual betters are wrong.'[39]

Income tax was a key symbolic and economic issue for the *Sunday Times*, which saw Reagan-style tax cuts as an ideal model. In a submission to the treasurer in 1988, the paper suggested that ultimately there should be a single flat tax rate.[40] That the *Sunday*

Times made such a submission shows how much Neil saw it as an independent political force in the country. A flat tax would bring practical benefits to many *Sunday Times* readers but also symbolised the neo-liberal campaign for small government. What better way to shrink the size of government than by cutting off the transfusion of tax pounds? When the 1988 budget cut the top rate of income from 60 to 40 per cent, the *Sunday Times* congratulated itself: 'For some time now the *Sunday Times* has been virtually a lone voice in championing the case for a top income tax rate of 40 percent. We have harried and badgered the Chancellor at every opportunity.' Responding to the *Financial Times* and the *Guardian*, which had criticised the tax cuts as unfair, Neil said that the centre left had 'stopped thinking; it reacts from the gut. It has stopped doing the necessary research to keep it well informed ... it is Britain's new "stupid party", a political stigma we used to reserve for the old Tory party.'[41] Again, there was the self-declared stance of the contrarian and iconoclast. The newspaper's tax-cutting zeal, he argued, 'flew in the face of the centre-left consensus which still regarded high taxes as a virility symbol of its belief in "justice" and "fairness" '.

Another campaign by Neil concerned Britain's closer integration with Europe. Once in favour of this, by 1991 the *Sunday Times* had begun to believe that Britain had to choose between the United States and Europe and the different models of society represented by them. The choice had suddenly become stark because of the collapse of the Soviet Union, the common enemy of Europe and the United States. Rejection of Europe later became a cardinal belief of Rupert Murdoch; in the 1990s it was a touchstone of Murdoch's attitude towards New Labour under Tony Blair. The *Sunday Times'* radical shift was marked by editorials in which Neil began to attack 'the consensus of the political establishment, on the left and right', which supported 'a social market economy in the European mould ... with market forces and government control in rough equality, a capitalist society tempered by a strong streak of collectivism'.[42] The *Sunday Times* stood for 'a radical alternative', starting from a recognition 'that the traditional European mixed economy is in deep trouble. European industry is reeling under the costs of overvalued currencies, expensive labour, inflexible work practices and too much government regulation.'

In its early years, the Thatcher government had considered changing Britain's education system by using educational vouchers, an idea proposed by the neo-liberal economist Milton Friedman. With such vouchers, parents would control the funding of schools and, it was argued, their market-like decisions would drive up the quality of education. But the plan was abandoned as impractical. Then, in the 1990s, opposition to government regulation began to extend beyond the strictly economic to social and cultural questions, such as education. Early in the decade the *Sunday Times* revived Thatcher's views, arguing that

> the idea of an internal market in education, with schools competing for pupils and their funding depending on the numbers they attract, is little understood and misrepresented . . . Those schools that build up strong reputations will prosper and grow; those with records that repel parents will wither and die, their pupils being distributed to better schools.[43]

This has continued to be one of Rupert Murdoch's main causes. While the ideological campaign for free market schooling took some time to develop, a more ambitious and dramatic campaign by the *Sunday Times* involved an attack on the British welfare state.

THE UNDERCLASS: A MONSTER IN OUR MIDST

Toward the end of the 1980s, the Thatcher revolution was beginning to run out of steam. Thatcher herself was losing popularity, and in spite of an initial spurt that accompanied deregulation, the economy slowed into a recession. Until then Neil's *Sunday Times* saw itself engaged in a struggle against a powerful economic orthodoxy that supported regulation and state ownership. But after ten years of Thatcher, what was once radical had hardened into an orthodoxy of its own. Yet, the instinct to combat orthodoxy persisted and Neil soon found new politically correct giants to slay. This time the target—the British welfare state—paralleled attacks by the early US neo-conservatives, who were dismayed at the social policies of the Johnson administration in the 1960s. The central figure in the crusade was the conservative American political scientist Charles Murray, a deeply ideological researcher based at the conservative think tank the American Enterprise Institute. He first published his ideas on welfare in 1982, in Irving Kristol's magazine *Public Interest*. They re-emerged in 1984 in his controversial and influential book *Losing Ground*, which argued that the social policies of the 1960s on unemployment, poverty, discrimination and one-parent families had worsened the problems they had been designed to ameliorate. In the 1980s, *Losing Ground* set a political and policy agenda for Ronald Reagan's administration. In the weeks following its publication, the *Washington Post* devoted three editorials to discussing its ideas. In 1985, Murray was considered by Reagan as a possible assistant secretary in the Health and Human Services administration.[44]

Andrew Neil had read Murray's book and had been impressed by 'the clarity of his thoughts on welfare dependency'.[45] Through Irwin Stelzer, Neil invited Murray to Britain in 1989. Stelzer was 'the godfather', Murray later told the *New York Times*.[46] Murray did a whirlwind study to explore whether Britain was also developing what he called an 'underclass'. In May, Murray twice met John Moore, the secretary of state for Social Security. In November, the *Sunday Times Magazine* published a long essay by Murray proclaiming the imminent arrival of an underclass in Britain. Murray defined this underclass as a 'population of working-aged, healthy people who live in a different world to other Britons . . . whose values are con-taminating the life of entire neighborhoods'.[47] Such people could be recognised by their tendencies to have children outside marriage, commit crimes and refuse to join the work force. Illegitimacy, a deliberately chosen term, was of particular concern, because the absence of fathers in families meant that the resulting families were less able to convey social and civic norms that prevented crime and encouraged work. These issues never emerged in public discussion, complained Murray, for a reason that was by now familiar to *Sunday Times* readers. What he described as 'the intellectual conventional wisdom' failed to recognise the symptoms. The Left and intellectuals refused to acknowledge that crime was a problem, he said, and assumed that the defeat of Margaret Thatcher's government would solve social issues. As for solutions, Murray could offer only the free market mantra that the government should get out of the way.

In an editorial, Neil welcomed Murray's 'study' and described how the underclass had been 'cut adrift from society and has no intention of rejoining it, no matter how generous the welfare state . . . it is characterized by drugs, casual violence, petty crime, illegitimate children, homelessness, work avoidance and contempt for conventional values'. He concluded that 'a monster is being created in our midst and public policy has no desire to confront it'.[48] Over the next few years the *Sunday Times* continued to refer to Murray's views, linking them to failure by schools to teach literacy and inculcate discipline, the spread of 'yob culture' and the squalor of 'sink' housing estates.[49]

Murray's *Sunday Times* article set off a major public debate in which the populist habit of blaming intellectuals was picked up. The 'poverty industry' was dominated by intellectuals who had 'stubbornly refused to recognize the extent of and damage done by increasing crime and soaring bastardry, *damage obvious to ordinary people*'[50] (emphasis added). Once again, this was framed as contrarian wisdom that rebelled against the restrictions of orthodox thinking.

The campaign by Murray and Neil against the welfare state accorded with the views of Rupert Murdoch, who told a business meeting at the time that 'it is a sorry fact that the media as a whole … unquestioningly embrace a welfare state which divides and embitters our society without helping the truly poor and needy'.[51] In fact, for Murdoch, the campaign probably did not go far enough. Neil recalled saying to Murdoch that, in spite of radical reform, there still had to be a safety net for everybody. Murdoch responded: 'Yeah, yeah maybe, but it should be very low'.[52] Later, Murdoch arranged for Murray to address one of his regular global meetings of news executives in Aspen.

In the early 1990s, when riots broke out in Britain's inner cities, the *Sunday Times* frequently endorsed Murray's analysis in editorials and published further articles espousing his views.[53] Murray also began to spell out the hair-raising implications of his opinions. In a 1993 *Sunday Times* article that he saw as 'defying the intellectual conventional wisdom', he advocated stopping all government finance for single mothers, legal penalties to promote marriage, the revival of child adoption and the establishment of 'well-equipped, carefully staffed orphanages' to deal with children whose mothers were unable to financially support them.[54] The Institute of Economic Affairs then ran a public campaign to revive adoption, which an 'IEA insider' described as 'the ultimate privatization, taking children out of care and the hands of the state'.[55] In the United States, Donna Shalala, the Democrat secretary of Health, compared Murray's ideas to Jonathan Swift's 'modest proposal' that the Irish eat their children in order to end starvation.[56]

MURDOCH'S THINK TANK

The visits by Charles Murray to Britain and the publicity for his views reflected an ideological alliance that developed in the 1990s between the *Sunday Times* and the free market think tank the Institute of Economic Affairs (IEA). Set up in the 1950s, the IEA originally represented a tiny minority strand of economic thought usually defined as 'economic liberalism'. Its central belief was in the overwhelming superiority of economic markets, and its chief ideologue was the Austrian economist and philosopher Friedrich Hayek. In the years immediately before Margaret Thatcher's election in 1979, the influence of the IEA grew as traditional economic levers began to fail. The IEA was crucial to Thatcher, who said that her government could never have achieved what it did without the institute's leadership.[57] Under Andrew Neil, the *Sunday Times* regularly publicised the IEA's activities and its polemical pamphlets.

When Charles Murray arrived in Britain he first addressed an IEA conference, blaming the breakdown of the family for football hooliganism. Welfare agencies also contributed to social breakdown and disorder, he said.[58] His first *Sunday Times* article was immediately reprinted as an IEA pamphlet, in the introduction to which the institute's David Green called for a return to stigmatisation of the poor, who he claimed were responsible for their situation.[59] Subsequent articles by Murray were also reprinted in pamphlet form, published jointly by the IEA and the *Sunday Times*, a remarkably public identification by a newspaper of its ideological stance. In addition, in 1993, Andrew Neil was the keynote speaker at the IEA's annual conference; and in the 1994 pamphlet *Underclass: the crisis deepens*, the *Sunday Times*' crest was prominent on the cover, and the newspaper sponsored a forum in London with the IEA that 1000 people attended.

This was more than Neil simply indulging his favourite right-wing think tank, however. The intellectual affinity and political alliance between the IEA and the *Sunday Times* continued for some years *after* Neil resigned, in 1994. In 1996, the IEA and the *Sunday Times* published *Charles Murray and the Underclass: the developing debate*, and other pamphlets with joint sponsorship continued to be published, such as *Does Prison Work?* in 1998. The connection was between the IEA and Rupert Murdoch.

Between 1988 and 2001, the founder and long-time director of the IEA, Lord Ralph Harris of High Cross, was an independent director of Times Newspapers Holdings, owned by Murdoch. The intellectual firepower of the IEA was also enrolled in Murdoch's campaign to expand into television: in 1990, Dr Cento Veljanovski, research and editorial director of the IEA, wrote *The Media in Britain Today*, which argued that the ownership of satellite television channels by an existing newspaper owner posed no threat to media diversity or competition. The author said he had a free brief to write the book and denied being influenced by News International, which published it.[60] A year later, Veljanovski denounced a leading academic who had argued that Murdoch's ownership of BSkyB added to 'the extraordinary concentration of UK media power in the hands of Rupert Murdoch'. According to Veljanovski, the United Kingdom had the most competitive national newspaper market in the world, and the academic had confused 'monopoly with success in business'.[61] The alliance between the IEA and News International, a major news media corporation, was remarkable, as it involved newspapers and television outlets being used as vehicles to publicise the think tank's political and intellectual agenda.

PRIVATISING THE BROADCASTING ESTABLISHMENT

The most engaging aspect of Rupert Murdoch's ideological stance is how he manages to combine the sincerity with which he propounds it, its appeal to the liberating values of freedom and the way in which it benefits Murdoch in terms of profit. In 1989, in a speech written with the help of Andrew Neil and Irwin Stelzer, Murdoch achieved this combination in a provocative call to overturn television broadcasting policy in Britain. Murdoch had been asked to give the prestigious MacTaggart Lecture at the Edinburgh International Television Festival. He opened his speech by paying tribute to Edinburgh's famous son Adam Smith, the eighteenth-century philosopher of free markets, and went on to argue that British broadcasting needed a radical market-based reformation to allow real choice. For too long, a broadcasting establishment had dominated British television and had operated on the assumption that the people could not be trusted to watch what they wanted to watch: television had to be controlled by those who knew what was good for them. 'The fact that those who control British TV have always worked in a non-market environment, protected by public subsidy and state privilege, is a major reason why they are innately unsympathetic to markets and competition,' he said. Britain's claim to produce some of the world's best television was weak, while US television had been 'disgracefully misrepresented by propagandists in this country'. Murdoch homed in on the key argument of those who favoured Britain's public broadcaster, the BBC, that quality would suffer in a deregulated, US-style multi-channel environment:

> Much of what passes for quality on British television really is no more than a reflection of the values of the narrow elite which controls it and which has always thought that its tastes are synonymous with quality . . . But this public service TV system has had debilitating effects on British society by producing TV output which is so often obsessed with class, dominated by anti-commercial attitudes and with a tendency to hark back to the past.

He decried up-market soap operas 'in which strangulated English accents dominate dramas which are played out in rigid, class-structured settings'. Several times, he attacked the notion of public interest:

> I have never heard of a convincing definition of what public service television really is, and I am suspicious of elites, including the British broadcasting elite, which argue for special privileges and favours because they are supposed to be in the public interest as a whole.[62]

Many dismissed the lecture as a blustering demand for Murdoch's company to be allowed to buy into terrestrial television. Six months earlier, Murdoch had launched the four satellite channels of Sky

Television. The barely disguised target of the speech was the BBC, which stood in the way of the privatised broadcasting system that Murdoch desired.

POPULIST CHAMPIONS

When Margaret Thatcher finally resigned, in 1990, Andrew Neil made the political position of the *Sunday Times* plain:

> On many of the big struggles *The Sunday Times* has stood shoulder to shoulder with her: the decision to go to war over the Falklands, the need for outright victory in the miners' strike (when others counseled compromise), the deployment of cruise missiles, the American raid on Tripoli launched from British bases . . . the privatization programme, the drastic cuts in marginal tax rates and a host of other steps taken to give Britain a competitive market economy on these and more, Mrs Thatcher's battles were our battles.

Yet the paper's ideology was deeper, more complex, than this. Under Neil, it promoted a political discourse best described as 'market populism' that has resonated ever since. It champions economic markets as the friend of ordinary people and damns critics of those markets as representatives of the self-interest of establishments and elites. It amounted to the view expressed by US writer Thomas Frank that 'markets expressed the popular will more articulately and more meaningfully than did mere elections'. Markets confer legitimacy.[63]

Sometimes assumed to be simply 'Thatcherism', these ideas emerged from the American Right, in which populism was part of a resurgence of republicanism after Richard Nixon.[64] Striking similarities existed between the political language used in the *Sunday Times* and that employed by the influential Republican ideologue Richard Viguerie in his 1983 book *The Establishment vs. The People*, which framed left-wing causes as those of an establishment elite that favoured high taxes and opposed the market.[65] The *Sunday Times'* discourse also echoed the language of another group of the Reaganite Right, the neo-conservatives, who constructed their political stance by attributing much of what was wrong with the United States to the emergence of the 'New Class', a vague yet contemptuous description of intellectuals whose policies they intensely disliked.[66] The New Class supported the welfare policies of the Johnson era and opposed the Vietnam war; they also adopted liberal political stances in the name of 'the people' or the public interest but were really interested only in promoting their own power: 'elitism disguised as social concern'.[67] In carrying out an ideological position in the *Sunday Times*, Andrew Neil and Rupert Murdoch clearly drank from the same neo-conservative stream.

CHAPTER 6
OUTFOXING THE LIBERALS

I don't know whether it happened with my friend Ted [Turner] marrying Jane Fonda or giving up lithium, but one thing or another [CNN] has changed very greatly in the last couple of years . . . [CNN has moved] further and further and further to the left . . . We think it is about time CNN is challenged.[1]

Rupert Murdoch, 1995

There is no 'after the Cold War' for me. So far from having ended, my cold war has increased in intensity, as sector after sector of American life has been ruthlessly corrupted by the liberal ethos . . . We have, I do believe reached a turning point in American democracy. Now that the other Cold War is over, the real cold war has begun.[2]

Irving Kristol, 1993

In June 1992, some of the United States' leading conservative intellectuals were taking part in a discussion panel at a conference centre in Aspen. As the speaker, a top television executive, addressed the audience, a handsome man walked onto the stage next to him and slowly began to remove his shirt, his pants and his underclothes until he was naked. Prominent Republican Lynne Cheney, who was moderating the panel, was stunned. Sitting in the audience was her husband, Dick Cheney, then Defense Secretary in the Bush administration, who was equally shocked. Some in the audience laughed nervously. Rupert Murdoch, sitting with his wife Anna close to the stripper, did not.

The discussion was part of an editorial conference held by News Corporation. Present were dozens of Murdoch's editors and television news directors, officials from 20th Century Fox, former adviser to Margaret Thatcher Sir Charles Powell, Australian ambassador to the United States Michael Cook, and free market futurist George Gilder. The speaker was the brash president of Murdoch's Fox Television, 36-year-old Steve Chao, a wunderkind responsible for some of Fox's blazing successes such as *Cops*, *America's Most Wanted* and the raunchy *Studs*. The stripper, arranged by Chao, was a conference centre staffer. Chao had been the author of many daring, sometimes shocking, innovations during his career. He had earned an MBA from Harvard, had worked for two years on the tabloid *National Inquirer* (for which he once visited Latin America on the trail of UFO sightings) and had reached the top in Fox Television in nine years. Much of the success of the network rode on his own success. That day in Aspen, Murdoch sacked him.

Some commentators pointed out the hypocrisy of dismissing Chao, seeing as News Corporation's *Sun* newspaper had been displaying photos of naked women for many years. Closer to home, Murdoch's free-to-air Fox Telvision had competed with the established networks CBS, NBC and ABC by using a mix of sexual titillation, violence and confronting drama. Conservative rumblings about the Fox network had already been audible. This contradiction had in fact been the subject of the panel discussion that the stripper had so stunningly disrupted. The Fox network's profitable business success was built on a libertarian cultural approach that broadcast programs showing sex and violence. But if you supported the libertarian economics of free markets, how could you censor popular culture? There was food for thought here, according to the man responsible for the intellectual agenda of the conference, Irwin Stelzer, a fellow of the American Enterprise Institute and a Murdoch adviser. He had expressed the dilemma in the title of the panel discussion: 'The threat to democratic capitalism posed by modern culture'.

The speakers on the panel made up a rollcall of ideological influences in and around News Corporation in the 1990s. One panel member was Michael Medved, the author of *Hollywood vs. America*, which charged Hollywood liberals with systematically and deliberately changing the United States' moral values. Also present was John O'Sullivan, formerly of the *New York Post* and at the time editor of *National Review*, the country's leading conservative magazine, and Irving Kristol, the 'godfather' of neo-conservatism and editor of *Public Interest*. Kristol argued that censorship was acceptable since it usually reflected the prevailing public morals. Popular culture on television had usurped parents' roles in values formation with their children. Medved agreed and pointed out that movies and television were influential; otherwise, why would corporations invest millions in advertising? But market success could not justify the emphasis on violence, he said, since R-rated movies did less well at the box office than PG movies. Medved implied that the values of the Hollywood entertainment elite were to blame for the spate of R-rated movies. Chao then argued against censorship, pointing out that actual violence was more obscene than nudity and sex; that was the point of the stripper. No powerful liberal entertainment elite dictated the content of television, he said.[3]

MURDOCH'S CULTURE WAR

The Aspen conference took place at a time when politics throughout the world was in flux. The Soviet Union had struggled to reform; then suddenly, one year before the conference, the 'evil empire' had collapsed. Many people sought a new beginning in a world free of cold war divisions. This was a spur to the election of a bright young president, Bill Clinton, a few months after the conference. But the end of the cold war had left conservatives divided. At the 1992 Republican convention, Pat Buchanan electrified the party in a call for a 'religious war for the soul of America' and condemned the 'raw sewage of pornography that pollutes our popular culture'. Buchanan backed the uninspiring George H. W. Bush as Republican presidential candidate, because the alternative was Bill Clinton, 'a draft-dodging, pro-gay, greenhorn married to a radical feminist'.

In the early 1990s, Rupert Murdoch was completely bereft of a political platform. He had bought the film studio 20th Century Fox in the mid 1980s at a bargain price and had become a US citizen in order to buy the television stations that formed the country's fourth national network. But after he lost his beloved *New York Post*, in 1988, Murdoch had no influence in the news media and thus little influence in politics. His television network and film studio produced entertainment, not editorials.

After Ronald Reagan's presidency, Murdoch's political stance had become more radically right-wing. In the primaries for the Republican candidate in the 1988 presidential election, he told colleagues that he preferred Pat Robertson, the champion of the religious Right. Robertson was 'right on all the issues'.[4] At that time, Robertson was claiming that the Russians had missiles in Cuba, and that he had direct access to God. He argued at one point that feminism encouraged women 'to leave their husbands, kill their children, practise witchcraft, destroy capitalism and become lesbians'.[5]

In the 1992 presidential election, Murdoch supported the right-wing maverick Ross Perot, whom Murdoch said he knew 'quite well'. Perot had opposed the 1991 Gulf war and urged massive spending cuts and protection of American jobs.[6] He ran a populist campaign, and his candidacy split the Republican vote and ensured Clinton's win.

But as the 1990s unrolled, Murdoch gradually created a stable of media outlets that gave him a powerful voice in US politics. In 1993 he repurchased the *New York Post*, based in the country's most powerful city; in 1995 he founded the *Weekly Standard*, based in Washington, DC, which became the flagship of the neo-conservatives; and in 1996 he launched Fox News, whose agenda-setting power has influenced US politics ever since. Each of these media start-ups was a gamble. Indeed, the *New York Post* and the *Weekly Standard* were guaranteed loss-makers from the beginning. But profits were not the point: Murdoch was interested in promoting his brand of conservatism. Only with Fox News was he eventually able to find a market niche that both popularised conservatism and made healthy profits.

Murdoch's news media strategy in the 1990s was paradoxical. The decade saw the emergence of a triumphalist conservative politics dubbed the 'Republican Revolution'. Within this revival, Murdoch's political instincts detected an opportunity. Many Americans had a deep-seated and growing suspicion of the established mass media. Although this was as likely to come from the Left as from the Right, it resonated with Murdoch's own hostility to the 'liberal media'. To take advantage of this suspicion, Murdoch created media that were anti-media, critics of the mainstream. His outlets, in true Murdochian fashion, railed against powerful elites, shouting their message from the rooftops with total belief in their own righteousness. By 1996, *Time* magazine described Murdoch as the fourth most influential man in the United States, after President Clinton, the chairperson of the Federal Reserve Board and Bill Gates of Microsoft.

Throughout 1992 and early 1993, Rupert Murdoch kept his eye on the agonising decline of his precious *New York Post*. After he had been forced to sell the paper, in 1988, it had been acquired by real estate developer Peter Kalikow. By 1993 it had been sold to a parking station builder, Abe Hirschfeld, whose editorial plans caused open revolt within its staff. After several days of turmoil in March 1993, the journalists defied their new owner. A *Post* front page screamed: '*Post* staff to Abe Hirschfeld . . . GET LOST!' On another page was the question: 'Who is this nut who's taken the

Post hostage?' Hirschfeld's financial difficulties offered Murdoch an opening. The Democrat governor Mario Cuomo, in a move he may later have regretted, urged that Murdoch be given a federal waiver to allow him to own both the *Post* and his New York television station. Several hundred jobs were at stake, and Murdoch was the only potential owner in sight.

A legal battle ensued but, on 29 March 1993, about 30 minutes after Hirschfeld's bankruptcy judge granted him control, Rupert Murdoch and his son Lachlan strode onto the newsroom floor of the *New York Post*. They were loudly applauded by the staff, including many who had kept the flame burning since the dark days of 1988. Standing on a packing crate in the newsroom, Murdoch spoke to them. 'Newspapers can do a lot toward creating informed debate,' he said. 'Publishing is not about making money; it's about achieving things and improving society.' The *Post*'s mission, he said, was to take on the big shots and be anti-establishment. He particularly wanted the paper to take on the *New York Times*, which he attacked for being 'elitist'.[7] One staff member who suffered the consequences of Murdoch's return was the *Post*'s liberal editor, Pete Hamill. Although he had led the journalists' revolt, he was quickly sacked because of 'political incompatibility'.[8] Murdoch was back in town.

The *Post* soon related Murdoch's words to its readers. His return meant that the paper would 'dedicate itself to providing an "alternative voice"' in public policy debate. Above all, it would 'eschew the Politically Correct path', unlike other newspapers.[9] Murdoch's coded references to elitist enemies formed part of the populist conservatism that increasingly dominated US political life in the 1990s. His vision of improving society rather than making money was sincere: the *Post* had lost $100 million during his first period of ownership, but in Murdoch's eyes it had improved public debate.[10]

The *New York Times* (which had supported calls to save the *Post*) retaliated against Murdoch's pot shots. Murdoch may have saved the *Post*, it said, 'but there should be no illusions that he is a healthy influence on American journalism'. The problem was not tabloid taste but that 'his newspaper journalism has often been, at bottom, politically and professionally dishonest. He used his papers to grind the axes of his political buddies [and] to promote a reflexive conservatism.'[11] Murdoch was either ignorant or indifferent to the ideals of ethical journalism, the *New York Times* argued.

Murdoch was furious. The next day, the *Post* responded with a long, angry and revealing editorial that encapsulated the meaning of Murdoch's return to the newspaper and signalled his stance for the years to come. Unusually, it began by admitting that Murdoch and the *Post* had an 'ideological orientation'. Then it accused the *New York Times* of hypocrisy and suggested that the 'liberals and leftists who dominate the American media universe can't face the fact that they themselves are likewise animated by ideological considerations'.[12] To prove this, the *Post* singled out the *Times'* editorial support for gay rights and affirmative action (the program designed to rectify past discrimination by favouring minorities and, in some cases, women). But even if the *Times* were to publish no editorials, its liberal bias would be evident in its news coverage, the *Post* said. By contrast, Murdoch freely admitted that his own political orientation would 'inform the character of this newspaper'. The *Post* saw the world in strictly ideological terms: everyone represented an ideological force, whether they knew it or not. It was a view with a curious and inverted Marxist ring. A few days later, Murdoch's name began to appear on the *Post's* masthead above the daily editorial. He was designated 'editor-in-chief', making clear his oft-stated and intense identification with the newspaper's politics.

Among Murdoch's immediate decisions were those to reinstate his ideological watchdog Eric Breindel as the editorial page editor and to add an extra page of opinion to the paper. For Murdoch, the editorial and opinion pages were the heart of the newspaper, and this made the *Post* a tabloid unlike any other. While its news pages remained classically sensational and celebrity-obsessed, its opinion pages were showcases of intellectual seriousness drawn from columnists based in think tanks such as the American Enterprise Institute, the Manhattan Institute and the Hoover Institution. Nothing like this existed in the *Post*'s counterpart in Britain, the *Sun*, whose opinion content was tiny in both size and intellect by comparison.

There had been some changes during Murdoch's absence. By 1993, the *Post* was no longer so candidly contemptuous of homosexual people. It now occasionally reported gay bashings, and an openly homosexual reporter had been given a column. Shortly after Murdoch's takeover, however, when a demonstration of several hundred thousand people converged on Washington demanding gay civil rights, a *Post* editorial protested that the movement sought 'to make Americans accept as normal certain practices—sexual practices—that most people have long regarded as aberrant'.[13] A few days earlier, another editorial had seized on a minor study that purported to show that homosexuals constituted only 1 per cent of the population rather than the higher figures generally accepted. *Post* columnists like Michael Medved argued that homosexuals were not interested in affirmative action for the simple reason that in many areas 'gays are already over-represented—and they know it'.[14] New York's program of AIDS education in schools alarmed another *Post* columnist, Mona Charen, who was also a speechwriter for the Reagan administration. She suggested that twelve year olds were being taught techniques for 'fisting' and golden showers. 'As for the lesbian stuff, it amounts to an advertisement, in repellent detail, for sadomasochism.'[15]

The Republican Revolution in late 1994, which saw that party take control of both houses of Congress, targeted many of the gains such as welfare support and health insurance for the poor, but abolishing affirmative action was a prime goal. The *New York Post* shared this aim, and its editorials damned Bill Clinton's administration for being selected on the basis of 'racial and gender quotas'. *Post* columnists decried affirmative action as 'ideologically repulsive'.[16]

Murdoch himself was deeply hostile to affirmative action. Just as he had secretly funded extreme anti-communists in the Thatcher era, so he quietly promoted his favoured causes during the culture war of the 1990s. In 1996, Eric Breindel introduced Murdoch to Ward Connerly, a regent at the University of California who had launched a state ballot to ban affirmative action.[17] As a result, Murdoch gave $1 million to the Californian Republicans to support their anti–affirmative action and presidential campaigns. The ballot succeeded in striking down support for minorities and was a win for the Right, marred by the success of Clinton in the presidential vote. Undaunted, Murdoch gave $300,000 in 2003 for a similar attempt to ban the collection of race-based data by state and local governments in California. This move failed and Murdoch fought hard to oppose the release of court documents detailing his political donation.[18]

Throughout the decade, the *New York Post* was unrelentingly hostile to President Clinton and his Democratic administration. One *Post* editorial at the time complained that 'the entire agenda [of the Democrats] is set by environmentalists, Congressional Black radicals, feminists and homosexuals; moderates have been written out of the party'. By contrast, it enthused, the Republicans were 'ideologically diverse'.[19] In 1994, the *Post*'s enmity towards the president was highlighted when one of its reporters caused a national sensation by suggesting that a key Clinton aide, Vince Foster, who had died the previous year, might have been killed rather than having committed suicide, as was widely accepted. The *Post* then reported that Foster had kept a 'secret apartment', from which his body had been moved to the park in which it had been found.[20] Several inquiries dismissed these claims as baseless speculations. But this story and others fuelled a torrent of rumours and conspiratorial gossip about the president, helped not least by his own affair with an intern. All of this fed a well-funded campaign by far right Republican supporters which was later revealed by an erstwhile activist, David Brock.[21] At the same time that it was publishing stories about secret political killings and 'Whitewatergate', a *Post* editorial complained that 'American public discourse is polluted by inflammatory declamations that have their origins in the precincts of the Left'.[22]

Despite the *Post*'s over-heated coverage of many Clinton 'scandals', however, its unique contribution to the 1990s was in fostering the deeper ideological offensive of the culture war, by showcasing a counter-establishment of conservative intellectuals. A prominent feature in this was a regular column by Pat Buchanan, the presidential hopeful of the militant Right. In his column he talked about 'winning the culture war'. He damned the 'decadent' art of bisexual photographer Robert Mapplethorpe and opposed multiculturalism, which he defined as an 'across-the-board assault on our own Anglo-American heritage'.[23]

The *Post* was also publishing columns by such iconic figures of the Right as William Buckley and Ronald Reagan's ambassador to the United Nations Jeane Kirkpatrick. A black conservative from the Hoover Institution, Thomas Sowell, regularly argued in the *Post* that every welfare state program designed to lower poverty or crime or to promote health had not only failed but had done the opposite of what had been intended. Other writers included the ubiquitous Murdoch adviser Irwin Stelzer, who joined the *Post* to give economic commentary, and Ben Wattenberg, who like Stelzer was a fellow of the American Enterprise Institute.

The most significant of the *Post*'s writers were warriors in the battle against the liberal media. One of these was Michael Medved, whose book *Hollywood vs. America* argued that the film industry promoted violence, crime, sex and vulgarity and deliberately undermined accepted values, and that Hollywood's political liberalism meant that its films were inevitably hostile to religion. In 1993, he became a film critic for the *Post*; his articles were as much about the rating system as they were about storylines and stars. Medved's crusade was taken up wholeheartedly by News Corporation both in the United States and in Britain. Published by Murdoch's HarperCollins, his book was serialised in the *Sunday Times*, which also sponsored a public debate between Medved and his critics. The *Times* published a positive editorial about the issues Medved raised.[24]

Hilton Kramer joined the *Post* in 1993, an embittered ex–art critic from the *New York Times*. In the conservative magazine *National Review*, he complained that the *Times*' arts pages had been turned over to 'pop music, television garbage [and] Hollywood gossip'; too much space was being lavished on the culture of minorities, while 'the serious painters and sculptors who really do constitute an endangered minority' were ignored.[25] In his *Post* column, Kramer focused solely on the despised *New York Times*: his column logo was styled 'Times Watch'. Week after week, he minutely examined the paper's journalistic reportage, internal gossip and liberal sins. He invariably concluded that the coverage 'of certain subjects dear to the editors' hearts—race, gays, "diversity", feminist politics etc—is regularly allowed to abandon the realm of disinterested reporting in favour of advocacy journalism'.[26]

Extraordinarily, the *Post* had not one but two media critics at the time. The second was Brent Bozell, who ran an organisation called the Media Research Center with a $2 million budget largely drawn from conservative foundations and corporations. While the centre attacked Hollywood's portrayal of sex and violence, its main target was the alleged political bias of the mainstream media.[27] Bozell did not do this from a lofty stance of neutrality but as a leading activist from the conservative wing of the Republican Party. The year before his *Post* column began, he was chief fundraiser for Pat Buchanan's unsuccessful bid for the 1992 Republican nomination for president.

Bozell's columns fuelled the extreme anti-Clinton campaign of the Right, claiming that the mainstream news media operated on the basis that 'if it hurts a conservative, run it; if it hurts a liberal, spike it'.[28] The news media, he said, 'have a lot of apologizing to do for all the personal garbage they've tossed out and spread about conservatives'. The news media were similarly biased in favour of the 'single-payer socialist system' of health care, because 'reporters aren't Republicans'. Network television, he claimed, refused to report bad economic news, as the blame could be attributed to Bill Clinton.[29]

THE REAL ORIGINS OF FOX NEWS

While the *New York Post* had clout in the United States' most important city, its reach was limited. So in the 1990s Rupert Murdoch began work on another project, which aimed to have a nation-wide impact on politics. The result was the successful and controversial cable channel Fox News, which mobilised support for George W. Bush in 2000, supported his attack on Iraq in 2003 and backed him again in the election of 2004. It also fuelled conservative contempt for Barack Obama both before and after he gained presidential office in 2009. Fox News has emerged as one of Murdoch's most powerful media voices, and while the channel claims to be 'fair and balanced' it is in fact an outlet for overwhelmingly conservative political voices.[30] Murdoch routinely denies this, but an examination of the origins of Fox News shows that it was designed from the start as a partisan vehicle to intervene in US politics and the news media.

Most accounts of Fox News begin with the recruitment of Roger Ailes, the wily chief executive officer who made the channel both profitable and politically influential. Ailes, who had been a media adviser to both Ronald Reagan's and George H. W. Bush's presidential campaigns, was recruited by Murdoch in late 1995. But the story begins at least six years prior to that. When Murdoch first met Ailes, he said that he had been 'trying to get a news channel started ... I've had a bunch of guys try'.[31] Between 1990 and 1995, Murdoch attempted to construct a news operation for his newly created Fox Broadcasting network. This was quite different from Fox News, but it was similarly driven by the desire to promote conservative interpretations of news under the guise of adding balance to the liberal media.

Alleged liberal bias in mainstream US newspapers and television had been an obsession of Murdoch's for many years, as we've seen. In 1984, he told a forum of the American Enterprise Institute that the press was trying to change the country's political agenda and 'traditional values'.[32] By the late 1980s Murdoch had created a fourth national television network, but, unlike the other big networks—ABC, CBS and NBC—the Fox network did not have its own independent news division. Its affiliated stations heavily relied on their own local news operations plus Ted Turner's Cable News Network (CNN).

In 1990, CNN's coverage of the Gulf War infuriated many conservatives, who denounced as unpatriotic the network's continued broadcasts from Baghdad after the war began. Murdoch watched CNN each morning and had a love–hate relationship with it. He began to plan a news service that would counteract the bias of the mainstream media but found himself plagued with problems. In his first attempt, he appointed a former Reagan speechwriter and journalist, Peter Robinson, to plan the fledgling news service, but this went nowhere and Robinson left to become a fellow at the Hoover Institution. Next, in 1992, Murdoch announced that he would create a network news service on Fox Broadcasting, called Fox News. He appointed Steve Chao to run the network, but Chao's sacking over the stripper incident at Aspen abruptly terminated the operation. Murdoch eventually decided to start from the ground up, using the existing stations owned and operated by Fox, each of which had its own small news division. Shortly after sacking Chao, he spoke to a meeting of local Fox affiliates and said that he wanted to forge a new identity for the network that would mean doing news reporting differently. The problem, he said, was with mainstream network television news: 'I honestly cannot distinguish one program from another . . . It's like every news director in the market place graduated from the same dumb journalism class.'[33] The key Fox station for the new operation was the Washington-based WTTG.

Journalists at WTTG soon began to have fears for the reputation of its news. One reporter at the station, David Burnett, recalled his introduction to the new style of politicised journalism. 'They wanted to bring in a more conservative newscast. They wanted, I think, to use us as a sort of experiment, to see how a conservative approach to the news might work.'[34] On one occasion, the WTTG news manager insisted on skewing a report on the nomination of Clarence Thomas to the Supreme Court, a key Republican campaign. News producer Diana Winthrop recalled management complaints over any story about 'gays, AIDS, race, affirmative action'. Journalists were told at one point to air a story that had little news value but attacked liberal senator Ted Kennedy.[35] Producer Frank O'Donnell resigned over this story. He later recalled:

> Those of us who had seen it, had seen it happen in Australia, we had seen it happen with the *New York Post*. We thought that eventually it might happen to us. And it was kind of like being in an office and seeing people come down with the flu around you. We knew the flu eventually might reach us, but we were hoping if we took enough vitamins that we'd never catch the flu, and so when it finally happened, we were stunned.[36]

In mid 1993, the pressure for a new type of conservative television news at WTTG was stepped up. The station's new director of news, Joe Robinowitz, drew up a memo to the chairman of Fox Television, Les Hinton:

> As we've discussed it is going to be a pleasure in coming months to replace WTTG news staff who are inept, politically correct, shallow and/or unsuitable

for the jobs we have here in our newsroom. Since I'm very much a newcomer to this market, I am relying on the expertise of the following individuals to help me in this regard.[37]

The list included Brent Bozell; Reed Irvine, the head of right-wing watchdog Accuracy in Media; former George H. W. Bush speech-writer Tony Snow, who later joined Fox News; and Herb Berkowitz, an official at the Heritage Foundation. When contacted by the *Washington Post*, which broke the story of the memo in September 1993, Bozell said that he had already complained about a 'liberal tilt' on the evening news of Robinowitz's television station. He had also spoken to people at the Fox network in the past and urged them to broadcast more conservative voices and story ideas. When asked by the *Post* about his memo, Robinowitz defended himself by saying that those individuals just happened to be the first on a list of 40 he planned to consult. 'Unfortunately, all six are right of centre,' he said. He added that he simply wanted 'balanced journalism,' a slogan that later became familiar at Fox News under Roger Ailes. A weekend anchor, David Burnett, said he felt sorry for Robinowitz, 'who was doing what he was told' and was being made a scapegoat.[38] Robinowitz quickly resigned, but the memo's suggestion about ongoing discussions with the head of Fox Broadcasting about journalists who were 'politically correct' sheds some light on the politicisation of news coverage within Rupert Murdoch's empire and its role in the operation that ultimately became Fox News.

The following year, Murdoch flew his former *Sunday Times* editor Andrew Neil to the United States to work on a program for his new television news operation. Murdoch at first wanted a magazine program to rival CBS's famous *Sixty Minutes*, then a weekday news show, and later a daily late-night news program. His indecision eventually caused a rift between him and Neil, who resigned late in the year. But there was agreement between them on the political tilt of the news programs. Neil had wanted to produce a 'politically incorrect' program different from mainstream network television. He told a journalist that there was a 'great soggy liberal consensus on the Big Three networks and we can challenge it and offer something new'. One idea was to 'expose the myth of AIDS . . . nobody in America dares take that on—except us'.[39] Citing the growing success of conservative talk radio, he said: 'I did not want to produce a "right wing" news magazine but I wanted one that was different [and] was not automatically hostile to the new ideas that were sweeping America from the right of the political spectrum.'[40]

Another story idea concerned the Endangered Species Act. 'We were going to show that at a cost of billions of dollars it had actually saved none—but was a serious infringement of individual property rights.' It was a great story, Neil said, because it was 'certain to outrage America's powerful environment lobby groups'.[41]

At a final meeting with Neil, Murdoch wondered aloud whether the famous anchor at NBC, Bryant Gumbel, might host a news program. But then he dismissed Gumbel as 'too left'. The program 'should be politically incorrect—not necessarily right wing or conservative but definitely not PC'.[42]

Finally, in 1995, Murdoch met Roger Ailes. His 24-hour cable news channel started broadcasting in late 1996. Shortly after Fox News began, Murdoch was interviewed by the magazine of the conservative American Enterprise Institute. It was a sympathetic interview, but the first question probed Murdoch's belief about the left-wing slant of US journalists. Given that Fox News would have to employ journalists from existing television networks, how would the station avoid importing the very problem it was designed to avoid? Murdoch responded: 'I don't think we employ those sort of people. Roger Ailes keeps a very close watch on that.'[43]

Before his name became synonymous with Fox News' style of aggressive conservative opinion, Roger Ailes was best known as a top Republican political strategist. His political career began with a role as a junior media adviser with Richard Nixon's campaign of 1968. By the 1980s, Ailes was working on many Republican congressional campaigns as well as producing the national advertising for Ronald Reagan's campaign in 1984 and working for George H. W. Bush's campaign in 1988, regarded as one of the dirtiest up to that point. After the Bush campaign, the *Washington Post* said Ailes had a 'slash and burn image' and a 'reputation as a master of gut-punching negative ads'.[44] The legendary Republican adviser Lee Atwater said Ailes had two speeds: attack and destroy. As campaign adviser to New York senator Alfonse D'Amato in 1986, Ailes at one point asked him 'Can you fly?' A puzzled D'Amato asked why. Ailes said: 'Because we are 42 stories up, and you're going to go out that window if you say one more word.'[45] D'Amato was a friend, not a foe. Ailes once said to politicians he was advising: 'You've got to understand that the media has no interest in substance . . . There are three ways to get on air: pictures, attacks and mistakes.'[46] A *Wall Street Journal* report described him as one of 'the nation's roughest Republican political consultants'.[47] After many years in politics, Ailes returned to television, briefly producing a program for conservative radio host Rush Limbaugh and then founding successful cable channels for NBC. When he rang Rupert Murdoch's office in late 1995 to offer his services, the response was instant: 'A secretary called back to say that Murdoch was arriving in New York that afternoon and could see Ailes at five.'[48] Later that day, they talked about their common view that mainstream media, including cable giant CNN, was 'too liberal'. Within an hour, Ailes had a deal to launch a news channel.

Murdoch had finally found the man who could design and execute the dream that had eluded him for many years. In January 1996, standing beside Ailes, Murdoch announced this dream to the world. The news operation would be an all-news cable station rather than a network news division within Fox, meaning that it would directly compete with CNN. Shortly before the launch Murdoch had attacked CNN, which, he said, was shifting 'further and further and further to the left'. Murdoch said: 'I don't know whether it happened with my friend Ted [Turner] marrying Jane Fonda or giving up lithium but . . . [CNN] has changed very greatly.'[49] His cable channel would compete with CNN and bring 'really objective' news to the airwaves. The next day, Turner said that he was 'looking forward to squishing Rupert like a bug'. Murdoch's response was to repeat that he would beat CNN by appealing to the public's dislike of the liberal 'media elite'.

Ailes was one among many staff with conservative views in the young cable channel. Although its marketing slogans were 'fair and balanced' and 'we report, you decide', the early high-profile staff were overwhelmingly skewed to the conservative and Republican side of politics. According to the president of Fox News, Joe Peyronnin, one of Ailes's first acts was to clean house.

> I had about forty people working for me and he asked some of them if they were liberal or not. There was a litmus test. He was going to figure out who was liberal or conservative when he came in, and try to get rid of the liberals.[50]

Peyronnin objected and soon resigned.

The man appointed as executive in charge of news, John Moody, had worked at *Time* magazine for many years, but even that venerable institution, he believed, had succumbed to an unconscious but powerful liberal bias.[51] At the start of Moody's job interview, Ailes told him: 'One of the problems we have to work on here together when we start this network is that most journalists are liberals . . . And we've got to fight that.'[52] Moody would later become famous for his political memos to Fox News staff that dictated the 'line' to be followed for the day's coverage, especially during the Iraq war (see Chapter 8).

The Washington-based Brit Hume was recruited as a key on-air journalist for Fox News in 1996. A veteran reporter for ABC News,

Hume had also written for conservative US publications such as the *National Review*, the *American Spectator* and Murdoch's own *Weekly Standard*. According to Hume, Washington reporters allowed their political attitudes to affect their judgement 'all the time'.[53] Other early recruits included Bill O'Reilly, a registered Republican, though he denied this for some time;[54] Catherine Crier, formerly an elected Republican judge from Texas; and Fred Barnes, a writer for Murdoch's *Weekly Standard*.

Fox News also used political criteria in recruiting less prominent journalists. In New York, the station expressed interest in employing an energetic city hall reporter, Andrew Kirtzman. The *Village Voice* reported at the time:

> FNC reviewed his tapes and liked what they saw but expressed concern over his political affiliation. 'They were afraid I was a Democrat' [said Kirtzman]. 'I did not think it was appropriate to give them that [information]. All employment discussion ended at that point.'[55]

Two years later, as Fox News' political character became ever more obvious, the *Columbia Journalism Review* spoke to a number of former employees who were among its 'severest critics'. Several complained of management interference in the writing and editing of stories to make them more palatable to conservative tastes. One said: 'I've worked at a lot of news organizations and never found that kind of manipulation.' Another declared that it was a 'tyrannical and horrible' place to work. 'I wanted to wipe off my shoe.'[56] One of the few shows in which genuine liberals regularly appeared was *Fox News Watch*, a weekend program that highlighted 'stories ignored by the dominant media'. Hosted by the *New York Post*'s Eric Breindel, the founding assumption of the program was of systematic political bias—in *other* news media.

Political criteria suffused the planning of the shows that would air on the channel, something that was unusual at the time. The centrepiece of Fox News' evening line-up was a program with two hosts, a conservative and a liberal. The conservative was chosen early on, and so for some time the planned program was referred to as 'Hannity and Liberal To Be Determined'. Sean Hannity was an acknowledged conservative with a domineering telegenic personality. The man ultimately chosen as his co-host was a moderate liberal, Alan Colmes, who was ineffectual and acted as a foil for the aggressive and forthright Hannity.

Early advertisements for the channel were aired on Rush Limbaugh's conservative radio program. Limbaugh boomed out: 'Check any recent polls and it's clear Americans think the media are biased. But now there's an alternative. Fox News is fair news.'[57] On mainstream television newscasts, Brit Hume warned viewers about bias on network television. Murdoch's comments about CNN suggested that the battle was for 'objective news', and Ailes played up to this. On the eve of the launch, he said that Fox News would be 'basically a hard-news network' providing 'straight, factual information to the American people so that they can make up their own minds, with less spin and less face time for anchors'.[58] But when Fox News commenced, in October 1996, Murdoch's competitors and critics discovered that it was not mainly about news at all. Certainly, the station carried regular daily news updates that were politically neutral, but this was not the distinctive edge that was the basis for its competition with news rivals. Ailes had turned the tables and produced a version of talk radio that relied on angry and articulate right-wing hosts who had lots of 'face time' and who flattered their conservative audience. The air time for news reporting was relatively small for an 'all-news' channel.

Rupert Murdoch has infuriated critics of Fox News by responding to every accusation of bias with the same routine mantra: Fox News is not biased, and the proof of this is that it regularly has guests who are Democrats, liberals and even critics of Fox News. The annoying thing is that this is partially true. Fox News has a distinct right-wing bias and it regularly has guests who are not right wing. Even more unusually, on occasions, it is *because* Fox creates 'balance' that it is right wing.

The use of balanced debate to foster political bias seems paradoxical, so deeply is the norm of balance ingrained in ethical discussion. But constructing a device of balance on some issues can strongly support a conservative view. It creates the perception of a public controversy where none exists. It can give legitimacy to one side of a debate since 'balance' presumes that both sides are equally legitimate. It can move the 'centre' of a debate to conservative territory by the choice of extreme parameters. Far from being automatically neutral, the construction of balance can be a key part of political agenda setting. The best example of this is the way in which Fox News created 'balance' on issues like climate change. Programs would feature one guest who supported the scientific findings on climate 'balanced' by a climate change sceptic who did not. In this 'balanced' framework, scientific findings would appear controversial, since the premise of the debate was politics: the sub-text was that support or opposition to climate science was a matter of political belief. Moreover, Fox's promotional slogans 'fair and balanced' and 'we report, you decide' acted as important signals for conservative viewers. 'By advertising its supposed objectivity, Fox was attacking perceived bias in rival news organisations,' said writer Scott Collins.[59]

In its first two years, Fox News lost $150 million. It seemed doomed in a limited market already crowded with news providers, with CNN as the king of cable news. But Fox News' conservative bias was the key to its financial success, not merely an accidental result of being owned by Rupert Murdoch. In an early, staccato memo, Roger Ailes said that he sought to 'position cable channel as haven for viewers looking for relief from the one-sided reporting by competition'.[60] Ailes identified the same phenomenon as

Republicans experienced in the 1990s: you could foster a populist revolt by depicting the commanding heights of the media, universities, politics and government bureaucracy as captive to liberals.

Murdoch's critics dismissed the founding assumption of Fox News, which was that a significant part of the US public distrusted the news media. But Murdoch was smarter than those critics imagined. The post–cold war 1990s saw the emergence of a more sceptical and fragmented society, and conservatives made up a significant slice of this pie. They provided the audience for a polarised, niche news media in a saturated news market. Murdoch and Ailes created a politicised business model that ultimately contributed both profits and political influence to News Corporation. It has been brilliantly successful and remains so today.

CHAPTER 7
THE REIGN OF THE
SUN KING

When you work for Rupert Murdoch you do not work for a company chairman or chief executive: you work for a Sun King . . . All life revolves around the Sun King: all authority comes from him . . . The Sun King is everywhere, even when he is nowhere. He rules over great distances through authority, loyalty, example and fear. He can be benign or ruthless, depending on his mood or the requirements of his empire.[1]

Andrew Neil, former *Sunday Times* editor, 1996

I have never met Mr Murdoch, but at times when I worked at Downing Street he seemed like the 24th member of the cabinet. His voice was rarely heard . . . but his presence was always felt.[2]

Lance Price, media adviser to Tony Blair, 2006

In July 1995 Alastair Campbell was on holiday in the south of France after an exhausting twelve months of working as media adviser for Labour's rising star, Tony Blair. Joining Campbell and his wife Fiona one warm night at the rented holiday house in Provence were Neil and Glenys Kinnock. As some vegetable kebabs were sizzling on the barbecue, a minor argument started over the meaning of a French word. But Campbell could see that something else was on Neil Kinnock's mind: 'His cheek muscles were flexing . . . as first he tried to keep his voice under control, but failed every six or seven words; the hand movements getting wilder.'[3] It became clear that the definition of that French word was not what had agitated Kinnock, who started to say sarcastically: 'Oh, Margaret Thatcher, not too bad you know, not such a bad person, quite a radical and, of course, you have to admire her determination and her leadership . . . radical my arse, that woman killed people!' But the object of Kinnock's rage was not Thatcher. He was angry about a recent speech by Tony Blair: 'It won't matter if we win, the bankers and stockbrokers have got us already, by the fucking balls, laughing their heads off. All that before you go and take your 30 pieces of silver.' Campbell hit back. 'What's *that* supposed to mean?' '*Murdoch,*' Kinnock raged. 'Tell me how I'm supposed to feel when I see you set off half way around the world to grease him up.'

Two weeks earlier Campbell had accompanied Tony Blair when he delivered a speech at an editorial conference of News Corporation on a luxury island in Australia. Because the conference was in the country of Murdoch's birth, for Kinnock, and many others, the irresistible image created was of a supplicant political leader travelling around the world to win the approval of a powerful media baron. But to some Labour supporters, out of office since 1979, Murdoch's softening attitude to the party was a welcome relief. Others felt, however, that it was not Murdoch who had softened his political position, but Blair and New Labour.

Throughout the three terms of Tony Blair's UK Labour prime ministership, Rupert Murdoch loomed as a shadowy presence in the government. His influence was exercised through personal contact with Blair and his chancellor, Gordon Brown, and through the *Sun* newspaper. The personal contact between Murdoch, Blair and Brown was something that neither side wished to publicise. Just as Murdoch's influence and requests for favours from Margaret Thatcher's government were secret until Woodrow Wyatt's diaries were published, so the full story of Murdoch's dealings with the British Labour government remained unknown until after its defeat, when diaries, insider accounts and Freedom of Information requests revealed the truth.

Former adviser in Blair's office Lance Price described Murdoch as seeming like

> the 24th member of cabinet. His voice was rarely heard ... but his presence was always felt. No big decision could ever be made inside Number Ten without taking into account the likely reaction of three men, Gordon Brown, [deputy prime minister] John Prescott and Rupert Murdoch.[4]

As a former civil servant, Price was obliged to submit the manuscript of his 2005 book, *The Spin Doctor's Diary*, to the Cabinet Office. One-third of the initial changes demanded concerned Murdoch's relationship with the Blair government. 'They were very, very sensitive about the number of times that the Prime Minister had met him.'[5]

All media owners had 'reasonably good access to the Prime Minister. But Rupert Murdoch could almost click his fingers and see Tony Blair whenever he wanted to,' recalled Price. Murdoch's relationship with the Labour leadership was even closer than that with Thatcher: he admitted to the *New Yorker*'s John Cassidy that the Conservative prime minister 'didn't go out of her way to develop a personal relationship with me', but that, by contrast, Blair and Brown had made efforts to be sociable, often inviting him to Downing Street when he was in London.[6] This attitude did not pass unnoticed by the other side: an executive from News International told the *Financial Times* that 'Rupert's access to the Prime Minister is pretty amazing. We were all a bit bowled over.'[7]

BURNT BY THE *SUN*

Murdoch observers have argued that the key to Murdoch's politics is that he likes winners, which explains his support for Blair in the 1997, 2001 and 2005 UK elections. But there is a glibness to this view that ignores Murdoch's heartfelt political passions. Bill Clinton was a winner in both the 1992 and the 1996 US presidential elections, but Murdoch backed his opponents. Nor did Murdoch support the likely winner in the 1992 UK election. For much of that campaign, Labour's Neil Kinnock was high in opinion polls, and Britain had been badly affected by the global economic recession of 1991–92, meaning unemployment had risen dramatically: these were perfect conditions for a Labour victory. If Murdoch had been a mere opportunist who loved winners, he would not have allowed the *Sun* to treat Neil Kinnock and Labour with the extreme journalist thuggery that it did. The 1992 campaign was burnt into Kinnock's memory and explained his rage at the barbecue in southern France. It was also seared into the memory of Tony Blair, but he drew quite different conclusions.

In the decisive seven final days of the 1992 election campaign, the *Sun* took no hostages. It began with an attack on Labour's Jack Straw: the front page proclaimed 'I'm alright Jack' and damned Straw as a hypocrite 'for preaching socialism from the luxury of THREE homes'. Inside, an article claimed that the interest paid on home loans 'would soar with Labour'. A microscopic story noted that two opinion polls gave Labour a seven-point lead. The next day, a front-page editorial backed Conservative John Major, with five pro-Major stories on page 2, including one reporting the prediction of a fortune teller.

Five days before the election, the *Sun* reported primary school children voting in a mock election that put the Monster Raving Loony Party ahead of Labour. A few pages later the paper played the race card, with a double page article that began: 'Tens of thousands of immigrants will be let into Britain if Labour win the election.' Maps bearing arrows showed an invasion of 'bogus refugees'.

Three days out from the election, the Labour team members were compared to the seven dwarfs, while a nearby article yelled:

'Don't sleepwalk to socialist nightmare'. An editorial called for the privatisation of the BBC. The next day the *Sun* published the 'Windbag tapes', in which someone who 'sounds like Neil Kinnock' promised higher taxes, 'implementation of EC rules on the width of cucumbers' and 'abolition of the armed forces'. Readers were urged to call a phone number to listen to the 'speech'.

On the day before the election, an extraordinary creation appeared in the paper: four consecutive double page spreads with the strap line 'Nightmare on Kinnock Street', a classic *Sun* parody based on the horror movie *Nightmare on Elm Street*. In the first spread, an official from the far-right Adam Smith Institute predicted evictions, rising interest rates and a crash in house prices if Labour won. Helpful tables indicated the potential rising costs of water, gas and electricity. The second spread attacked Labour's plans for a minimum wage. A photo of an attractive female factory worker was captioned 'Rag trade worker Kelly Simms is terrified of Labour's wage plans'. One article on 'loony councils' warned that town planners would be 'forced by law to consult homosexuals'. Another reported that the parents of a premature baby believed that their child would have died if Labour's reforms to health care had prevailed. On another page, the *Sun* repeated a device used in the 1987 election, reporting that a 'psychic' had found that Labour was backed by Mao Zedong, Karl Marx, Joseph Stalin and Leon Trotsky. John Major's Conservatives were backed by Queen Victoria, Elvis Presley and Winston Churchill.

On the day of the election, the *Sun*'s front page showed Neil Kinnock's head in a light bulb with the headline 'If Kinnock wins today will the last person to leave Britain please turn out the lights'. On page 3 was a photo of a leering, obese woman raunchily lowering her shoulder strap. The headline jeered: 'Here's how page 3 will look under Kinnock!' 'Lefties like [Labour MP] Clare Short want to ban pretty girls', the story claimed.

It had been a ruthless exercise, using all the tools of popular journalism. The attacks were punchy and inventive, their venomous message concealed inside a satirical sugar coating. The theme running through the crusade, as always, was that the *Sun* was on the side of ordinary people and against those who wanted to push them around and fool them. A few years later, a Murdoch editor admitted that at the time

> news stories were told from a Thatcherite perspective, features geared to further Thatcherite ideas . . . At election time, Tory tabloids turned themselves into the publishing arm of Tory Central Office. The newspapers were full of powerful, skilful, constant propaganda for the Tory cause.[8]

Two days after the Tories' victory, the *Sun*'s front-page headline crowed that 'It's the Sun wot won it'. The story reported Tory MPs rushing to thank the newspaper for its coverage in the previous ten days. Inside, an academic columnist proclaimed: 'We have beaten socialism'. A cartoon showed Neil Kinnock dangling from a hangman's rope, with his tongue protruding, recalling the crude ecstasy at the hanging of Nazi war criminals after World War Two.

Murdoch rejoiced over the *Sun*'s role in Labour's defeat. He told friends that the Tory campaign had been 'appalling' and emphasised 'how lucky they were to have got in and how they had been helped by the *Sun*'.[9] In the days following Labour's defeat, Murdoch circulated to friends a *Wall Street Journal* article bemoaning the departure of Margaret Thatcher and her 'unshakeable convictions'. Murdoch's and the *Sun*'s triumphalist claims of victory concluded one of the most ferocious and effective newspaper onslaughts against a political party in modern times.

The *Sun*'s campaign revealed Rupert Murdoch's preparedness to use his newspapers mercilessly to destroy Labour's chances of victory. The paper's ruthlessness, and the 'Sun wot won it' headline, sparked a major debate in British politics about the power of the news media. Later, some academic studies minimised the influence of the *Sun* on voters who might otherwise have voted Labour, but they failed to note that its hysterical last weeks of coverage formed the culmination of years of hostile vilification. Former assistant editor of the *Sun* Roy Greenslade said that the paper had a 'drip-drip' effect (called by academics an 'agenda-setting role').[10] Whatever the *Sun*'s actual role had been in destroying Labour, however, the infamous headline revealed its motivation and smug satisfaction at a job well done.

EMBRACING LABOUR

Having worked hard to return John Major and the Tories to Downing Street, Rupert Murdoch and the *Sun* quickly turned on them as they failed in government. In September 1992, a political and economic crisis engulfed the country. The pound collapsed, and Britain withdrew from the European Exchange Rate Mechanism. Prime Minister Major rang the *Sun* editor Kelvin MacKenzie and asked how his paper would report these events. MacKenzie's reply was: 'I've got a large bucket of shit lying on my desk and tomorrow morning I am going to pour it all over your head.'[11]

Major had failed in an issue that was close to Murdoch's heart: Europe. The *Sun* began to regularly accuse the prime minister of giving in to a 'Brussels power grab' and referred to the 'Eurobeast'.[12] Murdoch's hatred of Europe was mixed with an irrational desire for Margaret Thatcher to return to power. 'Quit now Major and bring back Maggie', said one *Sun* headline before the 1993 Tory conference.[13] The *Sun* was not alone in its pursuit of the Major government: all UK newspapers except the *Daily Express* ran multiple stories on government scandal, real and manufactured. Murdoch's *News of the World* frequently included reports about Tory ministers' affairs and the pregnancies of their mistresses, and about Tory MPs' 'homosexual romps'.[14]

However, while attention was focused on 'Tory sleaze' and Major's policy towards Europe, the prime minister's attitude on another issue was causing Murdoch's blood to reach boiling point. In the 1980s, like many people, Major had been appalled by the antics of the tabloid press, the *Sun* and the *News of the World* in particular. An inquiry into press behaviour had resulted in the creation of the Press Complaints Commission, and this had narrowly staved off the alternative: a privacy law. Murdoch had had little option but to accept this. But after the 1992 election, Major let it be known privately that he was toying with the idea of introducing a US-style law that foreigners could not own both newspapers and television stations. Murdoch would have to choose. Unfortunately for Major, his idea reached a Murdoch adviser who concluded that 'this would be totally ruinous to Rupert'.[15] When Major's report on media ownership was published in 1995, it examined the cross-ownership of television by newspaper publishers. Non-Murdoch newspaper groups had been jostling noisily to be allowed to expand into terrestrial and satellite television, and the report recommended a relaxation to allow this. Murdoch, however, was already too big in the report's eyes. When Major's government formulated its broadcasting bill, it allowed all newspaper publishers to expand into television *except* those who already held more than a 20 per cent market share. This was squarely targeted at News International and at the Mirror group, Labour's supporters on Fleet Street.

The combination of Tory sleaze and the government's hostile media policy made a tricky political dilemma for Murdoch. He despised Major and his scandal-prone government, but that would not have stopped him supporting the Conservatives if the alternative had been worse. His strategy in the lead up to the 1997 election, in which Labour returned to power, was remarkable; it demonstrated the lengths to which this major media owner, whose future expansion depended heavily on government, would go in order to exercise political influence as well as preserve his empire. One of the men who knew Murdoch best during this period described his 'megalomaniac moods [in which he] thinks he can choose the Prime Minister'.[16]

Murdoch's strategy had two tracks: one directed at Major's government, the other at Labour. The first track consisted of relentless pressure both in private and in the pages of the *Sun* against a party by whom Murdoch felt betrayed. The hostility was mutual: in February 1995, when Murdoch's newspapers reported an alleged affair between John Major's son and an older woman, Major confided that 'if I had a majority of a hundred and fifty, I would crush Rupert Murdoch and make sure he had no newspapers at all'.[17] A few months later the Tories released the report on media ownership. While generally loosening regulations, it would restrict the expansion of already large newspaper publishers into television. A witness to Murdoch's reaction saw him driven into 'a furious rage'.[18]

A year before the 1997 election, Murdoch met Major privately to pressure him to allow News International to expand into terrestrial television, but he found no joy: the Tories were 'sticking to their guns'.[19] Although he knew it would damage him in the election, Major, with a significant degree of courage, insisted on passing the broadcasting bill with its restrictions on large newspaper companies intact.

On the other hand, Murdoch was pleased to see that Labour was undergoing internal changes under its new leader, Tony Blair. In August 1994, Murdoch casually mentioned in an interview with *Der Spiegel* magazine that his newspapers had supported the election of the Labor government in Australia and said that he 'could even imagine supporting Tony Blair'.[20] A private meal followed between himself and Blair, after which Murdoch confided: 'Well, he is certainly saying all the right things, but we are certainly not letting our pants down just yet.'[21] Murdoch had good reason to be wary. At the beginning of 1995, well after Blair's ascension to the party leadership, a group of Labour MPs, including previous spokespeople on media policy, proposed a media bill that would have barred a newspaper publisher from owning more than one daily or Sunday newspaper. It also called for changes that would have forced Murdoch to sell his satellite television network BSkyB.[22] The group was a minority, but it was a reminder to Murdoch that behind Blair were parliamentarians who despised him and his power.

Murdoch's media did not rush to embrace Labour. Even after friendly meetings between Blair and its owner, the *Sun* continued to scorn the Labour leader. In March 1995, an editorial attacked him for managing to sound 'more Tory than the Tories'. It warned readers: 'Don't be fooled'.[23] When John Major resigned his party leadership and challenged his critics to stand against him in the ensuing leadership vote, Murdoch's press called for his defeat. But they did so because, as the *Sun* said in early July 1995, 'vote Major and you let Labour in'. The *Sun* was definitely not letting its pants down.

In spite of this, Murdoch continued to sound out the Labour leader. On several occasions he invited Blair to breakfast in his luxurious Mayfair flat, at which they once intensely discussed morality and family values.[24] Tony and Cherie Blair began to have social contact with Les Hinton, the head of News International in Britain and a member of Murdoch's Australian mafia. For Murdoch, the acquaintance was part insurance policy, part fascination with the new and pragmatic Labour leader. While John Major was actively restraining Murdoch's expansion, Blair said in early 1995: 'It's not a question of Murdoch being too powerful.' A few months later, when Labour launched its communications policy, it said nothing about restricting newspaper or television ownership. It was 'remarkably unthreatening for media tycoons like Murdoch', said one industry commentator.[25]

Then came an invitation in July 1995 for Blair to address the Australian editorial conferences that triggered Neil Kinnock's eruption of anger. In response to similar reactions by others in the Labour Party, Alastair Campbell replied that Labour had to work 'far harder cultivating the hostile press than the friendly press. They've done a lot of damage to Labour in the past.' Just before Blair and Campbell stepped on the plane to Australia, there was another straw in the wind. Murdoch had suddenly settled a long running legal case and agreed to pay damages to former Labour leader Michael Foot. Foot was the subject of a scurrilous story run by the *Sunday Times* that he had links with the Soviet KGB.

Introducing Blair to his senior staff, Murdoch commented: 'If the British press is to be believed, today is all part of a Blair-Murdoch flirtation. If that flirtation is ever consummated, Tony, I suspect we will end up making love like two porcupines—very carefully.'[26] Blair's speech argued that the Right had got economic policy correct but had failed to build the social order and stability needed in the revolution it had begun. The Thatcher–Reagan leadership, he said, 'got certain things right. A greater emphasis on enterprise. Rewarding not penalizing success. Breaking up vested interests. In that sense, Mrs Thatcher was a radical, not a Tory.' Many who supported the Tories were not really conservative, he said: 'they were anti-Establishment', echoing a Murdoch theme song from the *Sunday Times*. He showed most bravery in taking a pro-European stance, damning the Tories for being nationalistic. 'The Labour government I hope to lead will be outward-looking, internationalist and committed to free and open trade, not an outdated and misguided nationalism.'[27] Murdoch praised Blair's 'courage' in attending and afterwards loftily described him as 'a very bright young man [who] made a great speech'.

Blair and his adviser Alastair Campbell were also impressed when they saw Murdoch's power in action. When he spoke, they found the scene 'fascinating but a bit chilling, to watch all these grown men, and some women, hanging on every word and knowing that an inflection here or there would influence them one way or the other'.[28] Murdoch sent 'a chill down a few editors' spines when he went on about the failings of some editors, without naming names'.

When Murdoch emphasised the importance of Blair's speech to his editors of the *Sun* and the *Times*, they 'disappeared for a couple of minutes and told me proudly they had ordered London to give [the speech] a good show', Campbell recalled.[29] Even so, while the *Times* published Blair's speech, it also ran a critique of it.

In the eyes of some, Blair's presence at the event and Murdoch's speech sealed approval for a secret deal with New Labour, but this is a caricature both of the way in which Murdoch exercises power and how others respond to it. The invitation to Blair was as much an effort to pressure John Major as it was a gesture towards the potential prime minister. But as 1995 and 1996 rolled by, evidence of some sort of 'understanding' mounted. It became clear that Murdoch realised that, crucially, Blair presented less of threat to his newspaper and television ownership than Major. This was heavily underlined at the end of 1995, when a Labour shadow minister supported an inquiry by the Monopolies and Mergers Commission into Murdoch's dominance in cable and satellite television: he was immediately ordered to withdraw by Blair's office.[30] The following year, when Major persisted in laws restricting News International's move into television, Labour opposed him. It was hardly surprising that Labour opposed a Tory bill but, in this case, Major was on the side of maintaining diverse media ownership, while Labour supported an 'open and competitive market', which inevitably favoured an already dominant player such as News International.

Throughout the run-up to the 1997 election, the question of whether Murdoch would back Labour or the Tories loomed large. Blair and Campbell were acutely aware of Murdoch's power to dictate the editorial line of his newspapers. In March 1996, they had lunch with the top editors of the *Sun*. The most lasting impression was that while the right-wing journalists were hostile to Labour, they would do what Murdoch wanted. A portrait of Murdoch watched over the lunch, and Campbell thought the *Sun* journalists, like cult members, were 'all a bit Moonie-fied'.[31]

Until the last minute, Murdoch's decision was unclear. In late January 1997 the *Sun* was still hostile to Blair, contrasting him, 'the man with flexible convictions', with 'Mr Major who sticks to his convictions'. Blair and Campbell sent urgent messages through Murdoch's emissary Irwin Stelzer to ask 'what the hell is going on'.[32]

By February, Murdoch had made up his mind. The immediate price of his support was an article by Blair publicly distancing himself from pro-European sympathy. The *Sun* then made what it described as 'an historic announcement from Britain's No. 1 newspaper', claiming on its front page: 'The *Sun* backs Blair'. The Tories were 'tired, divided and rudderless', while Blair had vision, purpose and courage. A few days later, the paper's sentiments were more graphic. In 1992 it had used an obese semi-naked woman to warn that Labour would ban its 'page three lovelies'. In 1997 there was an echo for those who remembered. The *Sun*'s favourite pin-up girl was pictured lying naked on a beach; the headline read: 'Melinda Blairs it all'. Over at the *News of the World*, the story of an affair by shadow foreign secretary Robin Cook was suppressed before the election.[33]

Murdoch's backing for Blair in 1997 was unlike his support for the Tories in 1992. For the 1997 election there was no 'Nightmare on Major Street', and on election day the *Sun* published a column by one of Murdoch's Tory favourites, Norman Tebbit, supporting a Tory win. However, the front page showed a starry hand of God reaching down to anoint the head of Tony Blair: 'It must be you', said the headline. Inside, a gushing editorial emphasised Blair's pledge on Europe: 'Blair has promised to slay the dragon of Europe', by promising to hold a referendum on any deeper integration if it won. Britain needed the 'strong man instead of the wrong man in Number 10'.[34]

The day after Labour's landslide win, there was another echo of the 1992 election: the *Sun* trumpeted: 'It's the Sun wot swung it'. Blair was 'swift to give credit to our role' and 'had told party big wigs our support was vital'.[35] The *Sun's* grandiose claim to have 'swung it' was absurd, since Blair had been well ahead in the polls before the *Sun* backed him, but it was another crude reminder that Blair owed a debt to Murdoch. As well as self-important puffery, the *Sun* displayed an unmistakeable ideological element that day as well. Its editorial claimed that Blair had 'transformed Labour into a free market political force, the people's choice'.[36] A few days later, an official of the free market think tank the Adam Smith Institute praised Blair's plan to reform the welfare state along the same lines as Chile's. At the time, the Chilean experiment in personal pension funds was touted all over the world as the free market answer to government-guaranteed pensions.

When discussing powerful individuals such as Rupert Murdoch and governments like Tony Blair's, it is easy to fall into a comic book view of the world. Secret deals are struck, a price is agreed, promises are made and a soul is sold. Blair was acutely aware of this view of his government, and in his memoirs he satirically compared Faust's deal with Satan to the time when he announced to Labour traditionalists that he was going to Murdoch's editorial conference. Murdoch's support for Labour in 1997 did not involve the sale of Blair's soul for an agreed sum. For one thing, Murdoch's actual views barely changed. His support for Blair did not involve the vicious slurs and raucous jeers against the Tories that the *Sun* had directed against Labour in 1992. After 1997, his support for Labour was conditional: the influence he exercised over Blair was based on the assumption that he could never be taken for granted. The 'deal' between Blair and Murdoch never involved permanent support. In Murdoch's eyes, Labour had to prove its worth to him repeatedly.

GOAL SCORING

During the Blair government's period of office, Rupert Murdoch had three goals: to acquire regular personal access to Blair, to protect his newspaper and television empire and, perhaps most significantly, to influence Britain's foreign policy. He achieved them all.

In 1998, Murdoch was bidding for Silvio Berlusconi's giant Mediaset television network, hoping to add it to BSkyB. He realised the political sensitivities involved with a foreigner buying into Italian television and, as one of his colleagues told the *Financial Times*, 'said he would ring up the Prime Minister [Tony Blair] to see if he could help'. Murdoch asked Blair to question the Italian prime minister, Romano Prodi, about whether his government would have any objection to the takeover. Shortly afterwards, when Prodi made a routine call to Downing Street, Blair did just that and reported Prodi's answer—no real objection—back to Murdoch. When knowledge of the call became public, Alastair Campbell initially all but denied it had taken place then was forced to retreat. Blair protested: 'I treat Mr Murdoch no differently to anyone else,' to which News International added: 'It is perfectly common for major businesses to enlist heads of government on issues of this sort.' No doubt it was but, unofficially, News International executives told journalists how surprised they were by Murdoch's access to Blair.[37]

In the aftermath of the affair, Campbell was worried that attacks against himself could damage the Labour government. In his diary, he recorded: '[Blair] said he didn't fear them coming at him about me, but about the relationship with Murdoch. And he didn't fancy a sustained set of questions about whether Murdoch lobbied him.'[38] From that time on, Labour's contact with Murdoch was as discreet as possible. Years later, the Cabinet Office released a list of dates on which Blair and Murdoch had met or phoned each other over eight years, between 1998 and 2005. Fifteen formal contacts were recorded, and Campbell's diary recorded at least another three meetings. On top of that, there were further contacts such as a lunch at the *Sun* offices attended by Campbell and Blair in early 1999. At one point, Campbell and Lance Price cancelled a dinner Blair was due to go to with Murdoch on the grounds that it would 'look like we were pandering to him in a panic'.[39]

The Prodi affair highlighted another consequence of Murdoch's power: as the events unfolded, the Tories were reluctant to criticise Blair, unusual for an opposition. The reason, said one senior Tory off the record, was that they did not want to jeopardise their own party's attempt to improve relations with Murdoch's newspapers.[40] Murdoch used this both as an insurance policy in case the Conservatives were elected and as a threat to Labour that his support could not be assumed. For instance, in the two years before the 2001 election, the *Sun* praised the Conservative leader William Hague, but this was simply a strategic move: in October 2000, in a private meeting, Murdoch told Blair that 'the Tories were unelectable and that was that'.[41]

Labour had inherited John Major's Broadcasting Act with its restrictions on the expansion by large newspaper companies into terrestrial television (Murdoch already had satellite TV in BSkyB). Seeking to please Rupert Murdoch, the government watered down the Tories' restrictions, beginning in late 2001 after the election when Labour, citing technological change, decided to make new laws and issued a discussion paper on media ownership. News International wanted the ownership restrictions overturned and, when a draft communications bill was issued in May 2002, Labour did exactly that. Newspaper groups with more than 20 per cent of national circulation, the government proposed, could extend their power by buying Channel 5. The move sparked public criticism, with the provision dubbed the 'Murdoch clause'. The well-known filmmaker David Puttnam, who led the opposition to the provision in the House of Lords, commented scornfully: 'You cannot expect the government to tackle Murdoch when it needs the support of his newspapers.'[42]

Opposition to the bill forced the government to agree to a clause that allowed a minister to prevent a merger if it was not in the 'public interest'. But this was a meaningless sop, as documents leaked years later demonstrated. Behind the scenes, News International met the government six times during the bill's passage through parliament. Murdoch was worried that the law might mean that the new media regulator, Ofcom, could prevent News International from expanding into television. Minister Tessa Jowell privately assured Les Hinton that the company would be able to buy Channel 5 if it wanted to, and that minor changes to the new law were empty of any real meaning and would not be 'too onerous'.[43]

Yet the Conservatives' law was designed to prevent the emergence of monopolies in the media. This was essential to allow competition to operate and the market to flourish in a deregulated environment. Murdoch's lobbying of Labour on its Communications Act was entirely contrary to his professed belief in the market and competition. His actions actually favoured the emergence of a monopoly—his. The events were summed up in a comment made by Andrew Neil: 'Blair's attitude was quite clear . . . If the Murdoch press gave the Blair government a fair hearing, it would be left intact.'[44] In practice, it was even better: Murdoch was able to extract concessions to allow him to grab even more media outlets.

While protecting his media empire under Labour was no small achievement, Rupert Murdoch's biggest influence during this period was on British foreign policy. A popular (and academic) myth is that tabloidisation, or 'dumbing down', was the biggest consequence of Murdoch's rise as a newspaper and television mogul, but this would likely have happened without Murdoch. His influence on Britain's foreign policy is deeper and more lasting, a remarkable feat for a US citizen of Australian birth. His agenda was clear from the early 1980s, after he bought the *Times* and the *Sunday Times*. In that period, his most easily identifiable political cause was the strengthening of Britain's alliance with the United States which, in effect, meant the subordination of Britain to its senior partner. This was most obvious in the *Times*, which became a cheerleader for Ronald Reagan's foreign policy and thereafter more pro-American. Effectively, Murdoch wanted to curtail Britain's ability to chart its own independent foreign policy. Under New Labour, this developed into two causes: first, to oppose any deepening of Britain's relationship with Europe and, second, to urge Britain to support the disastrous US invasion of Iraq in early 2003. In the first, Murdoch's influence was considerable, even though he faced a prime minister who disagreed with him: Murdoch exercised a veto on pro-European moves by Labour. In the second, Murdoch and Blair were in unison; the problem was that ordinary Britons were reluctant to back the Iraq war. Murdoch's *Sun* helped to galvanise popular support for the invasion, supporting Labour's flawed policy and forever tarnishing Blair's reputation.

From the very start of Murdoch's support of Blair, in 1997, he was explicit that he wanted assurances that a Labour government would not favour further integration into Europe. The result was an interview in the *Sun* in which Blair engaged in double talk: 'Let me make my position on Europe absolutely clear. I will have no truck with a European super state. If there are moves to create that dragon I will slay it.'[45] After he retired, Blair complained bitterly about the 'truly hysterical behaviour of the Eurosceptic media' in which 'the Murdoch papers were especially virulent', but while in office he repeatedly allowed himself to be bullied.[46] Indeed, while Blair and his cabinet were largely pro-Europe and wanted to more closely integrate with the rest of the continent, this barely occurred during the ten years of his prime ministership.

Time and again, in raucous editorials and front-page stories, the *Sun* stated its opposition to the first act of closer integration, which was joining the European Monetary Union. The same message continued to be given to Blair when he met Murdoch privately. Campbell considered that 'it was faintly obscene that we even had to worry what they thought but we had to do what we could to get a better debate on Europe'.[47] Shortly afterwards, Blair and Campbell had lunch at the *Sun*, which Campbell later described as like being at a meeting of the British National Party, the extreme right-wing, anti-Europe group.[48] Less publicly, Murdoch's hostility to Europe meant that he helped fund a body called the New Atlantic Initiative, a project of the American Enterprise Institute. In May 1996, it held a gathering of 300 conservative figures whose overt purpose was to celebrate 'the achievements of Western civilisation' but whose practical task was to reinforce the pro-American conservatism in European politics. (In 2002–05 the New Atlantic Initiative was headed by Radek Sikorski, who worked for News Corporation in Europe and later became Poland's Defence Minister in 2005 and Foreign Minister in 2007.)

The key device by which Murdoch blocked any British move into Europe was his insistence on a commitment from Blair that he would call a referendum before joining the European Monetary Union. This would mean fighting out the issue in a public campaign in which Murdoch's popular newspapers would be at their loudest and most influential. Murdoch was by no means the only person who opposed closer ties with Europe; most of the Conservative Party agreed with him. Nor were his newspapers the only Eurosceptics, since the *Daily Mail* was just as hysterical as the *Sun*, and Conrad Black's *Daily Telegraph* was also adamantly opposed to Europe. But there was never any chance of the owners of these newspapers backing Labour at elections. Murdoch's bargaining chip was that he had backed Labour in 1997, and this gave him extra leverage.

Murdoch extracted promises of a referendum from Blair on several occasions, one of which was in late 2000, when Blair was riding high in the opinion polls and was expected to handsomely win the next election. This did not prevent the *Sun* from hysterical attacks on a minor decision by the government to join a European rapid reaction force in November 2000, which it said would destroy Britain's alliance with the Uited States. But, regardless of the *Sun*'s reflexive anti-Europe reactions, in 2001 Murdoch told his editors that the paper would endorse Labour at the election later that year. The *Sun* dutifully obeyed, saying: 'New Labour is not perfect. There is much to be done. And we will WANT results, Tony. We will demand them'.[49]

In 2002, when Blair began to signal that he still believed in closer ties with Europe, Murdoch publicly renewed the threat that his newspapers would campaign for a 'no' vote in a referendum. In case there was any doubt, the *Sun*'s editor predicted that holding a Euro referendum before the next election 'would be the biggest mistake of Tony Blair's career . . . I can't see the *Sun* campaigning for the Euro ever; [Mr Blair's] best hope—at some far off time in the future— might be that we simply don't oppose it'.[50] By this stage Murdoch was strongly backing Blair in his support for the invasion of Iraq, on which Blair had staked his entire reputation. Even this was not sufficient to guarantee Murdoch's long-term backing, however: shortly after the Iraq invasion, Murdoch made it clear that the issue of Europe would be enough to reverse his support for Blair.

In April 2004, Blair did a U-turn and publicly committed himself to a referendum on the European Union constitution, a decision made after a visit by Murdoch's emissary Irwin Stelzer a month earlier. This backdown was the price for Murdoch's support in the 2005 election. In the end, Blair didn't take Britain further into Europe. In his memoirs, he said that the anti-Europe hysteria had come from an alliance between the American Right and the British Right, who falsely framed the issue as a choice between being a United States ally or a Europe partner.[51] Although Blair didn't mention Murdoch explicitly, this exactly described the pro-American, anti-Europe policy that Murdoch had fostered in Britain since the early 1980s.

Murdoch's influence on the other big issue of Blair's foreign policy, Iraq, was exercised in a different way from that of Europe. Murdoch did not have to bully or cajole Blair on Iraq, because the prime minister embraced the disastrous course set by George W. Bush from the start. A month before the March 2003 invasion, Murdoch praised Blair as 'extraordinarily courageous and strong' and lauded his support for the coming war. 'It's not easy to do that living in a party which is largely composed of people that have a knee jerk anti-Americanism and are sort of pacifist,' said Murdoch, 'but he's shown great guts.'[52]

During the build-up to the war, the *Sun* was the leader of Blair's fan club and his fierce attack dog, savaging his critics. *Sun* editorials daily lavished fulsome praise on the prime minister. In July 2002, Blair was 'utterly steadfast'. In September, he was a 'statesman who inspires confidence that he will stick to his principles' whose 'stature as a world leader grows every day'. In October, after he attacked critics in his party, the *Sun* admired 'a supremely confident performance' in which he was 'at the peak of his form'. In January 2003, Blair's tough line against his party critics set 'exactly the right tone'. In February, the *Sun* urged 'the nation [to] rally behind the Prime Minister', whose performance had been 'faultless'. In March, on the day before the invasion, the *Sun* gushed that Blair had 'won his place in history alongside Churchill and Thatcher'.

Labour endured an agonising split as it rolled towards the invasion, and the *Sun* savaged those who opposed Blair. It urged that the 'squabblers and doubters' within his cabinet be silenced and attacked the 'misguided bleaters who have painted Bush and Blair as villains'. Special targets were newspapers and parts of the BBC that questioned the war. The *Sun* urged Blair to ignore 'the backslapping liberal media that has DISGRACED this country since September 11'. At times, the *Sun* even seemed shocked: 'The British broadcasting and print media has, in many areas, behaved appallingly. Even the Foreign Secretary is against an attack on Iraq'. The foreign secretary, Robin Cook, resigned honourably over Iraq, while Labour MPs such as Glenda Jackson helped to organise protests. The *Sun* described her and other Labour MPs as 'pumping out the anti-American poison over Iraq'. And when millions took part in February in a 'Stop the War' protest, the *Sun* petulantly pointed out that 'fifty-eight million other Brits DIDN'T march on London'.

But all this praise and patronage constructed a golden cage for Tony Blair. Behind the *Sun's* words was Rupert Murdoch's absolute commitment to George W. Bush's policy, not to Blair. If Blair had equivocated in his support for Bush, in the blink of an eye Murdoch would have switched his newspapers' support to the Tories, whose leader, Michael Howard, supported the war. This became crystal clear eight months after the invasion, in November 2003. Murdoch gave an interview to the BBC's *Ten O'Clock News* in which he was asked if Blair still had his support. He replied: 'Let's just say we have a friendly relationship as I do with Mr Howard, and the jury's out.' While he still praised Blair, he was not going to let gratitude over Iraq get in the way:

> We'll have to see how the Tory frontbench looks, if it looked like a viable alternative government, which it hasn't so far ... And we will not quickly forget the courage of Tony Blair in the international sphere in the last several months, so we may be torn in our decision. So let's wait and see.[53]

Blair must have been heartened that Murdoch was at least 'torn' between him and his opponent.

Rupert Murdoch was able to influence the Blair Labour government through a uniquely constructed veto. He used the leverage of having supported Labour in 1997 by threatening to withdraw his backing in the elections of 2001 and 2005. His ability to do this required complicity along with a lack of courage to confront a Murdoch-inspired, *Sun*-driven public campaign on Blair's part. In his memoirs, Blair obliquely acknowledged Murdoch's decisive influence and his own weakness. Writing about the party vote for a new leader (and prime minister) after his own resignation, Blair discussed the contenders. He had disliked Gordon Brown and ruled him out as a candidate; one alternative was the Labour MP John Reid, who Blair had thought would be good. But Reid's becoming leader proved impossible, because 'the Murdoch papers, I fear at Rupert's instigation, just wrote him off'.[54]

CHAPTER 8
THE ROAD TO BAGHDAD

We can't back down now where you hand over the whole of the Middle East to Saddam ... I think Bush is acting very morally, very correctly ... The greatest thing to come of this to the world economy, if you could put it that way, would be $US20 a barrel for oil.[1]

Rupert Murdoch, 2003

It won't be long before some people start to decry the uses of 'excessive force'. We won't be among that group ... Keep the Abu Graeb situation in perspective ... Let's be on the lookout for any statement from the Iraqi insurgents, who must be thrilled at the prospect of a Dem-controlled Congress.

Fox News, internal memos on Iraq coverage, 2005

On 20 March 2003 the long-expected invasion of Iraq began, with the night sky above Baghdad illuminated by sudden flashes as Tomahawk missiles and 'bunker buster' bombs rained down. Rupert Murdoch watched the attack on the panel of seven television screens mounted in the wall of his Los Angeles office. Then, during the first week of the war, he attended several of the 8 a.m. meetings of news producers at Fox News in New York. Sitting in a straight-backed chair, he would browse the newspapers and pepper the journalists with questions about the progress of the war. A senior Fox News executive recalled that week affectionately: 'He's got the bug. He is a newsman at heart.'[2]

By this time Fox News had been drumming up support for the war for over a year, later adopting the US government slogan

Operation Iraqi Freedom as its own. As the war began, on Fox News' flagship program *Special Report with Brit Hume*, the executive editor of the *Weekly Standard* Fred Barnes had enthusiastically compared the war to D-Day in 1944, 'with Patton and his tanks racing across the north of France. Thrilling.'[3] No less excited, the *Sun* told its readers two days later that 'a huge chemical weapons factory has been discovered', which would be 'a huge coup' for George W. Bush and Tony Blair.[4] Excitement also exuded from the pages of the *New York Post*; in a column headed 'Burn Baghdad burn' a *Post* editor, Adam Brodsky, commented on television reports of the bombing: 'I had no idea what Baghdad building was turning to rubble. But I didn't much care; it was a gleeful day, any way you cut it.'[5]

Murdoch's global news media outlets had been cheerleaders for the war ever since Iraq had surfaced as an opportune target of choice following the terrorist attack of September 11, 2001. In each of the three countries forming the key military allies for the Iraq invasion, the United States, Britain and Australia, News Corporation outlets were vital to mobilising public support for their leaders. This was a happy coincidence for George W. Bush, Tony Blair and the Australian conservative prime minister John Howard. No coincidence at all was the uniformity of News Corporation's media outlets' support for the war: Murdoch had insisted on it. Murdoch has never reflected publicly on whether he was wrong on Iraq, even though the reasons for the war, faithfully amplified by his news media, collapsed within a few months of the invasion.

Six weeks before the March 2003 attack, Murdoch's attitude to the war had been made plain. In a period in which intense global criticism was mounting, along with a sense of inevitability, he said: 'We can't back down now where you hand over the whole of the Middle East to Saddam and I think Bush is acting very morally, very correctly and I think he is going to go on with it.' Murdoch was confident that the United States would want to 'get out as soon as they can' after establishing a democratic regime. Flippantly, he added: 'The greatest thing to come of this to the world economy, if you could put it that way, would be $US20 a barrel for oil.'[6] In the weeks following the invasion, when the US action was being condemned widely, Murdoch spoke as an American citizen: 'We worry about what people think about us too much in this country. We have an inferiority complex, it seems. I think what's important is that the world respects us, much more important than they love us.' The US troops would soon be welcomed as liberators, he added.[7]

SUBSIDISING THE REPUBLICAN FUTURE

Murdoch's support for the Bush administration's plan for toppling Saddam Hussein arose from his identification with a group of influential US intellectuals who became known collectively as the neo-conservatives. In his frank memoir, former British ambassador to Washington Christopher Meyer recalled a revealing incident in early February 2001. He and his wife, Catherine, had been invited to dinner by Irwin Stelzer, Murdoch's adviser and liaison with Tony Blair. Meyer was surprised to see Murdoch himself present, along with 'salient members of the Republican Right'. These included Richard Perle, the notorious 'Prince of Darkness', and David Frum, a Bush speechwriter. Meyer described the result of his speaking about Britain's relations with Europe: 'I withstood a full frontal assault from all concerned against our alleged sell-out to the French. A low rumbling sound issued from Murdoch, in which the word "appeasement" could be identified.'[8] Murdoch's muttering of that particular word, with its echoes of the initially compliant British attitude to Hitler, would later become a leitmotiv in his media outlets' drive to war. The word was also part of the lexicon of the neo-conservatives as they made their urgent and uncompromising case for an invasion of Iraq.

Rupert Murdoch's connection with the neo-conservatives had begun in the 1990s, when his political game plan involved the quiet financial sponsorship of some highly ideological campaigns run by people who sought to drag the Republican Party in a more conservative direction. The Californian campaign against affirmative action, to which Murdoch gave $1 million, was one. Another was a project that aimed to revitalise the vision of the Republican Party after its defeat by Bill Clinton in the 1992 presidential election.[9]

The Project for a Republican Future was the brain child of Bill Kristol, an adviser to the US vice-president Dan Quayle. In 1993 Murdoch poured money into Kristol's group, which ended up playing a more influential role in US politics than anybody, including Murdoch, could ever have predicted. Ultimately, it was a powerful influence in taking the United States into Iraq.

Murdoch had long been a friend of Bill Kristol's father, Irving Kristol, who had taught his wife, Anna, at New York University. Like his father, Bill was an intellectual who combined ideological obsessions with practical politics. He had been part of the Reagan era, working as chief of staff to Education secretary William Bennett. Later, as chief of staff to George H. W. Bush's hapless vice-president Dan Quayle, he became a senior strategist for the Republicans. Kristol, a witty and affable man, was referred to as 'Dan Quayle's brain', as much for his own sharp intellect as for Quayle's obtuseness. Bill Clinton once called him 'the man who tells Republicans what to think'. His job, Kristol once remarked, was 'not to hum quietly, it's to change the world'.

Kristol supported Quayle's attack on the television series *Murphy Brown*, which portrayed its heroine, a single female journalist, choosing to have a child while remaining unwed. This epitomised the country's 'poverty of values', which explained the 1992 Los Angeles riots, Quayle claimed. His comments formed part of a generalised attack on cultural elites, who, Kristol said, were 'people who are contemptuous of mainstream values and try to impose their views on others'.[10]

With the defeat of George H. W. Bush in the presidential election of 1992, Kristol began to intervene in Republican politics through his Murdoch-funded Project for a Republican Future. He saw the Republicans' main problem as the absence of a Reagan-like leader. Ronald Reagan's strength had been that he was prepared 'to lead a populist crusade on behalf of the American national interest against the conventional wisdom of the elite'.[11] Kristol's reputation within the Republican Party soared when he played a crucial role in hardening Republican opposition to Bill Clinton's health care plan, which ultimately destroyed it. But he took a more careful position on abortion, steering the Republicans away from the more extreme religious Right.

In November 1994 the Republicans swept back into Congress, seizing control of the Senate and the House of Representatives, where they now held a majority for the first time in 40 years. In the afterglow of the 'Republican Revolution', Kristol, along with *New York Post* journalist John Podhoretz and the *New Republic's* Fred Barnes, decided to found a new conservative magazine, based in Washington. It was to be the 'interpreter, critic, expositor, and conscience of the new political era that began with the Republican triumph', said Podhoretz.[12]

With the help of Irwin Stelzer, the group initially approached Rupert Murdoch for a donation to the non-profit body that would own the magazine. Murdoch surprised them: he was not only happy to subsidise a new conservative magazine, he wanted to own it as a publication of News Corporation, a highly unusual move. Stelzer later said: 'People don't understand. Rupert is intensely intellectual and has intense beliefs that the Republican revolution is taking the country in the right direction . . . He wants to participate in ideas.'[13] Indeed he did. Before he was approached by Kristol and Podhoretz,

Murdoch had been looking for just such an opportunity. His earlier target had been the flagship of the US conservative movement, the *National Review*, founded by William Buckley, which Murdoch had offered to buy.[14]

For William Kristol the appointment to edit the *Weekly Standard* was a move from one Murdoch-supported project to another. In mid 1995 writers on the future *Weekly Standard* moved into the recently vacated offices of the Project for a Republican Future, which were housed in the 12-storey building of the American Enterprise Institute on 17th Street, Washington.

Murdoch initially invested $3 million to establish the *Weekly Standard*, and over the next fifteen years the magazine lost more than $30 million for News Corporation. While the *New York Post* and Fox News also lost money at the time, theoretically they had a chance of making profits. The *Weekly Standard* never had any such chance and was designed purely to exert influence both within the Republican Party and inside Washington. As executive editor Fred Barnes said, '[Murdoch] wants a presence here.'

The *Standard*'s unusual role as adviser and supporter of the newly triumphant Republicans drew sceptical comments from the editor of the rival *New Republic* and fellow conservative Andrew Sullivan.

> These are not new people or fresh voices . . . My idea of magazines is that you're always jousting against people in power. It's a little odd for a magazine to start specifically to celebrate the people who've just gotten in to power.[15]

But when it appeared, the magazine was more iconoclastic than Sullivan and many others had expected. Its first issue contained some criticism of the book *To Renew America*, written by the popular new speaker of the House of Representatives Newt Gingrich. Another article supported the moderate military figure General Colin Powell as the Republican nominee for the presidential election in 1996.

Later, the magazine needled the Republican nominee for president Robert Dole for being uninspiring and out of touch.

It soon became clear that the *Weekly Standard* was no ordinary magazine. Subsidised by a conservative billionaire, it boasted on its website that 'each issue is hand delivered—by request—every Sunday morning to an exclusive list of the most powerful men and women in government, politics and the media'. A vast number of those copies were free, courtesy of Rupert Murdoch. A rival conservative, Scott McConnell, commenting on the magazine's annual $3 million subsidy, noted that 'if Rupert Murdoch's purpose was to make things happen in Washington and in the world, he could not have leveraged it better. One could spend ten times that much on a political action committee without achieving anything comparable.'[16] While the magazine took pot shots at liberals and the Left, its actual purpose was to influence the Right. 'It's going to be more important for us to foster debate among conservatives than to keep shooting liberal clay pigeons,' said Kristol.[17]

Foreign policy was one such debate. Soon after the *Weekly Standard* began, Iraq became its defining theme. At the end of 1997, a special issue was published headlined 'Saddam must go', which attacked the policy of air strikes and sanctions against Iraq imposed by the Clinton administration. Rather than containment, Kristol and the *Standard*'s writers urged a pre-emptive war, to put US troops on the ground and impose 'regime change'. One article simply headed 'Overthrow him' was written by two figures who later became instrumental in the 2003 invasion of Iraq: future deputy Defense secretary Paul Wolfowitz and future US ambassador to Iraq Zalmay Khalilzad. Another frequent contributor on Iraq was John Bolton, later appointed by George W. Bush as under-secretary for Arms Control and International Security.

The *Weekly Standard* did more than simply offer a window into Washington politics to its owner. The main role of this elite magazine was to act as a platform on which its energetic editor and his co-thinkers could promote their extreme views on defence and foreign policy. Kristol was on a 'one-man media blitz', according to the *Washington Post*'s Howard Kurtz. In opinion pieces for the *New York Times* and the *Washington Post*, Kristol projected his campaign for committing ground troops to overthrow Saddam Hussein. In a single two-week period, he was a guest on CNN's *Capital Gang* and *Larry King Live*, Fox's *Special Report* and NBC's *Today* and *Meet the Press* (twice).[18] Kristol also made his pitch for a more aggressive foreign and military stance by the United States in the prestigious journal *Foreign Affairs*. Through all of these, he fostered a network of writers, activists and foreign policy specialists who agreed that US greatness had to be restored, along with its role of global policeman. The rallying point for these neo-conservatives was Rupert Murdoch's magazine.

In 1997, Bill Kristol founded the Project for a New American Century, a lobby group of neo-conservatives and hawks that called for 'a Reaganite policy of military strength and moral clarity'. Many of the original signatories to the project's 'Statement of principles' later worked for the Bush administration, including Vice-President Dick Cheney, Defense Secretary Donald Rumsfeld, Deputy Defense Secretary Paul Wolfowitz and Cheney's adviser 'Scooter' Libby. Another signatory was Jeb Bush, the younger brother of the future president. While Kristol's project and the *Weekly Standard* attacked cuts to defence spending under Clinton, their main purpose was to win an ideological struggle within US conservatism. The project's founding statement argued against 'isolationist impulses' within the Right and complained that 'conservatives have not confidently advanced a strategic vision of America's role in the world'.[19] Later, on principle, it supported Clinton's air strikes against Serbia, which many Republicans opposed.

Understanding Rupert Murdoch's attitude towards Iraq, shaped by Bill Kristol and the neo-conservatives, is crucial to understanding his overall political position. After September 11 the US Right, as well as the whole US polity, debated how to respond to the attack. As it became clear that the Bush administration intended to invade Iraq, the US Right split. The 'realists', some who had been influential figures in the administration of George H. W. Bush, and the paleo-conservatives became sceptical about the supposed justification for the invasion, while Murdoch unequivocally supported the neo-conservatives' call for war. Immediately after September 11 the *Weekly Standard* had seized the opportunity it had been waiting for. Its front cover, emblazoned with the word 'WANTED', showed a picture of Osama bin Laden and Saddam Hussein. Over the next year and a half, the magazine had furiously demanded an attack on Iraq. Articles claimed that its leader would soon have nuclear weapons that would be planted in major US cities and that the Iraqi dictator was linked to Al Qaeda. These utterly false claims were spread around the world by News Corporation's media outlets.

Conservative writers like Scott McConnell, who had worked on Murdoch's *Post*, were aware of the *Weekly Standard*'s role as agenda setter within the Right. In 2005, he argued that the magazine had misled the conservative movement and had capitalised on American shock and anger over September 11.

> Without the *Weekly Standard*, would the invasion of Iraq have taken place? It's impossible to know. Without the *Standard*, other voices—including those of the realist foreign-policy establishment . . . would have been on a more level playing field with the neocons. That would have made a difference.[20]

Most academic and professional observers of the news media are sceptical, however, of old-fashioned theories that emphasise the power of media owners to enforce a political line. More popular are subtler theories of power residing in values and culture, in which the audience is as much implicated as the media owners. Today, media owners are more often institutional investors rather than autocratic moguls. Not so with News Corporation: when Murdoch decided to support the Iraq war, a mighty global machine swung into action. The editorials of his media outlets were uniformly in favour. In the opinion pages of his quality dailies like the *Times* and the *Australian*, some debate on the war was permitted, but key tabloids like the *Sun* and the *New York Post* were wholly given over to drum-beating for war, as was their broadcast equivalent, Fox News. This went on for the eighteen months following September 11, and, in the last weeks before the invasion, it is no exaggeration to say that Murdoch's tabloids reached a state resembling frenzy. Throughout the period, their journalistic scepticism of official pronouncements—from governments in Washington, Whitehall and Canberra—evaporated. They reported uncritically and without reservation each and every claim made by Bush, Blair and Howard about Iraq's possession of weapons of mass destruction, its links with al Qaeda and its appalling human rights record. While the first two claims were empty, it was true that Saddam Hussein was every bit the cruel tyrant he was portrayed to be, but even a slightly critical journalist might have wondered what had changed since the United States had supplied him with weapons in the 1980s, when one of the post–September 11 Iraq hawks, Donald Rumsfeld, acted as Ronald Reagan's envoy to Saddam Hussein's regime. At that time, the Murdoch media backed US support for Iraq against Iran, portraying Iraq favourably, casting doubts on its use of chemical weapons, and when this was no longer possible minimising the fact for strategic reasons.[21]

LACHLAN MURDOCH'S JIHAD

The *New York Post* is regarded as the authentic voice of Rupert Murdoch. For many years, his name appeared as 'editor-in-chief' on the staff list above its daily editorials. But during much of the build-up to the Iraq invasion, his son Lachlan was the *Post*'s publisher and had appointed an Australian, Col Allan, as editor.

The *Post* was among the first news media to target Iraq over September 11. Nine days after the attacks, a *Post* editorial titled 'Saddam's fingerprints' argued that the 'evidence of the extent of Saddam Hussein's possible involvement in this latest outrage is too powerful to ignore'. This evidence, it explained, came from 'Israeli intelligence sources' that claimed that both Hezbollah and al Qaeda leaders had 'been meeting regularly with Iraqi intelligence for much of the past two years'.[22] A few days later, the *Post* told readers that there was 'growing evidence that Saddam played a role in the events of September 11'.[23] The following week, it claimed that there were 'several reports' connecting Osama bin Laden to Iraq[24] and, in succeeding weeks, that there was 'mounting evidence' linking Iraq to both September 11 and anthrax attacks within the United States. The newspaper attributed its claims to 'highly placed Iraqi defectors' and 'captured al Qaeda operatives'.[25]

Over the next eighteen months, the *New York Post* continually called for an attack on Iraq, its editorials twice urging that the Palestinian leader Yasser Arafat be included as a target.[26] Along the way, it foreshadowed the Bush administration's most discredited actions, arguing that fighting terrorism required kidnapping and torture. 'Human rights purists' would object, one editorial said. 'Too bad for the purists. They don't get it.'[27] Opponents of the war were attacked. The *Post* responded to mild criticism by Democrat Senate leader Tom Daschle, arguing that 'he should think twice before shooting off his mouth . . . Remember, there's no room for partisan politicking during wartime.'

In the view of Lachlan Murdoch and the *Post*, the US had been at war before 11 September 2001. In April 2002, it argued that 'the United States is most definitely at war—and has been for some time, even if most Americans didn't fully realize it until 9/11.'[28] Its concept of war was the neo-conservative 'culture war' in which the attack came from pre-modern Islamicists targeting Western enlightenment values. The *Post* argued that terrorist attacks in Africa, the Middle East and the Philippines 'were aimed at the classically liberal Western values which animate America'. Similar attacks were aimed at Israel, which was 'a beacon of Western enlightenment in one of the world's most benighted neighborhoods'. These were undertaken on behalf of a 'larger, more strategic goal: the expulsion from the region of Western values and influence'. Yet framing an attack on Iraq as a defence of Western values made no logical sense. In the Middle East, Iraq embodied one important 'Western value': it was a secular state. The real reason for the attack on Iraq was more likely to be the need to eliminate a relatively powerful threat to the interests of Israel and the United States, as conceived by the neo-conservatives. Among those sharing this world view was the former Israeli Prime Minister Benjamin Netanyahu, who addressed the editorial board of the *New York Post* in April 2002. The newspaper supported the Israeli political leader's protests against US pressure on Israel for military restraint.

The newspaper was also a player in the internal conflict within the Bush administration. It supported Defense Secretary Rumsfeld against Pentagon officials, whom it described as the 'surrender lobby'.[29] In a similar vein, its editorials called for 'fundamental reform' of the CIA and the sacking of its chief, George Tenet. The CIA in its current state 'simply isn't up to the job of taking the War on Terror to the enemy', it said.[30] As the debate proceeded, the *Post* scornfully disregarded 'predictable defeatists from the State Department and the *New York Times*' and attacked Republicans who opposed regime change. When solid right-wing Republicans, such as House Majority leader Dick Armey, opposed an 'unprovoked' attack on Iraq, the *Post* saw this as merely a communication failure on the part of the White House.[31]

At the end of 2002, in the midst of the *Post*'s hysterical Iraq campaign, Lachlan Murdoch endorsed its editorial page, which he said reflected both his and his father's views.[32]

THE ILLUSION OF BALANCE

During the build-up to the Iraq war, most of the US mainstream media were uncritical of the Bush administration's plans, but even in this atmosphere the bullying patriotism of Fox News stood out. It spoke about 'our troops', and its coverage of the war included an image of the Stars and Stripes in the corner of the screen. When this inevitably drew criticism, one host, Shepherd Smith, resented it. 'Fuck them . . . they are our troops . . . We needed a little something to rally around. I admit no apologies . . . Once we're in this war, it's us against them, and we're going to win.'[33] To help report the war Fox engaged Oliver North, a neo-conservative hero of the Iran–Contra scandal, as a military contributor. Fox News doubled its audience to almost 3.5 million viewers during evening prime time. Even more satisfying for Rupert Murdoch was that it beat its cable rival CNN.

Murdoch constantly denied that Fox News was partisan on Iraq. 'We're not in the least bit biased. We're a fair and balanced company . . . [Fox News] is full of Democrats, full of Republicans. The others, they only have Democrats. We don't take any position at all there.'[34] However, a count of pro- and anti-war guests on Fox's two key programs, *Hannity & Colmes* and *The O'Reilly Factor*, during the six months before the war showed that over six weeks a total of 108 guests appeared who debated Iraq, of whom 70 expressed pro-war views and 38 opposed the war.[35] Skewed at roughly two to one, this is hardly balanced. Another striking feature were the identities of the guests. Supporters of the looming war were frequently well-known figures, while opponents were far less well-known, in some cases obscure activists. In the two weeks just before the invasion, the nineteen pro-war guests on *Hannity & Colmes* included many former high-ranking officials from the Reagan administration, such as former Assistant Defense Secretary Richard Perle, Education Secretary William Bennett, Secretary of State Lawrence Eagleburger, Attorney-General Ed Meese and Secretary of State Al Haig. By contrast, the nine guests who articulated the case against the war were largely unknown individuals: two were anti-war activists, one of whom had just been arrested, and two were junior Democrat members of Congress.

In another two-week period, on *The O'Reilly Factor*, there were fifteen pro-war guests and eight anti-war guests. Bill O'Reilly began most programs with a personal editorial, called a 'Talking Points Memo'. On 5 March 2003, he warned the 37 per cent of Americans who opposed dislodging Saddam Hussein that 'we have entered the most dangerous period of American history ever. The terrorists will kill you and your family. The nations like Iraq and North Korea have the ability to provide those terrorists with doomsday weapons.' The comments made by the hosts to their guests often showed respect to those who were pro-war and disdain for those who were anti-war. On 11 March, Hannity was particularly aggressive towards Medea Benjamin, an anti-war activist, accusing her of making 'phony, false, ridiculous, hate-America accusations'. He introduced his next guest, neo-conservative Bill Kristol, with the oily comment 'I'm going to be a lot nicer to you than her.'

All of this mattered. One major study of public opinion found that many Americans held a number of false beliefs about Iraq and that these were highly skewed towards support for the war. While misperceptions existed in many viewers of network television, the study found that 'Fox was the news source whose viewers had the most misperceptions'. The belief that there were close links between al Qaeda and Iraq 'was substantially higher among those who get their news primarily from Fox'. Viewers of Fox also had the highest rate of belief that the United States had actually found weapons of mass destruction after its invasion of Iraq.[36]

WEASEL WORDS AROUND THE WORLD

News Corporation launched a worldwide campaign of support for the invasion of Iraq. When France and Germany opposed the invasion, the *New York Post* described them as the 'axis of weasels', a phrase taken up on Fox News and echoed in London by the *Sun*. France and Germany were 'weasels' who sought only to 'wring as much political and financial capital out of the conflict as they can'. Domestic critics of the war were described as the 'weasel voices of the wobblers'. The *Sun* mocked the 'UN weasels' for going 'soft on Iraq' and said that anti-war critics were 'traitors' and 'naïve pawns of the men who struck America'.[37] It falsely claimed that Iraq had a nuclear bomb or was making one on at least four occasions.[38] Like the *New York Post*, the *Sun* framed the war in neo-conservative terms of Churchill (Tony Blair) versus Hitler (Saddam Hussein), with critics of the war called 'appeasers'. This was also the language of the *Australian*, which heaped scorn on critics of the war such as the Labor Party and reprinted articles from the *New York Post* and the *Weekly Standard*. The *Australian*'s foreign editor Greg Sheridan claimed that Saddam Hussein would possess nuclear weapons 'within two or three years' and wrote a gushing account of his 'dizzying week' in Washington, which he described as 'imperial Rome without the vomitoriums, greater than London was at the height of the empire'. George W. Bush was 'really a modern Winston Churchill'. He also claimed that Iraq was co-operating with al Qaeda and that its diplomats had facilitated meetings with al Qaeda operatives.[39]

Within the Murdoch empire, some brave dissidents refused to toe the line. One was a feature writer on the *Sun*, Katy Weitz, who said that the paper had 'taken a sharp right-hand turn, launching into an aggressive anti-asylum seekers campaign'. Weitz had opposed the looming war for many months, and as the first bombs fell on Baghdad she had tried not to think about it. 'But then I picked up the *Sun*—a first edition copy—and the headline screamed out: "Show them no pity: they have stains on their souls." It was sickening . . . I felt ashamed.'[40]

For those dissidents who remained inside the company, there was a party line and there was discipline. In Australia, an editorial in Murdoch's Hobart *Mercury* argued in September 2002 that it 'would be wrong for the US to pre-emptively attack Iraq. It would be wrong for Australia to ride shotgun to any unilateral US assault on the hated regime of Saddam Hussein.' A written directive from company headquarters stamped on this, and a senior editorial writer refusing to follow the line was given different duties.[41] By January 2003, the *Mercury* was dutifully intoning: 'There comes a time when nations must take a stand. And that time is now'.

THE FOXIFICATION OF REALITY

The first few months after the March 2003 attack on Baghdad formed a period of unsullied victory for the Bush administration and its supporters. Saddam Hussein was gone, and many Iraqis rejoiced. Further 'regime change' in the Middle East was on the agenda. Perhaps democracy could be exported to Syria? Or to Iran?

Among Rupert Murdoch's top editorial staff, a dizzy triumph-alism prevailed. The *Sun*'s columnist Richard Littlejohn gloated that 'the Not in My Name crowd and the Starbucks Strategists got it hopelessly, ridiculously wrong'.[42] A week after the invasion, Fox News presenters Cal Thomas and Sean Hannity helped to host a fundraiser for a conservative group that targeted 'liberal bias' in the media. Thomas explained that the purpose of the night was to deliver 'to the liberal press our version of shock and awe'.[43] The 800-strong audience applauded as Brent Bozell, former columnist on the *New York Post*, roared: 'They're aligned with the protest army, we're aligned with the US Army.' The *Weekly Standard* gloated about 'the stupidity of antiwar doomsayers' and the *Australian* mocked critics of the war, whom it described as 'the coalition of the whining'. 'Remember the quagmire?' it sneered.

The quagmire duly arrived in the shape of multiple car bombings, looting and the raw hatred of ethnic and religious rivalry. Other problems, more prosaic, also emerged. Repairs to electricity and water supply dragged on. Twelve months after the invasion, Iraq had descended into full-blown chaos. Murdoch did a radio interview to reaffirm his commitment to Bush's policy in Iraq. Australia had no choice but to 'see the job through', he said. The situation in Iraq had been 'misrepresented'; however, 'there's tremendous progress in Iraq. All the kids are back at school, 10 percent more than when Saddam Hussein was there. There's 100 percent more fresh water.' He added: 'Most of Iraq is doing extremely well.' Rather than there having been a disastrous policy on Iraq, the real problem was the liberal media, which insisted on highlighting the negatives in a situation of otherwise 'tremendous progress'.[44] A few days before Murdoch's complaint about 'misrepresentation', Fox News' vice-president for news John Moody had issued a memo to the newsroom claiming that the situation was improving in Iraq but that this was being overshadowed in the media. 'As is often the case, the real news in Iraq is being obscured by temporary tragedy,' Moody wrote.

Iraq's tragedy was far from temporary, however. Ten days later, a bloody US operation in the city of Fallujah drew this comment from Moody in another memo: 'We will cover this hour by hour today, explaining repeatedly why it is happening. It won't be long before some people start to decry the uses of "excessive force". *We won't be among that group*' (emphasis added). As the United States floundered, Moody's injunctions on Iraq became more stark. 'Do not fall into the easy trap of mourning the loss of US lives and asking out loud why are we there?' he instructed. The United States intended to set Iraq on the path to democracy. 'Some people in Iraq don't want that to happen. That is why American GIs are dying. And what *we should remind our viewers*' (emphasis added). A few weeks later, Moody urged his news crew to refer to US marines as 'sharpshooters', not 'snipers', 'which carries a negative connotation'. When the first photos emerged of the assaults and humiliation of prisoners at Abu Ghraib, Moody urged that 'we keep the Abu Graeb [*sic*] situation in perspective'.

The importance of such daily memos within Fox News was explained by a Fox producer, Charles Reina, who resigned in April 2003 after six years with the company. They had begun with Roger Ailes, Reina said.

> Roger is such a high profile and partisan political operative that everyone in the newsroom knows what his political feelings are and acts accordingly. I'd never worked in a newsroom like that. At ABC I never knew what management or my bosses' political views were, much less felt pressure from them to make things come out a certain way.[45]

Reina singled out the daily memos from top management as one of the key factors. 'The Memo is the Bible,' he said.

> One day this past Spring, just after the US invaded Iraq, the memo warned us that anti-war protestors would be "whining" about US bombs killing Iraqi civilians and suggested they could tell that to the families of American soldiers dying there. Editing copy that morning, I was not surprised when an eager young producer killed a correspondent's report on the day's fighting—simply because it included a brief shot of children in an Iraqi hospital.[46]

A Fox News spokesman described these as 'the rantings of a bitter, disgruntled former employee'.

In July 2004, four former Fox journalists publicly criticised the network and released further memos, which featured in the documentary *Outfoxed*.[47] Three months after the Iraq invasion, a memo from Moody noting that President Bush had spoken to an Arab peace summit suggested: 'His political courage and tactical cunning are worth noting in our reporting through the day.' By 2004 the insurgency in Iraq was in full swing, and the case for invading the country had fallen apart. In Washington, a Senate inquiry was conducting an exhaustive research into the intelligence failures before September 11. In March, Moody instructed staff: '*Do not turn this into Watergate.* Remember the fleeting sense of national unity that emerged from this tragedy. Let's not desecrate that' (emphasis added). The following day, he added: 'Remember that while there are obvious political implications for Bush, the commission is looking at eight years of the Clinton administration versus eight months (the time prior to 9/11 that Bush was in office) for the incumbent.' It was an election year and Bush's rival was Democrat John Kerry, who was 'starting to feel the heat for his flip-flop voting record', said another memo. And in 2006, when the Democrats did well in congressional elections, a memo noted: 'Let's be on the lookout for any statements from the Iraqi insurgents, who must be thrilled at the prospect of a Dem-controlled Congress.'[48]

VINDICATION OF A PRESIDENT

In April 2004, Rupert Murdoch confidently predicted that George W. Bush would be re-elected as president at the end of that year. Americans, he said, supported Bush's efforts to combat terrorism as well as his invasion of Iraq. 'They're with him on that, completely. He's going to walk it in,' he claimed, adding that the US economy was 'doing extremely well'. The only real problem in Iraq was confined to 'one small part where the Sunnis are, which were the people who supported Saddam'.[49] Murdoch's jaunty confidence was simply whistling in the dark. US intelligence teams had desperately searched for evidence of Saddam Hussein's possession of chemical and biological weapons and had found none. In his 'Mission accomplished' speech aboard the USS *Abraham Lincoln* in May 2003, Bush had claimed that they had 'removed an ally of al-Qaeda', but no evidence had been discovered to prove a working relationship between the organisation and Iraq.

One hope remained of justifying the disaster that had followed the invasion, and it was here that Murdoch could help. A number of intelligence reports from Iraqi defectors and others suggested that Iraq and al Qaeda had, in fact, had various contacts over the previous thirteen years. 'Contacts' do not justify the claim that Iraq had a close operational relationship with al Qaeda, but with careful promotion this evidence could save Bush's reputation by suggesting that Iraq was linked to al Qaeda which, of course, had carried out the September 11 attacks. Hints of a close relationship were repeatedly aired in the *Weekly Standard* by one of its journalists, Stephen Hayes. In November 2003, he wrote an article based on a memo prepared for the Senate Intelligence Committee by an under- secretary for Defense, Douglas Feith, to justify his claims that such a relationship had existed. The Feith memo was a set of cherry-picked data based on alleged contacts between Iraq's intelligence service and al Qaeda. Hayes' article created a minor storm in the serious press and on television talk shows and was reprinted in other parts of the Murdoch group, such as the *Australian* newspaper. In the United States, the article proved politically useful. Vice-President Dick Cheney recommended it as 'the best source of information' on the relationship between Saddam Hussein and al Qaeda.[50] (Later, Hayes was to become Cheney's official biographer.) Almost as soon as the article was published, however, its claims were discredited. A piece in *Newsweek* reported that the memo was

> mostly based on unverified claims that were first advanced by some top Bush administration officials more than a year ago—and were largely discounted at the time by the US intelligence community, according to current and former US intelligence officials.[51]

A former top CIA analyst said the article was a sign of desperation: 'To me they had to leak something like this because the neo-conservatives have nothing to stand on.'[52] Then, a former head of counter-terrorism for the National Security Council poured cold water on Hayes' claims and argued that the article's real target had been 'the consensus among journalists and experts that there were no substantive ties between Baghdad and Al Qaeda' and that its purpose was 'to shore up the rickety argument that Baathist Iraq had posed a real national security threat'.[53]

But News Corporation took Hayes' discredited claims very seriously. His assertions were published in a book, *The Connection: how al Qaeda's collaboration with Saddam Hussein has endangered America*, by HarperCollins, Murdoch's book company. The dust jacket of the hard-cover version repeated Dick Cheney's claim that Hayes' article had been the 'best source of information' on the connections between Iraq and al Qaeda. Publication of the book gave Hayes a platform on national television and radio, and the book was reviewed in many newspapers. On Fox News, Hayes was a guest five times immediately after publication.

Whatever the book's failings, its political effect was to support George W. Bush and undermine the Democratic candidate in a presidential election year. In it, Hayes accused some Democrats of having 'politicised the issue' and criticised the Democratic presidential candidate John Kerry's view that the attack on Iraq was a distraction from the war on terror, not a contribution to it.[54] The book generated continued debate about these false claims and thereby breathed life into the final possible justification for the Iraq war, a vital part of the campaign to have Bush re-elected in 2004.

The final word on the basis of Hayes' claims in his article and then in *The Connection* appeared in a 2007 report from the Pentagon inspector general that examined the Feith memo. The report said that Feith had developed 'alternative' assessments of intelligence that contradicted the intelligence community and had drawn conclusions 'that were not supported by the available intelligence'. Feith's claims had formed part of a pre-war briefing at the White House about the alleged connection between Iraq and al Qaeda from which the CIA had been deliberately excluded. In the wake of the damning report, the remaining task, said the *New York Times*, was 'to finally determine how old, inconclusive, unsubstantiated and false intelligence was transformed into fresh, reliable and definitive reports—and then used by Mr. Bush and other top officials to drag the country into a disastrous and unnecessary war'.[55] The *Times* could have added a further question: how, from the initial calls for an attack on Iraq in the late 1990s through the 2003 invasion to its ex post facto justification, the partisan media organisation owned by Rupert Murdoch had been able to be involved at every stage in promoting that 'old, inconclusive, unsubstantiated and false information'.

Three years after it began, Murdoch had no regrets over supporting the Iraq war. 'The death toll, certainly of Americans there, by the terms of any previous war are quite minute,' he said in November 2006. 'Of course no one likes any death toll, but the war now, at the moment, it's certainly trying to prevent a civil war and to prevent Iraqis killing each other.'[56] At that stage, 2832 US soldiers had died, along with an estimated 65,000 Iraqis.[57]

CHAPTER 9
FALSE DAWN ON
CLIMATE CHANGE

I am no scientist but I do know how to assess a risk—and this one is clear: climate change poses clear catastrophic threats . . . the climate problem will not be solved without mass participation by the general public . . . [News Corporation] need to reach them in a sustained way. To weave this issue into our content—make it dramatic, make it vivid, even sometimes make it fun. We want to inspire people to change their behaviour . . . [We want to] tell the story in a new way.[1]

Rupert Murdoch, 2007

In late July 2006, Rupert Murdoch and his editors and executives assembled at an exclusive resort at Pebble Beach on California's scenic coast. The meeting, on the theme of synergies between new and old media, was one of the global conferences held regularly by News Corporation since the late 1980s. As we have seen, the speakers at these meetings have often been drawn from the Right, sometimes from the more extreme wing of the US Republican Right. This occasion was different: one guest was former Democratic presidential candidate Al Gore, who screened his documentary on climate change, *An Inconvenient Truth*. Others known for their warnings about climate change were the British prime minister Tony Blair and Californian governor Arnold Schwarzenegger. Surprisingly, no current member of the Bush administration was present at the event, though prominent Republicans John McCain and Newt Gingrich did speak.[2]

Choosing the speakers for the Pebble Beach conference had been the responsibility of James Murdoch, the likely successor in News Corporation to his father. The new look had been signalled shortly before the meeting, in an interview with James, who had explained that his television company, BSkyB, had been moving towards carbon neutrality for some time.[3] It was important for the company to get its house in order, so that it could talk to its customers about the need to save energy, the younger Murdoch had said. On this score, BSkyB had made a documentary series, *Final Chance to Save*, about animal extinction. At Pebble Beach, during his presentation, Gore praised James Murdoch for his efforts.

It wasn't all sweetness and light at the meeting with the unprecedented green tinge. After Gore's speech, during question time, vociferous climate change sceptic and Melbourne *Herald Sun* columnist Andrew Bolt congratulated Gore on his performance but then began to attack claims made by Gore in his film. Soon, according to one onlooker, 'the pair were involved in "a full-on barney". Gore ended up shouting at Bolt.' One onlooker thought it was 'brilliant'; another described it as 'embarrassing'.[4]

Before the Pebble Beach meeting, Bolt had written often about climate change and attacked those who accepted the science, frequently in an abusive tone. They were 'green scaremongers', 'alarmists' and 'doomsayers'. In 2004, he quoted a critic who described green activists as having 'too many of the hallmarks of the Hitler Youth'. When cold, unseasonal weather blanketed his home town, Bolt insisted that claims of global warming were thereby disproved. In 2005, he argued that scientists who warned about global warming demonstrated that 'reason is dead. Facts no longer matter. Superstition rules.' In a number of columns, he cited the handful of actual scientists who were climate change sceptics, such as Patrick Michaels and Richard Lindzen. Bolt could be said to represent a certain type within News Corporation: columnists and commentators, mostly male, who were angry about, and scornful and dismissive of, claims of human-induced climate change. On Fox News, there was Sean Hannity and Glenn Beck; at the London *Sun*, Jeremy Clarkson and Richard Littlejohn; at the *New York Post*, Steve Dunleavy; at the *Daily Telegraph* in Sydney, Piers Akerman; and at the *Australian*, Christopher Pearson and Frank Devine. All were vocal sceptics, often framing climate change not as a scientific issue but as an ideological issue, between Left and Right. When the London *Sun*, after Pebble Beach, announced in an editorial that 'too many of us have spent too long in denial over the threat from global warming', it was referring to News Corporation's own journalists as much as to other climate change deniers.[5] So, after Al Gore was invited to the Pebble Beach meeting, the question was: what would happen to these right-wing Murdoch loyalists if company policy on climate change made a radical switch?

Company policy did change. In May 2007, Rupert Murdoch surprised his critics by announcing in a global broadcast to all his employees: 'I am no scientist but I do know how to assess a risk and this one is clear. Climate change poses clear catastrophic threats.' As a result, News Corporation, which he said was responsible for annual carbon emissions of 641,150 tons, would go carbon neutral by 2010. Some measures had already been taken: hybrid cars at News America, solar-powered vehicles at the Fox lot, replacement of wasteful incandescent lighting at the *New York Post*, buying bulk electricity from renewable sources. 'I've started myself,' he added. 'I bought a hybrid car a few months ago.' Any energy that could not be obtained from renewable sources would be paid for by carbon offsets, such as planting trees.[6]

This was remarkable, but there was more. News Corporation, he said, could spread the word about global warming and make an impact through its huge audiences. 'We need to reach them in a sustained way, to weave this issue into our content, make it dramatic, make it vivid, even sometimes make it fun. We want to inspire people to change their behaviour.' News Corporation needed to 'tell the story in a new way'. He warned against preaching and said that 'if we are genuine, we can change the way the public thinks about these issues'. He then added: 'There will always be journalists—including some of our own—who are sceptical which is natural and healthy. But the debate is shifting from whether climate change is really happening to how to solve it.'[7]

There is no reason to believe that Murdoch was anything but sincere when he delivered his speech. And, while some accused him of jumping on a green public relations bandwagon, the speech marked an extraordinary reversal in the ideas and attitudes that he and his news media had been promoting for years.

THE VOICE OF CLIMATE CHANGE DENIAL

News Corporation had been a major outlet of climate change denial in the ten years before its owner's 2007 'conversion'. Moreover, Murdoch himself had been personally involved in the Cato Institute, a Washington-based think tank that specialised in the denial; in 1997, he had joined its board. The Cato Institute was co-founded by Charles Koch, a zealously ideological businessman and the owner of the second largest private company in the United States, which had extensive oil interests.[8] Perhaps not surprisingly, the Cato Institute ran a campaign of climate change denial, as did oil companies such as ExxonMobil. While Murdoch was on the board of Cato, the *Columbia Journalism Review* carried a long article on the then recently established Fox News channel that revealed something of Murdoch's attitudes. In it, senior vice-president of News Corporation Eric Breindel said that Murdoch felt strongly that there was a pattern of liberal bias on most television news, 'so much so that the people who run these channels aren't aware that they're governed by a bias. It is to them, for example, wholly natural that global warming be reported as a fact, not a controversy.'[9] Convincing the public that global warming was a controversy and not a fact had been a long-running aim of the Cato Institute. A few years before Murdoch joined its board, the think tank had published a book by one of its so-called 'senior fellows', Dr Patrick Michaels, an academic at the University of Virginia. The book, *Sound and Fury*, argued that 'the popular vision of an approaching apocalypse caused by global warming has no scientific foundation'.[10] Cato later published two more denialist books by Michaels on climate change as well as similar publications by others.[11] Sponsored by oil interests, Michaels admitted to also having received funding from coal interests in the 1990s.[12] He has been a regular guest on Fox News for many years.

Another climate change denial campaigner sponsored by Cato at the time of Murdoch's involvement was Steven Milloy. Cato published three of Milloy's books, including *Silencing Science*, which argued that 'real science'—which involved scepticism about climate change—was being silenced by the withdrawal of funding, and by social pressure and intimidation. As well as being an 'adjunct fellow' at the Cato Institute, Milloy was a recipient of ExxonMobil's largesse.[13] At an earlier stage, he had helped the American Petroleum Institute to develop a plan to promote doubts about climate change science in the mass media.[14] More significantly, Milloy was at the same time a regular 'Fox News contributor' (a title designated by the channel to its regular commentators) and a columnist for foxnews.com, on which he was presented as a journalist and commentator, even though he wrote about industries from which he received payment, such as the tobacco industry. Indeed, Fox News continued to publish Milloy's columns even after it was told of the money he had received from these industries.[15]

Although it is unlikely that Murdoch personally suggested that Michaels and Milloy be invited as guests or associates of his US media outlets, these outlets proved willing to embrace the campaign of scepticism that the pair represented. If Milloy and Michaels had been the only voices of climate change denial on Fox News it would have been a matter of little importance, but this was not the case.

In the decade before Murdoch's 2007 climate change 'conversion', almost all of Fox News' 'voice-of-authority' program hosts routinely scorned the idea of global warming and criticised those who accepted it. Climate change was presented as merely a political issue. As host Bill O'Reilly of *The O'Reilly Factor* said on one occasion: '[Global warming] has become an intense issue between liberals and conservatives with libs saying pollution is ruining the earth and some right-wingers claiming the warming is simply nature evolving.'[16] Talk show host Sean Hannity suggested that any warming was the result of a natural rise and fall in global temperatures. The problem of climate change was part of 'a socialist agenda'. It was all about 'global warming hysteria and indoctrination', he said.[17]

Because Fox News insisted that climate change was a political, not a scientific, issue, it was able to argue that it was obliged to seek 'balance' in discussions about it. In practice, this meant that it frequently invited two guests with opposing positions to debate climate change; Fox News was fulfilling its marketing slogan 'fair and balanced',[18] while scientific findings could appear controversial, since guests spoke according to political beliefs. No special expertise was needed to debate a political issue, simply two people who happened to disagree. By contrast, seeing the issue as one involving scientific expertise meant employing the methods of traditional journalism, which stipulate that journalists seek out authoritative and credible sources. It was as if the link between tobacco smoking and cancer was still being debated by medical researchers and lobbyists in the pay of the tobacco companies, with the resulting discussion regarded as 'balanced'. Climate change deniers pursued a strategy summed up by a memo from the Brown & Williamson tobacco company, which stated that the object was not to prove tobacco harmless; rather, 'doubt is our product since it is the best means of competing with the "body of fact" that exists in the mind of the general public. It is also the means of establishing a controversy.'[19]

Fox News also often framed the issue as a battle between two evenly matched groups of scientists. Thus, O'Reilly could claim: 'Some scientists say emissions from the earth are making the planet hotter. Other scientists say sun spots or some other natural occurrence is in motion and the heat will soon subside.'[20] Hannity, introducing a debate on climate change in 2004, said: 'Even though *scientists still can't agree* on whether the global warming is scientific fact or fiction, the vanquished Vice President, Al Gore, is using the film [*The Day After Tomorrow*] as an excuse to bash President Bush one more time.'[21] (emphasis added) But Fox News' claims to balance were not always achieved. When climate scientists were meeting in Paris in January 2007 prior to releasing a report by the Intergovernmental Panel on Climate Change, the *Hannity & Colmes* program hosted two well-known climate change sceptics. Hannity introduced the item by asking: 'Is the growing panic over global warming based on fact or fiction?' Unsurprisingly, both guests denied that climate change was caused by burning carbon. Hannity commented: 'I know they're claiming *on the left*, and Al Gore leading the way, that the polar ice caps and glaciers will melt.' He then returned to Gore, asking: 'Is he *lying* to the American people? Is he politicizing this topic for some type of political agenda?'[22] (emphasis added)

The story was similar at Murdoch's other major news outlet in the United States. The *New York Post* repeatedly sneered at concern about climate change. During the 2000 presidential election campaign, an editorial reassured readers that fears about the melting of the polar ice caps were 'overblown and unjustified'. It claimed that 'a couple of scientists with a definite agenda saw an opportunity to advance the discredited—but very politically correct—notion that humans are irreparably destroying the environment'.[23] Later *Post* editorials endorsed George W. Bush's rejection of what it several times called the 'ill-advised Kyoto protocol'.[24] When Bush visited Western Europe in 2001 and was criticised for his rejection of Kyoto, one of the *Post*'s leading columnists, Steve Dunleavy, asked: 'Does global warming really exist? Really exist? I couldn't see it last winter when I was freezing my rear end off.' Dunleavy then quoted well-known sceptical scientist Richard Lindzen, saying that 'the climate is always changing . . . change is the norm'.[25] The newspaper continued the attack on the science of climate change in a 2004 editorial opposing a move by the state of New York to sue several power companies, claiming: 'It can't be repeated enough, there is serious scientific disagreement over what global warming is—or even if it exists.'[26]

As on Fox News, particular *Post* targets were Al Gore and his film *An Inconvenient Truth*. A *Post* columnist described Gore as 'a dangerous evangelist', saying his claims were 'absurd'; Gore 'assesses the trade off between the economy and the environment with the kind of buffoonery you'd expect from a Marxist comic book.' A few months later, an editorial declaimed: 'Everyone knows global warming causes cancer, kills puppies . . . It snarls rush-hour traffic and breaks up happy homes . . . Al Gore says so.' When Gore won an Oscar for his film, a *Post* editorial responded with an attack claiming that his personal consumption of energy was high—a favourite theme of the climate change denial movement.[27]

Murdochian climate change scepticism was not confined to the United States. The *Australian* strongly supported the conservative Howard government's refusal to sign the Kyoto agreement, which aped the treaty's rejection by Bush. The newspaper was not as consistent as the relentless voices of climate change denial in the

United States, however: it was confused and erratic. At one point, it grudgingly accepted that global warming was occurring and that greenhouse gases were responsible. In 2005, it stated clearly that there was 'no doubt that coal-fired power stations make an enormous contribution to global warming'.[28] But shortly afterwards, it argued that

> while environmental activists say science shows fossil fuels are responsible for a global warming crisis, which may be right, they could just as easily be wrong. It seems certain the world is warming but no one knows how long the trend will continue or why it is happening.

It added that 'support for Kyoto cloaks the green movement's real desire: to see capitalism stop succeeding'.[29] Strangely, as Rupert Murdoch began to accept that climate change was real and posed threats, the *Australian* reversed its previous acceptance and became more sceptical.

The heart of the *Australian*'s campaign against climate change science was situated among its highly opinionated pundits and columnists, almost all of whom scorned it. One regular columnist was business consultant Alan Oxley, whose organisation, the APEC Study Centre, hosted a 2005 conference of fossil fuel companies and climate change sceptics in Canberra. In his column, he told readers that at the conference 'leading scientists also explained how the science on which Kyoto is based was unravelling and argued that the cataclysmic threat of global warming is oversold'.[30] Another regular columnist, Christopher Pearson, frequently praised climate change scepticism. In 2006, when even the Howard government finally began to acknowledge publicly that carbon emissions were linked to dangerous climate change, he felt 'bitter disappointment' about curbs on 'what will turn out to be, in all probability, a perfectly harmless gas'.[31]

In Britain, Murdoch's newspapers took another approach. Their editorials rarely expressed an opinion, but they had several columnists who were climate change sceptics. For instance, in the *Sun*, motoring writer Jeremy Clarkson repeated various sceptical claims, including that those who warned about climate change were hypocrites either because they drove 'gas guzzling' cars or were 'in it for the money'; that climate change was merely an excuse for raising taxes; and that the widely accepted science of climate change was false. In 2000, he managed to combine all of these themes in one article, lamenting that 'now people will face a rise in their car tax because half a dozen scientists say carbon dioxide emissions from cars are causing global warming and that we'll all melt. It's rubbish.' He added that scientists 'have to spread scare stories because that way they'll get more money'.[32] The only scientists whom Clarkson mentioned were the same well-known figures in the climate change denial campaign that his colleagues in the United States were quoting, such as Richard Lindzen and Patrick Michaels. Much of Clarkson's commentary was simply abuse. He railed at 'eco-mentalists [who] say we must stop burning oil and gas immediately and go back to living in caves'.[33] The *Sun*'s popular columnist Richard Littlejohn wrote that George W. Bush was 'right not to endorse the Kyoto Treaty which was simply another excuse for European politicians to raise taxes'.[34]

FALSE DAWN

Rupert Murdoch has acknowledged that he changed his mind on climate change and committed his organisation to carbon neutrality largely because he was convinced to do so by his son James; given his commitment to conservative ideas, it was not a conclusion he would likely have reached on his own. After Murdoch donated $500,000 to the Clinton Global Initiative on climate change and made his remarkable speech in 2007, the hopes of many around the world were raised. Here was the global media owner who had earlier backed the call to invade Iraq, and whose newspapers and television channels had promoted the pro-war message in an influential campaign around the world. Whatever they had previously thought of Murdoch, the people concerned with the threat of climate change celebrated the recruitment of the influential media lord to their side. But, while Murdoch had rallied his editors and journalists to campaign on Iraq, he did nothing like this on climate change. Initially, there was a flurry of public relations claims from News Corporation celebrating its own 'conversion' and its commitment to reduce carbon emissions. But the main consequence in the company's news media was that, for two years following Murdoch's speech, they merely muted their enthusiasm for denying climate change. Editorials on the topic in the *New York Post* ceased, though the paper contained barely suppressed barbs against 'carbon kooks' and 'global warming hypocrites'.[35] On Fox News, there were fewer and less angry claims about climate change, but the channel still insisted that there was a continuing debate over whether climate change existed, and it invited industry-funded climate change sceptics to discuss the issue. It also used climate change issues as vehicles for 'infotainment'. In May 2008, the *Hannity & Colmes* show seized on a study suggesting that fossil fuel use had increased because the average weight of people in industrialised countries had increased. 'Obese people cause global warming,' said Rich Lowry, a leading conservative and guest anchor. Later, he suggested that 'you should encourage anorexia'.[36] Bill O'Reilly also took up the theme. One guest, Republican strategist Andrea Tantaros, claimed that 'under this logic, anorexics are environmental champions'.[37]

The suppression cracked in late 2009, when thousands of emails from a British climate change research institute were released on the internet in an event dubbed 'Climategate'. Although the researchers were subsequently cleared of any scientific malpractice, their loosely worded private emails elated sceptics around the world, including those chafing within Murdoch's news organisations. The *New York Post* exploded with a flurry of editorials about 'growing doubt' over the science that underlay 'the carbon-cut scam'.[38] President Barack

Obama was trying 'unilaterally to lower the Earth's temperature—
or kill the US economy trying'. The consequences for the country
would be 'extreme', the paper said, quoting the chief of the American
Petroleum Institute without blinking.[39] In December, a *Post* editorial
celebrated the failure of the Copenhagen climate change conference
which, it said, 'deserved to die ignominiously'. The *Post*'s Washington
bureau chief railed against environmentalists 'who want to dismantle
capitalism and bleed America dry'.[40]

On the eve of the Copenhagen climate change conference a senior
Fox News official had sent an email to journalists and producers,
directing their coverage of the issues. It stated:

> We should refrain from asserting that the planet has warmed (or cooled) in any
> given period without IMMEDIATELY pointing out that such theories are based
> upon data that critics have called into question. It is not our place as journalists
> to assert such notions as facts, especially as this debate intensifies.[41]

Yet the warming of the planet is not a 'notion' but rather an established
scientific fact that some sceptics accept even though they dispute
that its cause is the burning of fossil fuel.

Fox News talk show hosts needed no encouragement. After the
leaking of the emails, Sean Hannity gloated that 'this institute, in
fact, was hiding from the people of Great Britain and the world
that, in fact, climate change is a hoax. Something I've been saying
for a long time.'[42] When blizzards hit Washington in early 2010, he
attacked 'the alarmists [who] manufactured science' and who had
been 'lying to the public'.[43] In April 2010, he announced that global
warming was 'a myth cooked up by alarmists' and warmly welcomed
the author of a new book who had argued that 'the global warming
hype is really just a form of communism rooted in the principles of
Karl Marx'.[44] Nor was it just Hannity. The channel's website, foxnews.
com, published 'Five reasons the planet may not be its hottest ever'.

Hannity's continued scepticism may have surprised Murdoch.
After his 2007 speech, Murdoch had been asked whether the

host's views might change, and he had replied: 'Probably Sean's first reaction will be that this is some liberal cause or something, you know? But he is a very reasonable, very intelligent man. He'll see, he'll understand it.'[45] Hannity never did so, but he did not go as far as another militant climate change sceptic on Fox News, Glenn Beck, who frequently dismissed scientific findings on climate change as deliberate lies. In January 2011, he ranted to his audience: 'Do I believe scientists? No. They lied to us about global warming.'[46] Just two months later Rupert Murdoch made a public announcement that News Corporation was officially 'carbon neutral', rather a hollow gesture given the outpourings of his news media and their undoubted effect on public debate.

In Murdoch's Australian news outlets, equally bizarre things were happening. His flagship newspaper, the *Australian*, seemed actively determined to hollow out any real commitment by Murdoch to 'tell the story in a new way'. After Murdoch's pledge on climate change the newspaper started to intensify its support for climate change scepticism. In 2009, the newspaper widely publicised a book by a leading Australian climate change sceptic, professor of geology Ian Plimer. An editorial agreed with him that 'the science on global warming is certainly not settled', accusing environmental activists of believing that any challenge to their 'prophecies of planetary peril' was 'heresy'.[47] Leading public intellectual Robert Manne pointed out that Plimer's book was 'self-evidently extreme' in its claims and its description of the climate change science community as 'the forces of darkness'. The newspaper had made a grave mistake in its enthusiastic coverage of Plimer's work, Manne said.[48] The *Australian* rejected the criticism and defended Plimer, arguing that 'the evidence for man-made global warming is equivocal'. It added that, 'given that the levels of carbon emissions have been measured only relatively recently, it remains to be proved that their rise is the major driver of global warming'.[49] A few months after this editorial, editor-in-chief Chris Mitchell won an 'Award for Media Excellence' for his newspaper's coverage of climate change. The award was issued by Australia's oil and gas exploration body, whose spokesperson said that the newspaper's coverage was thoughtful and balanced.[50]

Perhaps buoyed by this, the *Australian*'s campaign of scepticism continued relentlessly. In the following year, an editorial suggested that it was time to disband the Intergovernmental Panel on Climate Change in favour of a 'less political body'.[51] By that time, some leading climate scientists were refusing to engage with the newspaper. The chief climatologist at the Bureau of Meteorology, Dr Michael Coughlan, gave up talking to the *Australian* because of its sponsorship of crude climate change scepticism. He told one journalist:

> The *Australian* clearly has an editorial policy. No matter how many times the scientific community refutes these arguments, they persist in putting them out—to the point where we believe there's little to be gained in the use of our time in responding.[52]

The campaign wasn't confined to editorials: one article in the newspaper's glossy weekend magazine said: 'Extreme greenies would have us all embrace a radical new regime. So what would life be like under their rules?'[53] Countless other hostile articles sneered at and dismissed anyone who was concerned with climate change as a 'doomsayer' or 'alarmist'. Such editorials and articles hollowed out the commitment to carbon neutrality adopted by News Corporation.

DENYING THE CLIMATE CHANGE ORTHODOXY

When Rupert Murdoch promised his son James in 2006 that News Corporation would show leadership on climate change issues, he was undoubtedly sincere. He also committed actual dollars and cents to reducing the carbon pollution emitted by his company. But when he tried to encourage his editors and journalists to accept the reality of climate change, he received only a half-hearted agreement to keep quiet. Perhaps they sensed that their boss was not as committed as he appeared. Rather than accept scientific findings, many of his columnists and commentators continued to present climate change as an orthodoxy of the liberal elite. This meant that, as the evidence of human-caused climate change strengthened, an even more sceptical response emanated from News Corporation's conservative warriors: the growing scientific consensus was seen as the strengthening of the orthodoxy. Climate change deniers and sceptics, regardless of their lack of evidence or scientific qualifications, were elevated to the status of brave dissidents against an oppressive doctrine. Then the issue became one of 'balance'. Would the brave critics be 'censored'? Would there be tolerance for 'different views' on climate change?

Opposition to orthodoxy—fighting establishments—is the story of Rupert Murdoch's life. It fits in with his self-image and his world view. All his life, he has seen himself as an outsider, a contrarian, an opponent of orthodoxies and elites. The term 'sceptic' could have been designed to name Murdoch's form of conservative politics. Murdoch's commitment to his son to 'tell the story in a new way' proved to be extraordinarily shallow. When the 'Climategate' emails were released, just before the Copenhagen conference, the extent of his commitment was reached. Or perhaps Murdoch *has* seen the light on climate change but no longer imposes his views on his editors. It just happened to coincide with his simultaneous adoption of the view that climate change was a threat. Whatever the sequence of events, climate change sceptics barely missed a beat within his news media.

In 2011, Murdoch announced that his company had achieved 'its first sustainability milestone' and had become carbon neutral. He proudly pointed out that the British arm now bought all of its energy from hydroelectric dams in Scotland and that his US company Dow Jones, which owns the *Wall Street Journal*, had built the largest solar-power system in the United States. Moreover, he said, 20th Century Fox's movie *Avatar* had proved 'that passionate environmental messages can be fodder for both blockbusters and real world action'. As far as News Corporation was concerned, 'we are well on the way to becoming the innovative, regenerative business we want to be. In the long term, we aim to grow our business without growing our carbon footprint, to power our operations with clean electricity.'[54] Shortly before Murdoch wrote these fine words, the *New York Post* had railed against 'job killing' laws designed to stop climate change, and a *Wall Street Journal* editorial had attacked 'global warming alarmism'.[55]

Murdoch's announcement on achieving carbon neutrality drew some praise from the president of the Union of Concerned Scientists. 'It's admirable that Rupert Murdoch sees the value of limiting his own company's carbon emissions,' said Kevin Knobloch. He went on: 'But that effort is an empty gesture if he fails to take action to stem the efforts of his flagship US news organisation to mislead the American public about a critical scientific and policy issue.' All of this posed an obvious question: 'If carbon neutrality is good for NewsCorp, why isn't Fox News pointing out why that's good for the rest of us, too?' Future generations will not remember that Murdoch made News Corporation carbon neutral, but if Fox News continues to deceive the public they will certainly remember that Rupert Murdoch's company was part of a policy to deny and delay action on climate change.[56]

FACTS AND POLITICAL CORRECTNESS

Rupert Murdoch's erratic stand on climate change is revealing on many levels. At its most basic, it demonstrates that News Corporation adopts policy attitudes to particular issues and then campaigns on those issues. When the parent company and its CEO announce such attitudes, it is expected to affect the kind of news and opinion published or broadcast by its media outlets. Otherwise, why take a public stance on an issue?

Just a few years before his climate commitment, Murdoch rallied his troops on a different cause. The war in Iraq saw the mobilisation of his editorialists, commentators and journalists in a global crusade to convince waverers that the Iraq invasion was justified. They uncritically repeated government claims that Saddam Hussein had weapons of mass destruction that he would not hesitate to use against local enemies or pass on to terrorist outfits such as al Qaeda.

The evidence to confirm Iraq's possession of weapons of mass destruction, cobbled together over a couple of years by intelligence agencies, was deemed adequate enough to mobilise News Corporation's full might to support the invasion. The result was over 100,000 dead and, within a few months of the invasion, the collapse of the evidence on which the war was based. As well as embracing the argument that Iraq has weapons of mass destruction and might soon have nuclear weapons, News Corporation actively promoted the even wilder claims that Iraq had a meaningful connection with the 9/11 bombers from al Qaeda. It simply bypassed the normal process of trying to establish facts, understand them and convey them to readers.

In the case of climate change, the overwhelming evidence accumulated over more than twenty years by the best minds in the field is treated very differently to the 'evidence' about Iraq. For many years, this evidence meant nothing to the columnists and editorialists who joined the campaign to deny climate science. Concern about climate change was seen as merely another claim from a liberal social movement. The trouble with this is obvious. The aims of political and social movement, such as feminism or multiculturalism, can be debated, accepted or rejected. But climate science and the people and institutions that produce it are not political or social movements. To reject their conclusions means resorting to a curiously postmodern argument that the knowledge derived from climate science is simply socially constructed and has no special claim on our beliefs. This is the kind of logic that has led parts of the American Right to support creationism and deny Darwinian evolution.

In 2007, when Rupert Murdoch announced his decision to go carbon neutral and 'tell the story in a new way', there was an interlude in which News Corporation toned down its campaign of climate science denial. But this was not because the strength of the evidence finally convinced its editors. Rather, it was because of a sudden change of corporate policy, imposed from the top. In turn, this had more to do with the inner dynamics of the Murdoch family and a father's hope that he would be succeeded by his son. In this situation, key outlets such as the *New York Post* and Fox News simply played it safe and remained silent rather than encouraging a genuine debate on what to do about climate change. At the first opportunity the climate change deniers re-asserted themselves, with Rupert Murdoch's acquiescence. Today, to varying degrees, News Corporation has returned to its more comfortable role providing a platform for climate change scepticism, particularly in the US and Australia.

EPILOGUE
THE ONCE AND FUTURE MURDOCH DYNASTY?

You've seen great companies go by the wayside because there's been no major shareholders. They have a bad year or two and the Wall St piranhas move in and some one else takes it over and maybe wrecks it ... You may say that's the marketplace working. I think there is a great thing to be said for a media company to have stability of leadership.[1]

Rupert Murdoch explaining why he wants his children to succeed him

The phone hacking scandal in Britain shook Rupert Murdoch's public reputation and badly wounded his son and designated successor, James Murdoch. The sweeping police investigation has seen a string of his journalists, editors and executives arrested and charged. Trials will continue for some years and Rupert Murdoch's reputation will be forever tainted, at least in Britain. The financial cost has also been enormous. Apart from the legal costs and compensation paid to hacking victims it includes the loss of revenue from the *News of the World* and the failure of the takeover of satellite TV provider BSkyB.

The biggest consequence of the hacking scandal has been the splitting of News Corporation into two, with most TV, cinema and entertainment grouped in one company, with newspapers and book publishing into another. This separates the money spinners of TV and movies from the less profitable news and book-publishing enterprises. It also means that the vehicles through which political and intellectual influences can be exercised must stand alone. Among other things, this will spotlight the loss-making newspapers which Murdoch has previously subsidised in exchange for political influence. These include the London *Times* (reliant for a long while on the *Sunday Times*), the *New York Post* (which has never made a profit in twenty years) and the *Australian* whose annual losses are estimated at $25 million a year.

Yet the scandal is unlikely to end Murdoch's ability or desire to influence politics. In 2012, his key American media outlet, Fox News, was part of the selection process to choose the Republican candidate for the presidential election. Fox News is also influential in setting the political agenda for American conservatives and it was a factor in the 2012 presidential election. In 2015, Britain is scheduled to hold another general election. Unless Rupert Murdoch completely changes his life-long fascination with politics, it is hard to imagine that he could resist dabbling in British politics. If he retains the credibility to allow him to exercise any public influence, then the political parties will seek his support, in spite of his tarnished reputation. But for the moment, while politics still enthrals him, Murdoch is fighting to contain the damage to his global media corporation, News Corporation. There is, however, one other issue which he presses to resolve.

Rupert Murdoch comes from a media family. His widely respected mother, Dame Elisabeth, reached 100 years of age, long enough to see the humiliation of her family because of the phone hacking scandal. And while Rupert Murdoch may also live to a similar age, he is keen to ensure that his children continue the family tradition in the media business. Also, Murdoch faces what might be called a philosophical problem. In one part of his mind, he supports markets and opposes establishments, including monarchies such as the British Royal Family. He and his tabloids have repeatedly been scathing about the system of inherited class privilege, of which royalty is the pinnacle. Yet when it comes to the future of News Corporation, no amount of blustering can conceal that the Murdoch family is part of an establishment and an elite both within the company and in the wider world. Rupert

Murdoch, now in his ninth decade, intends to establish a hereditary dynasty by promoting his sons James and Lachlan, as well as his daughter Elisabeth, to senior positions in News Corporation. These appointments are not subject to any sort of market competition. Indeed, Murdoch fears that, after he dies, 'the Wall Street piranhas' could move in and wreck the company. 'You may say that's the market place working but I think there is a great thing to be said for a media company to have stability of leadership,' he has said.[2] Murdoch's hopes for his children are perfectly understandable on a human level. No doubt he wants to avoid the difficulties and confusion which followed his own father's death. Nevertheless, his plans demonstrate a significant degree of hypocrisy.

All this has been complicated by the phone hacking scandal which has emphasised that, while News Corporation is legally a shareholder-run public corporation traded on the New York Stock Exchange, it is actually a family business. Rupert Murdoch and his family control around 40 per cent of the voting stock and, until 2011, other shareholders were happy to let him run the business as if it were his own, including promoting his children to very senior positions. Family businesses are quite unlike any others: they have a primal element and are at their most vulnerable at the point of inheritance and generational change. One crisis has already occurred, triggered by Murdoch's marriage to Wendi Deng, which has produced two children. His divorce from his second wife of 31 years, Anna Murdoch, caused a massive upheaval that had implications for the viability and future control of News Corporation. As part of the marriage settlement, it was agreed that control of the family stake in News Corporation would be passed on to Anna's children, Lachlan, Elisabeth and James, along with Prudence, the child of Murdoch's first marriage. Securing her children's future was Anna Murdoch's price for avoiding an even messier and much more expensive divorce. Rupert Murdoch later unsuccessfully tried to change the arrangement to make *all* his children (including his two young children with Wendi Deng) equal shareholders and voters in the family trust that controls the Murdoch stake in the company.[3] This precipitated the abrupt resignation of his eldest son, Lachlan, from a very senior post in News Corporation in 2005. Having been groomed for ten years within the company, Lachlan left New York and moved to Australia, though he retained his seat on the board of News Corporation.

A similar but less dramatic separation had occurred in 2000 when Elisabeth resigned her senior position in the satellite broadcaster, BSkyB. 'I think he was a little surprised and a little bit hurt,' she recalled. Elisabeth went on to build her own TV production company, Shine, outside the family orbit. 'In some ways it's easier to be a Murdoch outside News [Corporation] than inside,' she said after this move. In 2011, Rupert Murdoch arranged for News Corporation to purchase Elisabeth's TV company and promised her a seat on the board with her brothers. However, since the phone hacking scandal, Elisabeth has consciously distanced herself from the company and not yet taken up the offer of a board seat.

James Murdoch was initially Rupert's most rebellious son and seemed the least likely to join the family business. After dropping out of Harvard, he started a short-lived underground record company, Rawkus Records, that specialised in hip hop. He soon joined the family company, however, and has stayed in it the longest. Until recently, it was assumed he would automatically inherit the position of chief executive officer of News Corporation. But the phone hacking scandal has taken its toll on relations within the family. James and his father are said to have had a number of fierce arguments after which both men have not been on speaking terms for periods.[4] This follows earlier disagreements between them. But though badly wounded by the scandal, that James will not ultimately assume the top position is hard to imagine.

While the time is overdue for News Corporation to undergo historic generational change, there are still several obstacles. The first is that while Rupert Murdoch has talked frequently about how much he desires his children to take over, this can only occur if he retires. This is self-evident, but difficult to imagine. In one of his few comments hinting at the reasons for his marriage break-up with Anna, he told a television interviewer that she had been urging him to retire, so they could spend time together and play golf. 'Retirement was something that was not on my radar screen and still isn't,' he said.[5] In the same interview he suggested with a smile that maybe he will live until he is 100 or even older, like his mother. The point is that Rupert Murdoch has no life outside News Corporation. Retirement must seem like a kind of death to him and it is an option he has been unwilling to consider. Actual death or incapacitation would initiate generational change, but he has cultivated a robust good health for many years. When Lachlan Murdoch was interviewed by biographer Michael Wolff, he explained that family businesses are 'fraught with difficulties' and, in a stumbling attempt to explain his family's dilemma finally said: 'I'm not really answering your question but, uh, don't you know that my Dad's never going to die?'[6]

The second obstacle to a smooth succession is the corporate culture of News Corporation. Every former editor or executive who has gone on the record has attested to its utter dependence on the personality, mood and political preferences of Rupert Murdoch himself. The company has a paternalistic culture, with intense group loyalty built around that single personality. The news division especially fosters a group-think that even prides itself on being disliked by outsiders. At senior management levels, genuine independence of mind is not valued, while yes-men and 'team players' are embraced. An 'Australian mafia' of Murdoch's old friends and trusted mates inhabits the senior layers of management in New York, London and Los Angeles. This corporate culture in which Murdoch alone makes the key decisions and plots corporate strategy has given News Corporation enormous strength. It has allowed the company to be decisive, fast and nimble. It has also created one of the most aggressive corporate cultures in the world.[7] But with any intimation of mortality, it becomes clear that this strength conceals an inner fragility, because so much relies on the decisions of one man.

The persistence of this corporate culture makes a smooth generational transition difficult. With the splitting of News Corporation into two companies, Murdoch has indicated that he will chair the new publishing group but he will not be its CEO. This will be an interesting experiment because it will require that Rupert Murdoch deny himself the right to directly interfere in the most political of his ventures. It is difficult to imagine him presiding with equanimity over decisions with which he disagreed but this could be a first time, especially if a family member became the CEO of the new publishing group.

LOOKING FORWARD

But it is in the political culture fostered by Murdoch and his news media outlets that we find the greatest potential for a rupture in any transition. His children grew up in a different political era to their father. Murdoch's politics were forged in the Cold War and by opposition to the social changes of the 1960s. He scorned the new ideas and social customs of feminism, environmentalism and gay liberation as 'political correctness'. His children have grown up in a different world where many of these ideas are accepted.

Politically speaking, Lachlan is the child most like his father. He loves newspapers and treasures a photo of himself as a 6-year-old, clutching a copy of the *New York Post* while dressed in a baggy newspaper-seller's apron. He hero-worships his father (or did) and shares his right wing Republican values. When Lachlan was the publisher of the *New York Post*, it was at its mouth-frothing worst in campaigning for the invasion of Iraq. In 2002, Lachlan gave a speech to journalists and media bosses that could have come straight from his father's lips. He attacked 'the orthodoxy of the media elite' which, he claimed, disparaged profit making in the news media. He said that 'the dangers of elitism' was one of the 'three fundamental beliefs of News Corporation'. [8] Yet it was Lachlan who had the most explosive disagreement with his father. It is intriguing to wonder whether this has given him reason to reflect on his own and his father's political attitudes.

Elisabeth Murdoch is the child whose political views are most clearly different from those of her father. In April 2008, she hosted a party in her London home that raised over $500,000 for Barack Obama's campaign for the Democratic nomination for the US presidency. This was no passing fad: after Obama had won the nomination and the presidency, she hosted an inauguration party in a London cinema at which guests watched the Washington inauguration ceremony live on screen. Elisabeth said she found Obama 'very inspiring'. She also has some knowledge of the sting of racism. When she married her first husband, Elkin Pianim, a Ghanaian economist and son of a political prisoner, she said she had become aware of racial prejudice: 'Elkin will open my eyes to the fact that people may be being rude to us not because they don't happen to like us but because he's black.' [9] She had two children with Pianim and she has presumably thought a great deal about the likelihood that these children will experience racism.

Like her brother James, Elisabeth supported the election of the Conservative Party under David Cameron in Britain in 2010, while carefully expressing respect for Labour under Gordon Brown. As well, she has been happy to go on record praising the BBC, which has long been attacked by her father and his British newspapers. When Elisabeth's second husband, Matthew Freud, harshly and publicly criticised Fox News for its right-wing propaganda, she emailed the Fox News chief, Roger Ailes. While she distanced herself from Freud's comments, she made the point that she didn't 'agree with everything in the political commentary [on Fox News]'. She then added: 'I am a big supporter of the achievements you've had.'[10]

James is perhaps the most difficult Murdoch to read politically. His early adult years involved a cultural rebellion but since then he has been the most loyal member of the clan, if loyalty is measured in continuity of service to the family business. He joined News Corporation after it bought out Rawkus Records. In 1998, he headed the company's digital program, then became head of the Asia-based Star TV in 2000; in 2003, he became chief executive of BSkyB despite some shareholder opposition. In 2011, he was appointed deputy chief operating officer of News Corporation, the position his brother Lachlan had held before he suddenly resigned. James' public stance has been immaculately corporate, especially under close public questioning during the hacking inquiries. He shares his father's libertarian beliefs about the media business, opposing public broadcasting. In 2009, he accused the BBC of 'dumping free, state-sponsored news on the market' thus making it harder for News Corporation to erect 'pay walls' around its online newspapers.[11] Like his father, he opposes the regulation of the media using the language of commercial populism, labelling governments who want regulation 'elites who are terrified by the people taking power from them'.[12] In his view, the decisions of governments, elected by the people, are not as legitimate as the choices of television subscribers.

However, the overtly political side of James Murdoch is markedly different from that of his father. He has been a supporter of Bill Clinton and Al Gore. On one issue close to his father's heart, Israel, he was not afraid to show his disagreement. When visiting Prime Minister Tony Blair in 2002, James told his father in front of their host that he was 'talking fucking nonsense' on Israel, according to Blair's adviser Alastair Campbell.[13] But it is on climate change that he most differs from his father. James understands the science of climate change and in a revealing 2009 interview warned that 'all of the climate prediction models suggest we are on a worst case trajectory and some cases worse than the worst case. That's my depressing take on it.'[14] He describes much of the policy making in this area as 'totally gutless' with no mandated standards to measure carbon emissions which, he says, is 'crazy'. His wife Kathryn Hufschmid works for the Clinton Climate Initiative.

In 2006, James arranged for Al Gore to show his documentary *An Inconvenient Truth* to a News Corporation editorial gathering in California and he convinced his father to pledge that the company would become 'carbon neutral'. If he has any conscience, and he appears to, then James Murdoch will take very seriously the use of his family's media businesses as megaphones by climate sceptics. This would place the future of outlets such as Fox News squarely at the centre of any negotiated transition from Rupert Murdoch's control of the business to control by his heirs. Here another problem arises. The cable networks overall, of which Fox News is a part, are now responsible for half of News Corporation's profits and Fox News itself has tripled its profits in recent years.[15] James, Elisabeth and Lachlan Murdoch will be forced to make the old, old choice between money and principles, between self-interest and regard for others.

So far there is no sign of Rupert Murdoch genuinely stepping aside. His previous attempt to hand over power to his eldest son Lachlan went off the rails, as did his 2007 pledge to James Murdoch that News Corporation would become a voice for sanity in the debate on climate change. Given these and his oft-repeated rejection of retirement, Rupert Murdoch is likely to remain a powerful figure capable of influencing world politics for a considerable time to come.

ACKNOWLEDGEMENTS

In the course of this project, I received support and encouragement from many people and institutions. I am grateful to the two universities at which I worked during my research: the University of Technology, Sydney and the University of New South Wales. Good libraries are necessary in order to write substantial books, and I thank the staff at Fisher Library, University of Sydney, and the library of the University of New South Wales. Staff at the Library of Congress in Washington, the Butler Library at Columbia University in New York and the BBC library in London were also very helpful. Much of the original research for this book was funded by a Discovery Project grant (DP0774025) from Australia's national research funding body, the Australian Research Council, for which I am grateful.

In particular, I would like to thank Jane Mills for her wise advice and support, as well as Rod Tiffen, Elizabeth Weiss, Peter Botsman, Penny Mansley and Julie Clarke. For research support, thanks to Bob Burton, Shant Fabricatorian, John Fisher, Madelaine Healy, Mitchell Hobbs, Craig Maclean, David Smith and Alex Stuart. I would particularly like to record my deep appreciation for assistance from the late Cathy Carey. For interviews, advice or other support, thanks to Roger Alton, Steve Barnett, Neil Chenoweth, Chris Fogg, Gerard Goggin, Murray Goot, Chris Hird, Godfrey Hodgson, Mark Hollingsworth, Joyce Kirk, Phillip Knightly, Rod Lever, Catharine

Lumby, Brian MacArthur, Brian McNair, Denis MacShane, Robert Manne, Patrick Masters, Adrian Monck, Richard Neville, Penny O'Donnell, Bruce Page, Robin Ramsay, Matthew Ricketson, David Rowe, Lindsay Tuffin, Sean Tunney and Graeme Turner. I would also like to thank the many people who have worked for News Corporation and who helped me but who prefer to retain their anonymity here.

NOTES

FOREWORD

1 Michael Wolff, *The Man Who Owns the News: Inside the secret world of Rupert Murdoch*, Broadway Books, New York, 2008, p. 282.

2 Kaplan left CNN soon thereafter: Robert McChesney in conversation with Rick Kaplan, March 2002. For a detailed discussion of this period, see Scott Collins, *Crazy Like a Fox: The inside story of how Fox News beat CNN*, Portfolio, New York, 2004, ch. 11.

3 Kathleen Hall Jamieson and Joseph N. Cappella, *Echo Chamber: Rush Limbaugh and the conservative media establishment*, Oxford University Press, New York, 2008, pp. x, 240.

4 Eric Alterman provides a compendium of prominent conservatives like Pat Buchanan, William Kristol and James Baker acknowledging the liberal bias of the news is BS. See Eric Alterman, *What Liberal Media?*, Basic Books, New York, 2003, p. 2. Ralph Reed has said the same. See Joe Conason, *Big Lies*, St. Martin's Press, New York, 2003, p. 34.

5 The groups Fairness & Accuracy In Reporting and Media Matters for America have both done rigorous work fact-checking and analysis of conservative news media, and their mountains of resultant work is fire-tested for credibility. The picture is not pretty. FAIR also applies the exact same standard to mainstream news media, and finds much that is flawed there as well.

6 'Some news leaves people knowing less', Fairleigh Dickinson University's PublicMind Poll, press release, 21 November 2011.

7   Jon Stewart says those who watch Fox News are the 'most consistently misinformed media viewers', PolitiFact.com, 20 June 2011 <http://www.politifact.com/truth-o-meter/statements/2011/jun/20/jon-stewart/jon-stewart-says-those-who-watch-fox-news-are-most>.

8   Mark Howard, 'Study confirms that Fox News makes you stupid', AlterNet, 15 December 2010 <http://www.alternet.org/story/149193/study_confirms_that_fox_news_makes_you_stupid>.

INTRODUCTION

1   Ken Auletta, 'The pirate', *New Yorker*, 13 November 1995.

2   Lloyd Grove, 'Rupe's attack dog gets bitten, keeps barking', *New York*, 10 September 2007.

3   See <www.levesoninquiry.org.uk>.

4   Chris Mullin, 'Rupert Murdoch, Tony Blair and me', *Guardian*, 25 August 2011.

5   Transcript of Morning Hearing, 25 April 2012, pp. 9–13.

6   Transcript, 25 April, pp. 47–50.

7   Transcript, 25 April, p. 52.

8   Transcript of Morning Hearing, 12 June 2012, Evidence, Leveson Inquiry.

9   Transcript of Morning Hearing, 28 May 2012, Evidence, Leveson Inquiry.

10 Lance Price, 'Rupert Murdoch is effectively a member of Blair's cabinet', *Guardian*, 1 July 2006.

11 Transcript of Morning Hearing, 14 June 2012, Evidence, Leveson Inquiry.

12 That is, in June, August and October. Exhibit DC1, 'Meetings with media figures as Prime Minister', Leveson Inquiry.

13 Andrew Neil, *Full Disclosure*, Macmillan, London, 1996, p. 172.

14 Jane Mayer, 'Australia's Murdoch is getting his kicks in US political races', *Wall St Journal*, 2 November 1984.

15 Amy Keller, 'Inaugural donor list released', *Roll Call*, 21 April 2005.

16 AAP, 'Bush bad communicator: Murdoch', *Sydney Morning Herald*, 25 April 2007.

17 Tim Dickenson, 'Rupert Murdoch's American scandals', *Rolling Stone*, 18 August 2011.

18 'Pols on the payroll', *New York*, 31 July 2011.

19 Jonathan D. Salant, 'Santorum paid almost $900,000 by Fox News, other interests, last year', *Bloomberg*, 26 October 2011.

20 Matea Gold, 'Fox News pulls Newt Gingrich, Rick Santorum off the air because of their interest in running for president', *LA Times*, 2 March 2011.

21 Beth Fouhy, 'Rupert Murdoch steps up visibility in US politics', *Huffington Post*, 6 July 2012.

22 'News and its critics', *Wall Street Journal*, 18 July 2011.

23 Nick Davies, 'Scam rocks Murdoch's flagship title', *Guardian*, 13 October, 2011.

CHAPTER 1 CRUSADING CORPORATION

1 Ken Auletta, 'The pirate', *New Yorker*, vol. 76, no. 6, 13 November 1995.

2 'Fox's political agenda', *Television Digest*, 4 March 1996.

3 See Alan Murray, 'As in the olden days, US media reflect the partisan divide', *Wall Street Journal*, 14 September 2004.

4 Michael Wolff, 'Tuesdays with Rupert', *Vanity Fair*, 1 October 2008.

5 'Heritage's Luce Award goes to Fox chairman Ailes', press release, Heritage Foundation, Washington, DC, 9 April 2011.

6 Murdoch sold the *Weekly Standard* in mid 2009 to fellow billionaire Philip F. Anschutz, for a reported $1 million.

7 Andrew Clark, 'Murdoch takes pot shot at Obama's anti-business reputation', *Guardian*, 16 October 2009.

8 'Leaked email: Fox boss caught slanting news reporting', Media matters, Washington, DC, 9 December 2010, <http://mediamatters. org/blog/201012090003>. See also Paul Farhi, 'Fox News criticised over email', *Washington Post*, 16 December 2010.

9 David Carr and Tim Arango, 'A Fox chief at the pinnacle of media and politics', *New York Times*, 10 January 2010.

10 William Shawcross, *Rupert Murdoch: ringmaster of the information circus*, Chatto & Windus, London, 1992, p. 302.

11 Auletta, 'The Pirate'.

12 Steve Stecklow, Aaron Patrick, Martin Peers and Andrew Higgins, 'In Murdoch's career, a hand on the news', *Wall Street Journal*, 5 June 2007.

13 Stephen Brook, 'Times and Sunday Times losses rise', *Guardian*, 23 March 2010.

14 Stecklow et al., 'In Murdoch's career'.

15 Andrew Neil, *Full Disclosure*, Macmillan, London, 1996, pp. 169–71.

16 Ken Auletta, 'Promises, promises: What might the *Wall Street Journal* become if Rupert Murdoch owned it?', *New Yorker*, 2 July 2007.

17 Bruce Dover, *Rupert's Adventure in China: how Murdoch lost a fortune and gained a wife*, Viking, Camberwell, 2008, pp. 31–2.

18 Steven Barnett and Ivor Gaber, *Westminster Tales: the twenty-first-century crisis in political journalism*, Continuum, London, 2001, pp. 66–7.

19 Sarah Ellison, *War At* The Wall Street Journal*: how Rupert Murdoch bought an American icon*, Text Publishing, Melbourne, 2010, p. 242.

20 Julie Bosman, 'HarperCollins to start conservative imprint', *New York Times*, 27 September 2010.

21 A selection of these includes Dan Quayle's *Standing Firm: a vice-presidential memoir* (1994); senior Republicans Jack Kemp and Bob Dole's *Trusting the People: the Dole–Kemp plan to free the economy and create a better America* (1996); Republican senator Arlen Specter's *Passion For Truth: from finding JFK's single bullet to questioning Anita Hill to impeaching Clinton* (2000); Republican senator Trent Lott's *Herding Cats: a life in politics* (2005); Republican senator Kay Bailey Hutchinson's *American Heroines: the spirited women who shaped our country* (2005); Bob Dole's *One Soldier's Story: a memoir* (2005); and Republican senator Chuck Hagel's *America: our next chapter* (2008).

22 For example, Peggy Noonan's *The Case Against Hillary Clinton* (2000); and Jerry Oppenheimer's *State of the Union: inside the complex marriage of Bill and Hillary Clinton* (2000).

23 Two examples are Eric Breindel's *A Passion for Truth: the selected writings of Eric Breindel* (1999) (Breindel was a militantly ideological opinion editor at the *New York Post*); and Stephen Hayes' *The Connection: how al Qaeda's collaboration with Saddam Hussein has endangered America* (2004).

24 Auletta, 'Promises, promises'.

25 Christian Berthelsen, 'Prop. 54's big-money backers revealed', *San Francisco Chronicle*, 19 May 2005; Ward Connerly, *Creating Equal: my fight against race preferences*, Encounter Books, San Francisco, 2000, pp. 169–73.

26 The subsidy to *Quadrant* took the form of free printing done by a company that owed money to News Corporation, according to former *Quadrant* editor Robert Manne.

27 Harold Evans, *Good Times, Bad Times*, Weidenfeld & Nicolson, London, 1983, pp. 160–1.

28 Shawcross, *Rupert Murdoch*, pp. 395–6.

29 Bruce Guthrie, *Man Bites Murdoch*, Melbourne University Press, Carlton, 2010, p. 87.

30 Auletta, 'Promises, promises'.

31 *The Real Rupert Murdoch*, a television documentary written and directed by Simon Berthon, Channel 4, London, November 1998.

32 Manuel Castells, *Communication Power*, Oxford University Press, New York, 2009.

33 Peter Johnson, 'Amanour: CNN practised self-censorship', *USA Today*, 15 September 2003.

34 Martin Dunn, 'How to survive Rupert Murdoch', *British Journalism Review*, vol. 18, no. 4, 2007.

35 Dover, *Rupert's Adventures in China*, p. 149.

36 Jo Becker, 'Murdoch, ruler of a vast empire, reaches out for even more', *New York Times*, 25 June 2007.

37 Frank Giles, *Sundry Times*, John Murray Publishers, London, 1986, p. 209.

38 Neil, *Full Disclosure*, p. 164.

39 Viv Groskop, 'Rupert Murdoch is a closet liberal', *London Evening Standard*, 29 March 2010.

40 Guthrie, *Man Bites Murdoch*, p. 7.

41 Shawcross, *Rupert Murdoch*, p. 550.

42 Bob Burton, *Inside Spin: the dark underbelly of the PR industry*, Allen & Unwin, Sydney, 2007, p. 107; Ron Brunton, 'Little more than fiction', *Courier Mail*, 28 April 2001. Murdoch appears as a member of the advisory council of the Institute of Public Affairs from 1987 to 2000 in its annual financial statements and reports lodged with the Australian Securities and Investment Commission.

43 Shortly before Murdoch joined Cato's board, the think tank had published a book that argued that 'the popular vision of an approaching apocalypse caused by global warming has no scientific foundation' (Patrick Michaels, *Sound and Fury*, Cato Institute, Washington, 1992). This was the first of a number of such books published by Cato.

44 David McKnight, 'The *Sunday Times* and Andrew Neil: the cultivation of market populism', *Journalism Studies*, vol. 10, no. 6, 2009, pp. 754–68.

45 Lord Harris of High Cross, obituary, *Times*, 20 October 2006.

46 Editorial, 'Ideas matter', *New York Post*, 30 January 2003.

47 David McKnight, 'Murdoch and the culture war', in Robert Manne (ed.), *Do Not Disturb: is the media failing Australia?*, Black Inc., Melbourne, 2005, pp. 58–9.

48 Eric Alterman, *What Liberal Media? The truth about bias and the news*, Basic Books, New York, 2004.

49 Nick Thimmesch (ed.), *A Liberal Media Elite? A conference sponsored by the American Enterprise Institute for Public Policy Research*, AEIPPR, Washington, DC, 1985.

50 Editorial, 'ABC of management', *Australian*, 6 July 2006, p. 13.

51 Editorial, 'Bundles of optimism', *Australian*, 21 November 2005, p. 9; Editorial, 'One step at a time', *Australian*, 13 September 2005, p. 13.

52 'Rupert Murdoch has potential', *Esquire*, 15 September 2008.

53 Tony Blair, *A Journey*, Hutchison, London, 2010, p. 98.

54 Margaret Canovan, *Populism*, Junction Books, London, 1981.

55 Rick Perlstein, *Nixonland: the rise of a president and the fracturing of America*, Scribner, New York, 2008, p. 277; Godfrey Hodgson, *The World Turned Right Side Up: a history of the conservative ascendancy in America*, Houghton Mifflin, New York, 1996.

56 Richard Perez-Pena, 'News Corp. completes takeover of Dow Jones', *New York Times*, 14 December 2007, p. 4.

57 Trip Gabriel, 'Many charter schools, varied grades', *New York Times*, 2 May 2010; Georg Szalai, 'Murdoch takes on NYC leaders', *Hollywood Reporter*, 29 June 2004.

58 Andrew Edgecliffe-Johnson, 'News Corp buys education software company', *Financial Times*, 23 November 2010.

59 Nat Ives, 'What to expect as NewsCorp dives into business of education', *Advertising Age*, 15 November 2010.

60 Jennifer Medina, 'Little progress for city schools on national test', *New York Times*, 16 November 2007.

61 Diane Ravitch, *The Death and Life of the Great American School System: how testing and choice are undermining education*, Basic Books, New York, 2010.

CHAPTER 2 THE OUTSIDER

1 Anna Carugati, 'Rupert Murdoch', *World Screen*, April 2005, p. 70.

2 John Menadue, *Things You Learn Along the Way*, David Lovell Publishing, Melbourne, 1999, p. 90.

3 Much of this section and the next relies on previous books on Murdoch, such as William Shawcross, *Rupert Murdoch: ringmaster of the information circus*, Chatto & Windus, London, 1992; and George Munster, *A Paper Prince*, Viking, Ringwood, 1985.

4 Shawcross, *Rupert Murdoch*, p. 45.

5 ibid., pp. 54–5.

6 Russel Ward, *The Australian Legend*, Oxford University Press, Melbourne, 1978, pp. 16–17.

7 Phillip Knightley, *A Hack's Progress*, Random House, Sydney, 1997, p. 27.

8 Shawcross, *Rupert Murdoch*, p. 29.

9 Gerard Henderson, *Australian Answers*, Random House, Sydney, 1990, p. 252.

10 Munster, *A Paper Prince*, p. 34.

11 Shawcross, *Rupert Murdoch*, p. 66.

12 Alan Ramsey, 'Once a Laborite and as zealous as ever', *Sydney Morning Herald*, 28–29 April 2001.

13 This section relies on accounts by Shawcross and Munster (see note 3, above).

14 Rod Lever, emails to author, 22 February 2003.

15 Munster, *A Paper Prince*, p. 85.

16 Interview between author and Adrian Deamer, 27 September 1996.

17 Menadue, *Things You Learn Along the Way*, p. 90.

18 Thomas Kiernan, *Citizen Murdoch*, Dodd, Mead & Co., New York, 1986, pp. 113–14.

19 Carugati, 'Rupert Murdoch', p. 70.

20 Munster, *A Paper Prince*, p. 135.

21 Simon Regan, *Rupert Murdoch: a business biography*, Angus & Robertson, Sydney, 1976, pp. 98–100.

22 Shawcross, *Rupert Murdoch*, pp. 209–11.

23 Interview with Adrian Deamer, 27 September 1996.

24 Munster, *A Paper Prince*, p. 95.

25 Regan, *Rupert Murdoch*, p. 101.

26 Laurie Oakes and David Solomon, *The Making of an Australian Prime Minister*, Cheshire, Melboure, 1973, p. 278.

27 Shawcross, *Rupert Murdoch*, pp. 162–3.

28 ibid., p. 169.

29 Kiernan, *Citizen Murdoch*, p. 172.

30 Paul Kelly, *November 1975: the inside story on Australia's greatest political crisis*, Allen & Unwin, Sydney, 1995, p. 244.

31 Murdoch denies the claims made in this account. Menadue, *Things You Learn Along the Way*, pp. 156–8.

32 This account is based on Kiernan, *Citizen Murdoch*, pp. 142ff.

33 ibid., p. 144.

34 Shawcross, *Rupert Murdoch*, p. 266.

35 Kiernan, *Citizen Murdoch*, p. 145.

36 Dan Glaister, 'Media mogul's guest speakers', *Guardian*, 20 March 2004.

37 *The Real Rupert Murdoch*, television documentary, Channel 4, London, November 1998.

38 James Thomas, *Popular Newspapers, the Labour Party and British Politics*, Routledge, Oxford, 2005, p. 77.

CHAPTER 3 AT THE BARRICADES OF THE REAGAN REVOLUTION

1 Jonathan Friendly, 'Ethics of Murdoch papers under scrutiny', *New York Times*, 12 February 1981.

2 Charles Wick to William P. Clark, 'Request for the president to host a dinner', USIA memo, 7 March 1983, National Security Archive, Washington, DC, item no. IC00076.

3 Cited in USIA Memo from Wick.

4 'Talking Points for meeting with Charles Wick and private sector donors', confidential memo from Walter Raymond to William P.

Clark, National Security Council, 18 March 1983 (item no. IC00078), on National Security Archive website <www.nsarchive.chadwyck.com/home.do>.

5   *Weekly Report*, from Walter Raymond to William P. Clark, 20 May 1983. This document (item no. IC00104) can be found on the website of the National Security Archive, Washington, <www.nsarchive.chadwyck.com/home.do>.

6   Jane Perlez and William Safire, 'Head of USIA secretly taped top Reagan aide', *New York Times*, 4 January 1984.

7   Roy Cohn to Edwin Meese, James Baker and Michael Deaver, letter, 27 January 1983, WHORM Subject File, Reagan Library, National Archives and Records Administration, Washington, DC, TR066 123905.

8   Richard Belfield, Christopher Hird and Sharon Kelly, *Murdoch: the great escape*, Warner Books, London, 1994, p. 32.

9   Fay Wiley, 'Carter blasts Rupert Murdoch', *Newsweek*, 27 October 1980.

10 Frank Lynn, 'Tie to Reagan may win Koch a White House key', *New York Times*, 23 December 1980.

11 Friendly, 'Ethics of Murdoch papers under scrutiny'.

12 Andrew Neil, *Full Disclosure*, Macmillan, London, 1996, p. 172.

13 Frank Giles, *Sundry Times*, John Murray Publishers, London, 1986, pp. 202–3, 206.

14 Hugo Young, 'Rupert Murdoch and the *Sunday Times*: a lamp goes out', *Political Quarterly*, vol. 55, no. 4, October–December 1984.

15 Editorial, *New York Post*, 26 & 28 October 1983.

16 Giles, *Sundry Times*, p. 229.

17 Kiernan, *Citizen Murdoch*, p. 287.

18 Geoffrey Stokes, 'The Post papers', *Village Voice*, 4 December 1984.

19 Thomas Kiernan, *Citizen Murdoch*, Dodd, Mead & Co., New York, 1986, pp. 289–90.

20 Jane Mayer, 'Australia's Murdoch is getting his kicks in US political races', *Wall Street Journal*, 2 November 1984.

21 Steven Cuozzo, *It's Alive: how America's oldest newspaper cheated death and why it matters*, Times Books, New York, 1996, pp. 127–8.

22 Mayer, 'Australia's Murdoch is getting his kicks'.

23 Kiernan, *Citizen Murdoch*, p. 288.

24 Nick Thimmesch (ed.), *A Liberal Media Elite? A conference sponsored by the American Enterprise Institute for Public Policy Research*, AEIPPR, Washington, DC, 1985, p. 10.

25 'Reagan to networks: try airing good news', *Boston Herald*, 4 March 1983.

26 Dorothy Rabinowitz 'Network forums for the Left', *New York Post*, 5 May 1983.

27 Dorothy Rabinowitz, 'Soviet TV has some familiar views', *New York Post*, 11 January 1985.

28 'Cord Meyer's trek', *Washington Post*, 7 February 1978; 'CIA: secret shaper of opinion', *New York Times*, 26 December 1977.

29 Steve Cuozzo, *It's Alive*, p. 101.

30 ibid., p. 103.

31 Pat Buchanan, 'Privileged in protest', *New York Post*, 9 March 1982.

32 Letters to and from Milton Friedman, Maxwell Newton Papers, National Library of Australia, Canberra, folder 24, including Friedman to Roger Wood, 8 November 1984.

33 According to Eric Alterman, at a private meeting 'Kissinger revealed that Murdoch also kicked in for half the upkeep of Podhoretz pere's sinecure at *Commentary* when that tiny publication was about to die a well-deserved death' (*Nation*, 23 June 1997).

34 'The wisdom of Norman Podhoretz', *New York Post*, 5 March 1985.

35 'The friends of Norman Podhoretz', *New York Post*, 6 March 1985.

36 Norman Podhoretz, 'Now for the left-wing dictators', *New York Post*, 4 March 1986.

37 'For whom does Tutu speak, anyway?', *New York Post*, 2 October 1986.

38 'Sullivan abandons his principles', *New York Post*, 8 June 1987.

39 Woodrow Wyatt noted that 'Rupert was arguing that America should support Marcos and we should support America in doing so' (Sarah Curtis (ed.)), *The Journals of Woodrow Wyatt*, vol. 1, Macmillan, London, 1991, p. 91.

40 Norman Podhoretz, 'We risk losing the Philippines if US abandons Marcos', *Chicago Sun-Times*, 30 November 1985.

41 Editorial, *New York Post*, 10 March 1986.

42 Editorial, *New York Post*, 19 March 1986.

43 'The case for mandatory testing', *New York Post*, 2 June 1987.

44 'At last, a realistic sex message', *New York Post*, 9 June 1987.

45   Cuozzo, *It's Alive!*, p. 110.

46   Neil, *Full Disclosure*, p. 168.

47   Editorial, *New York Post*, 1 October 1986.

48   Dorothy Rabinowitz, 'Of elves and fairy tales', *New York Post*, 3 October 1986; Norman Podhoretz, 'How Reagan succeeds', *New York Post*, 7 October 1986.

49   'Glasnost is less than an open book', *New York Post*, 12 September 1987.

50   Eric Breindel, 'US licks red boots', *New York Post*, 19 September 1987.

51   Cuozzo, *It's Alive!*, pp. 137, 179.

52   John Podhoretz (ed.), *A Passion for Truth: selected writings of Eric Breindel*, HarperCollins, New York, 1999.

53   Cuozzo, *It's Alive!*, p. 147.

54   Elisabeth Bumiller, 'Reagan team, a bit grayer, gathers again', *New York Times*, 10 June 2004.

CHAPTER 4 GATECRASHING THE BRITISH ESTABLISHMENT

1   Viv Groskop, 'Rupert Murdoch is a closet liberal', *London Evening Standard*, 29 March 2010.

2   Jo Becker, 'An empire builder, Murdoch still playing tough', *New York Times*, 25 June 2007.

3   Much of the following section relies on the diaries, published in Sarah Curtis (ed.), *The Journals of Woodrow Wyatt*, vols 1 & 2, Macmillan, London, 1991.

4   Thomas Kiernan, *Citizen Murdoch*, Dodd, Mead & Co., New York, 1986, p. 311.

5   Curtis, *The Journals of Woodrow Wyatt*, vol. 1, p. 372.

6   ibid., vol. 2, pp. 264–5.

7   ibid., vol. 1, p. 55.

8   ibid., vol. 1, p. 64.

9   ibid., vol. 1, p. 157.

10   ibid., vol. 1, p. 40.

11   ibid., vol. 1, p. 125.

12   ibid., vol. 1, p. 200.

13   ibid., vol. 1, p. 203.

14   ibid., vol. 1, p. 316.

15 ibid., vol. 1, p. 339.

16 ibid., vol. 1, p. 347.

17 ibid., vol. 1, p. 359.

18 Frank Giles, *Sundry Times*, John Murray Publishing, London, 1986, p. 203.

19 Hugo Young, 'Rupert Murdoch and the *Sunday Times*: a lamp goes out', *Political Quarterly*, vol. 55, no. 4, October–December 1984, p. 385.

20 Giles, *Sundry Times*, pp. 208–9.

21 Giles, *Sundry Times*, p. 224.

22 Harold Evans, *Good Times, Bad Times*, Weidenfeld & Nicolson, London, 1983, p. 283.

23 ibid., pp. 235–6.

24 'Mr Reagan's monetarism', *Times*, 10 June 1981, p. 15.

25 'The price of floating', *Times*, 8 July 1981, p. 17.

26 Harold Lever, 'The world's currency casino', *Times*, 15 July 1981, p. 12; Harold Lever, 'We need a new international bank', *Times*, 16 July 1981, p. 12.

27 'Down from Fudge Mountain', *Times*, 23 July 1981, p. 15.

28 'European economic laboratory', *Times*, 27 August 1981, p. 9.

29 James Tobin, 'The perils in Britain's economic experiment', *Times*, 14 October 1981, p. 16.

30 Evans, *Good Times, Bad Times*, p. 288.

31 'Biting the Polish bullet', *Times*, 13 January 1982.

32 'The state of the alliance', *Times*, 31 December 1981.

33 Richard Davy, email to author, 1 December 2009.

34 'The Times and its editorship', *Times*, 13 March 1982, p. 1.

35 'Thatcher airs doubts in invasion', *Globe and Mail*, 26 October 1983.

36 Editorial, *Times*, 26 October 1983.

37 Editorial, *Times*, 4 November 1983.

38 'Dr Kissinger's jolt', *Times*, 23 January 1982.

39 'Dialogue not détente', *Times*, 17 January 1984, p. 13.

40 'The unending threat', *Times*, 2 June 1984.

41 'Power and superpower', *Times*, 26 November 1984, p. 15.

42 Richard Davy, email to author, 1 December 2009.

43 Henry Stanhope, 'Howe underlines risks in Star Wars', *Times*, 16 March 1985.

44 'Howe's UDI from SDI', *Times*, 18 March 1985.

45 'Howe sees envoy over Star Wars', *Financial Times*, 21 March 1985.

46 Richard Perle, 'Arms: too serious to fudge', *Times*, 21 March 1985.

47 Andrew Neil, Minutes of Evidence, Select Committee on Communications, House of Lords, London, 23 January 2008, p. 5.

48 Richard Davy, email to author, 1 December 2009.

49 Editorial, *Times*, 1 June 1985 & 17 September 1985.

50 Advertisement, *Sun*, 11 June 1987.

51 David Hart, 'Help the miners beat Scargill', *Times*, 6 July 1984.

52 Seumas Milne, *The Enemy Within: MI5, Maxwell and the Scargill affair*, Verso, London, 1995, p. 266.

53 David Hart, 'Nothing short of victory', *Times*, 26 January 1985; David Hart, 'Coal: don't let the victory slip away', *Times*, 12 April 1985.

54 Sheila Gunn, 'Crusade from the radical Right', *Times*, 23 June 1987.

55 David Hart, 'Radical is as radical does', *Times*, 8 October 1987.

56 Richard Norton-Taylor and David Rose, 'PM adviser in smear campaign', *Guardian*, 14 December 1989.

57 David Rose, 'Murdoch funded Kinnock smears', *Guardian*, 23 December 1990.

58 Norton-Taylor and Rose, 'PM adviser in smear campaign'.

59 ibid.

60 David Rose, 'Murdoch secretly funds smear group,' *Observer*, 9 December 1990, p. 3.

61 Richard Norton-Taylor, 'David Hart receives financial support from News International', *Guardian*, 10 December 1990.

62 Tom Condon, 'At the Hart of changing *Times*', *Scotland on Sunday*, 18 September 1994.

63 ibid.

64 Brian Crozier, *Free Agent: the unseen war, 1941–1991*, HarperCollins, London, 1994 (paperback edition), p. 90.

65 Brian Crozier, 'Pipeline and party line', *Times*, 7 September 1982.

66 Arthur Gavshon, Mark Shapiro, David Corn and George Black, 'Conservative International: US funds British groups', *New Statesman*, 29 May 1987. A similar account was published in the *Nation* (New York), 6 June 1987.

67 Crozier, *Free Agent*, pp. 187, 245–6.

68 Arnold Beichman, *Free Agent*, book review, *National Review*, 7 March 1994.

69 Rose, 'Murdoch funded Kinnock smears'.

70 Andrew Neil, *Full Disclosure*, Macmillan, London, 1996, pp. 244–50.

71 Curtis, *The Journals of Woodrow Wyatt*, vol. 2, p. 380.

72 ibid., vol. 2, p. 395.

CHAPTER 5 ORTHODOXY IN THE BLOOD

1 Gerard Henderson, *Australian Answers*, Random House, Sydney, 1990, p. 249.

2 William Shawcross, *Rupert Murdoch: ringmaster of the information circus*, Chatto & Windus, London, 1992, p. 266–7.

3 Deirdre Fernand, 'Don't believe the hype', *Sunday Times*, 1 March 1992.

4 Neville Hodgkinson, 'Focus—AIDS—can we be positive?', *Sunday Times*, 26 April 1992.

5 Sun quotes cited in Robin McKie, 'Comforters of a free-for-all lifestyle eat their cheery words', *Observer*, 28 June 1992.

6 Cited in William Leith, 'Kenny and Holly find positive ways to face up to a new kind of fame', *Independent on Sunday*, 11 April 1993.

7 Editorial, 'AIDS and truth', *Times*, 11 May 1992.

8 Neville Hodgkinson, 'Epidemic of AIDS in Africa "a tragic myth"', *Sunday Times*, 21 March 1993; Neville Hodgkinson, 'New doubts over AIDS infection as HIV test declared invalid', *Sunday Times*, 1 August 1993.

9 Neville Hodgkinson, 'New realism puts brakes on HIV bandwagon', *Sunday Times*, 9 May 1993.

10 Neville Hodgkinson, 'The plague that never was', *Sunday Times*, 3 October 1993.

11 Neville Hodgkinson, 'AIDS—the emperor's clothes', *Sunday Times*, 28 November 1993.

12 John Moore, 'AIDS: striking the happy media', *Nature*, vol. 363, 3 June 1993.

13 'New-style abuse of press freedom', *Nature*, vol. 366, 9 December 1993.

14 Neville Hodgkinson, 'AIDS—why we won't be silenced', *Sunday Times*, 12 December 1993.

15 Neville Hodgkinson, 'Conspiracy of silence—scientists question the cause of AIDS', *Sunday Times*, 3 April 1994; Neville Hodgkinson, 'Research disputes epidemic of AIDS', *Sunday Times*, 22 May 1994.

16 Andrew Neil, *Full Disclosure*, Macmillan, London, 1996, p. 20.

17 ibid., pp. 25, 26.

18 ibid., pp. 165–6.

19 Paul Brown, 'Surprise choice as *Sunday Times* editor', *Guardian*, 22 June 1983.

20 Neil, *Full Disclosure*, pp. 35, 52.

21 'Sir Perry, libel star, foul-mouthed TV guest and LSD fan, is sacked', *Guardian*, 9 January 1997.

22 Interview with Brian MacArthur, present at the meeting.

23 Maggie Brown, 'Neil and his Sunday best', *Independent*, 20 July 1988.

24 'What the summit did', *Sunday Times*, 10 June 1984.

25 'Jane Turpin, unlikely industrial spy—part 1', *Sunday Times*, 17 June 1990; Neil, *Full Disclosure*, pp. 328–9. See also 'The dirty tricks campaign', *Sunday Times*, 10 January 1993.

26 Neil, *Full Disclosure*, pp. 334–5.

27 'NHS in crisis: an investigation into the NHS in crisis', *Sunday Times*, 24 & 31 January 1988.

28 Nick Rufford, David Leppard, Ian Burrell, 'Farmers paid £126m a year in subsidies', *Sunday Times*, 1 December 1991.

29 'Revealed—how Europe squanders our money', *Sunday Times*, 6 December 1992.

30 Brian MacArthur, *Deadline Sunday: a life in the week of the Sunday Times*, Hodder & Stoughton, London, 1991, p. 70.

31 Les Daly, 'Nightmare on Fleet Street', *Media Week*, 8 February 1985, pp. 20–2.

32 Neil, *Full Disclosure*, p. 385.

33 MacArthur, *Deadline Sunday*, p. 152.

34 Neil, *Full Disclosure*, p. 364.

35 Editorial, 'What a carry on, doctor', *Sunday Times*, 3 September 1989.

36 Editorial, 'The true view from afar', *Sunday Times*, 1 May 1988.

37 Hugo Young, 'Rupert Murdoch and the *Sunday Times*: a lamp goes out', *Political Quarterly*, vol. 55, no. 4, October–December 1984.

38 Editorial, 'Britain's breed apart', *Sunday Times*, 20 September 1987.

39 Editorial, 'Blimpish Britain', *Sunday Times*, 23 February 1986.

40 Editorial, 'Towards a flat rate tax', *Sunday Times*, 14 February 1988.

41 Editorial, 'The watershed budget', *Sunday Times*, 20 March 1988.

42 Editorial, 'Darling buds of Major', *Sunday Times*, 7 February 1993.

43 Editorial, 'Scandal and betrayal', *Sunday Times*, 22 November 1992.

44 'Inside: Health and Human Services new name emerges', *Washington Post*, 22 February 1985.

45 Neil, *Full Disclosure*, p. 381. Neil mistakenly refers to the book as 'Common Ground'.

46 Jason DeParle, 'Daring research or social science pornography?', *New York Times*, 9 October 1994, p. 48.

47 Charles Murray, 'Underclass: the alienated poor are devastating America's cities', *Sunday Times Magazine*, 26 November 1989.

48 Editorial, 'The British underclass', *Sunday Times*, 26 November 1989.

49 Editorial, 'Return of the family', *Sunday Times*, 28 February 1993; Editorial, 'Darling buds of Major'.

50 Digby Anderson, 'Poverty is a rich industry', *Sunday Times*, 10 December 1989.

51 Shawcross, *Rupert Murdoch*, pp. 266–7.

52 Neil, *Full Disclosure*, p. 166.

53 See editorials on 21 February & 28 February, 14 November 1993; Charles Murray, 'Two-parent families—why they are the only real cure for ghetto children', *Sunday Times*, 10 May 1992.

54 Charles Murray, 'Keep it in the family', *Sunday Times*, 14 November 1993.

55 Catherine Pepinster, 'Think tank urges lone parents to give up their children', *Independent on Sunday*, 5 March 1995.

56 DeParle, 'Daring research or social science pornography?'.

57 David Hughes and Maurice Chittenden, 'Radical Tories seek to strip Queen of her power', *Sunday Times*, 30 September 1990.

58 Nicholas Wood, 'High price paid for family breakdown', *Times*, 16 May 1989.

59 Murray, 'Underclass'; Charles Murray, *The emerging British underclass*, IEA Health & Welfare Unit, London, 1990.

60 Richard Evans, 'Cross-ownership of media no threat', *Times*, 18 January 1990.

61 Cento Veljanovski, letter to the editor, *Financial Times*, 5 January 1991.

62 Rupert Murdoch, MacTaggart Lecture, Edinburgh International Television Festival, Edinburgh, 25 August 1989. Extracts of the speech appeared in the *Times*, the *Financial Times* and the *Independent*, 26 August 1989; and in *Ariel*, 29 August 1989.

63 Thomas Frank, *One Market Under God: extreme capitalism, market populism and the end of economic democracy*, Vintage, London, 2002, p. xiv.

64 Rick Perlstein, *Nixonland: The rise of a president and the fracturing of America*, Scribner, New York, 2008, p. 277; Godfrey Hodgson, *The World Turned Right Side Up: A history of the conservative ascendancy in America*, Houghton Mifflin, New York, 1996, pp. 12–17.

65 Richard A. Viguerie, *The Establishment vs. The People: is a new populist revolt on the way?*, Regnery Gateway, Chicago, 1983, pp. 1–3.

66 Hodgson, *The World Turned Right Side Up*, p. 136.

67 Peter Steinfels, *The Neoconservatives: the men who are changing America's politics*, Simon & Schuster, New York, 1979, pp. 194–5.

CHAPTER 6 OUTFOXING THE LIBERALS

1 Jon Auerbach, 'Murdoch plans 24-hour news network', *Boston Globe*, 29 November 1995.

2 Irving Kristol, 'Why I am still fighting my cold war', *Times*, 9 April 1993.

3 The best outline of the discussion at the forum is in Erich Eichman, 'Fox on the run', *American Spectator*, September 1992.

4 Andrew Neil, *Full Disclosure*, Macmillan, London, 1996, p. 166.

5 Neil Chenoweth, *Virtual Murdoch: reality wars on the information highway*, Vintage, Sydney, 2002, p. 211.

6 Sarah Curtis (ed.), *The Journals of Woodrow Wyatt*, vol. 3, Macmillan, London, 1991, p. 36.

7 Colin Miner, 'Welcome home! Murdoch takes over *Post*', *New York Post*, 30 March 1993.

8 Steve Cuozzo, *It's Alive! How America's oldest newspaper cheated death and why it matters*, Times Books, New York, 1996, p. 310.

9 Editorial, 'A new beginning', *New York Post*, 30 March 1993.

10 Ken Auletta, 'The Pirate', *New Yorker*, 13 November 1995.

11 Editorial, 'Teaching Mr Murdoch', *New York Times*, 31 March 1993.

12 Editorial, 'The Times and Rupert Murdoch', *New York Post*, 1 April 1993.

13 Editorial, 'The gay march on Washington', *New York Post*, 24 April 1993.

14 Michael Medved, 'The missing demand', *New York Post*, 10 May 1993.

15 Mona Charen, 'Move over, rainbow curriculum', *New York Post*, 14 March 1994.

16 Editorial, 'Straight talk from a Democrat', *New York Post*, 11 March 1995; Hilton Kramer, 'Patience is a virtue', *New York Post*, 7 March 1995.

17 Ward Connerly, *Creating Equal: my fight against race preferences*, Encounter Books, San Francisco, 2000, pp. 169–73.

18 Christian Berthelsen, 'Prop 54's big money backers revealed', *San Francisco Chronicle*, 19 May 2005.

19 Editorial, 'Sam Nunn steps down', *New York Post*, 11 October 1995.

20 Eric Reichmann, 'Tabs tangle over Foster death', *Wall Street Journal*, 21 March 1994; Ellen Pollock, 'Vince Foster's death is a lively business for conspiracy buffs', *Wall Street Journal*, 23 March 1995.

21 David Brock, *Blinded by the Right: the conscience of an ex-conservative*, Scribe Publications, Melbourne, 2002.

22 Editorial, 'Al Gore as demagogue', *New York Post*, 6 October 1995.

23 Pat Buchanan, 'The cultural war goes on', *New York Post*, 19 May 1993.

24 Editorial, 'Turn again, Hollywood', *Times*, 11 March 1993.

25 Hilton Kramer, 'Hold the arts page', *National Review*, 21 June 1993.

26 Hilton Kramer, 'Not a pretty sight', *New York Post*, 5 March 1996.

27 Howard Kurtz, 'A crusade to right left-leaning news media', *Washington Post*, 6 June 1996.

28 Brent Bozell, 'Paula Jones vs. Anita Hill', *New York Post*, 3 March 1994.

29 Brent Bozell, 'The dos and don'ts of covering Medicare', *New York Post*, 4 October 1995; Brent Bozell, 'It's no longer the economy, stupid!', *New York Post*, 6 March 1996.

30 This has been shown by academic studies such as the article by Steven Kull, Clay Ramsay and Evan Lewis, 'Misperceptions, the media and the Iraq war', *Political Science Quarterly*, vol. 118, no. 4, 2003–04, pp. 569–98; see also Mike Conway, Maria Elizabeth Grabe and Kevin

Grieves, 'Villains, victims and the virtuous in Bill O'Reilly's "no spin zone" ', *Journalism Studies*, vol. 8, no. 2, 2007, pp. 197–223.

31 Ken Auletta, 'Vox Fox', *New Yorker*, 26 May 2003.

32 Nick Thimmesch (ed.), *A Liberal Media Elite? A conference sponsored by the American Enterprise Institute for Public Policy Research*, AEIPPR, Washington, DC, 1985.

33 Steve Coe, 'Murdoch blasts traditional news', *Broadcasting*, 29 June 1992.

34 Alexandra Kitty, *OutFoxed: Rupert Murdoch's war on journalism*, Disinformation, New York, 2005, p. 30.

35 Frank O'Donnell, 'Confessions of a news producer', *Regardie's Magazine*, February 1992.

36 Kitty, *OutFoxed*, pp. 28–9.

37 Howard Kurtz, 'Weeding out liberals at WTTG?', *Washington Post*, 9 September 1993.

38 Howard Kurtz, 'Fox News boss out after trashing staff', *Washington Post*, 10 September 1993.

39 Martin Walker, 'Why Andy's backing Bambi', *Guardian*, 19 September 1994.

40 Neil, *Full Disclosure*, p. 444.

41 ibid., p. 456.

42 ibid., p. 467.

43 Karl Zinsmeister, 'Live: Rupert Murdoch interviewed by Karl Zinsmeister', *American Enterprise*, September–October 1997.

44 T. R. Reid, 'Media consultant fights bad boy image', *Washington Post*, 29 July 1989.

45 Lloyd Grove, 'The image shaker', *Washington Post*, 20 June 1988.

46 'His lessons to Madison Avenue', *USA Today*, 15 November 1988.

47 James M. Perry, 'Roger vs Roger', *Wall Street Journal*, 20 March 1990.

48 Auletta, 'Vox Fox'.

49 Auerbach, 'Murdoch plans 24-hour news network'.

50 Al Franken, *Lies (and the Lying Liars Who Tell Them): a fair and balanced look at the Right*, Penguin Books, London, 2004, p. 66.

51 Auletta, 'Vox Fox'.

52 Scott Collins, *Crazy Like a Fox: the inside story of how Fox News beat CNN*, Portfolio, New York, 2004, p. 73.

53 John Meroney, 'The Fox News gamble', *American Enterprise*, September–October 1997.

54 Al Franken, *Lies (and the Lying Liars Who Tell Them)*, pp. 78–9.

55 James Ledbetter, 'FNC equals GOP?', *Village Voice*, 15 October 1996.

56 Neil Hickey, 'Is Fox News fair?', *Columbia Journalism Review*, 1 March 1998.

57 Meroney, 'The Fox News gamble'.

58 Jane Hall, 'News channel aims to out fox pessimists', *Oregonian*, 5 October 1996.

59 Collins, *Crazy Like a Fox*, p. 78.

60 Marshall Sella, 'The red state network', *New York Times Magazine*, 24 June 2001.

CHAPTER 7 THE REIGN OF THE *SUN* KING

1 Andrew Neil, *Full Disclosure*, Macmillan, London, 1996, p. 160.

2 Lance Price, 'Rupert Murdoch is effectively a member of Blair's cabinet', *Guardian*, 1 July 2006.

3 Alastair Campbell and Richard Stott (eds), *The Blair Years: extracts from the Alastair Campbell diaries*, Hutchison, London, 2007, p. 77.

4 Lance Price, 'Rupert Murdoch is effectively a member of Blair's cabinet'.

5 *The Media Report*, radio program, ABC Radio National, Sydney, 28 June 2007.

6 John Cassidy, 'Murdoch's game', *New Yorker*, 16 October 2006.

7 Robert Preston, 'Murdoch call raises questions over Blair link', *Financial Times*, 26 March 1998.

8 Andrew Neil, 'Blair's huge new asset—a defecting tory press', *Sunday Times*, 9 July 1995.

9 Sarah Curtis (ed.), *The Journals of Woodrow Wyatt*, Macmillan, London, 1991, vol. 3, p. 3.

10 Roy Greenslade, *Press Gang: how newspapers make profits from propaganda*, Macmillan, London, 2003, p. 607.

11 Neil, *Full Disclosure*, p. 9.

12 *Sun*, 16 & 17 March 1994.

13 Greenslade, *Press Gang*, p. 616.

14 ibid., pp. 617–18.

15 Curtis, *The Journals of Woodrow Wyatt*, vol. 3, p. 139.

16 ibid., vol. 3, p. 443.

17 ibid., vol. 3, p. 481.

18 ibid., vol. 3, p. 511.

19 ibid., vol. 3, p. 602.

20 Robert Shrimsley, 'Murdoch hints he might support Blair', *Daily Telegraph*, 9 August 1994.

21 Neil, *Full Disclosure*, p. 170.

22 Sean Tunney, *Labour and the Press: from New Left to New Labour*, Sussex Academic Press, Eastbourne, 2007, p. 109.

23 Editorial, *Sun*, 24 March 1995.

24 Stephen Castle, 'How Labour wooed and won the Sun', *Independent on Sunday*, 23 March 1997.

25 Raymond Snoddy, 'Murdoch's love for Labour', *Marketing*, 20 July 1995.

26 Fran Abrams and Anthony Bevins, 'Murdoch's courtship to Blair finally pays off', *Independent*, 11 February 1998.

27 'Is Labour the true heir to Thatcher?', *Times*, 17 July 1995.

28 Alastair Campbell, *The Blair Years*, p. 76.

29 ibid., p. 75.

30 Andy McSmith, 'Charmer Blair tries wooing tory press', *Observer*, 2 February 1997.

31 Campbell and Stott, *The Blair Years*, p. 111.

32 ibid., p. 156.

33 Confidential interview with *News of the World* journalist, London, 2007.

34 Editorial, *Sun*, 1 May 1997.

35 David Wooding, 'It's the *Sun* wot swung it', *Sun*, 2 May 1997.

36 'Now we have a leader again', *Sun*, 2 May 1997.

37 Preston, 'Murdoch call raises questions over Blair link'.

38 Campbell and Stott, *The Blair Years*, p. 287.

39 Lance Price, *Spin Doctor's Diary: inside Number Ten with New Labour*, Hodder & Stoughton, London, 2005, pp. 86, 119.

40 Robert Preston and Liam Halligan, 'Government pressed on newspaper market', *Financial Times*, 25 March 1998.

41 Campbell and Stott, *The Blair Years*, p. 477.

42 Tunney, *Labour and the Press*, p. 130.

43 ibid., pp. 134–5; David Leigh and Rob Evans, 'Files show extent of Murdoch lobbying', *Guardian*, 3 January 2005.

44 Jo Becker, 'Murdoch, ruler of a vast empire, reaches out for even more', *New York Times*, 25 June 2007.

45 Peter Oborne, *The Rise of Political Lying*, Free Press, London, 2005, p. 44.

46 Tony Blair, *A Journey*, Hutchison, London, 2010, p. 533.

47 Campbell and Stott, *The Blair Years*, p. 363.

48 Price, *The Spin Doctor's Diary*, p. 86.

49 Editorial, 'It's in the bag, Tony', *Sun*, 8 March 2001.

50 Tim Burt, 'Sun editor cautions Blair on pitfalls of Euro vote', *Financial Times*, 15 October 2002.

51 Blair, *The Journey*, pp. 533–4.

52 Nigel Morris, 'The threat of war', *Independent*, 12 February 2003.

53 Matt Wells, 'Murdoch papers may switch', *Guardian*, 15 November 2003.

54 Blair, *A Journey*, p. 655.

CHAPTER 8 THE ROAD TO BAGHDAD

1 Max Walsh, 'The Murdoch interview', *Bulletin*, 12 February 2003.

2 David Kirkpatrick, 'Mr. Murdoch's war', *New York Times*, 7 April 2003.

3 'All Stars discuss progress of war in Iraq', *Special Report with Brit Hume*, television program, Fox News, New York, 22 March 2003.

4 Brian Flynn, 'Chemical weapons plant is found', *Sun*, 24 March 2003.

5 Adam Brodsky, 'Burn Baghdad burn', *New York Post*, 29 March 2003.

6 Walsh, 'The Murdoch interview'.

7 Gary Gentile, 'Murdoch: Iraqis will welcome US troops', Associated Press, 3 April 2003.

8 Christopher Meyer, *DC Confidential*, Phoenix, London, 2005, p. 172.

9 Paul Starobin, 'If you like their publications … will you like their politics?', *National Journal*, 3 June 1995; see also Howard Kurtz, 'Magazine for the right-minded', *Washington Post*, 9 September 1995.

10 James M. Perry and John Harwood, 'Kristol, White House's smartest guy, is leading Quayle defender', *Wall Street Journal*, 30 July 1992.

11 John King, 'Conservatives form another group to save GOP', Associated Press, 22 October 1993.

12 Tim Bogardus, 'A new standard', *Folio*, 15 May 1996.

13 Starobin, 'If you like their publications'.

14 Richard Brookhiser, *Right Time, Right Place*, Basic Books, New York, 2009, pp. 200–1.

15 Kurtz, 'Magazine for the right-minded'.

16 Scott McConnell, 'The *Weekly Standard*'s war', *American Conservative*, 21 November 2005.

17 Jonathan Freedland, 'Rupert's push on Capitol Hill', *Guardian*, 21 August 1995.

18 Howard Kurtz, 'Right face, right time', *Washington Post*, 1 February 2000.

19 'Statement of principles', Project for a New American Century, Washington, DC, 3 June 1997, <www.newamericancentury.org/statementofprinciples.htm>.

20 McConnell, 'The *Weekly Standard*'s war'.

21 Eddie Davers, 'Our Australian: Murdoch's flagship and shifting US attitudes to Iraq', *Overland*, no. 170, autumn 2003.

22 'Saddam's fingerprints', *New York Post*, 20 September 2001.

23 'An alliance to fit the task', *New York Post*, 23 September 2001.

24 'Now more than ever', *New York Post*, 7 October 2001.

25 Editorial, *New York Post*, 25 September, 7 October & 9 November 2001.

26 Editorial, 'The task at hand', *New York Post*, 16 September 2001; Editorial, 'No exceptions for Arafat', *New York Post*, 20 November 2001.

27 Editorial, 'To protect the innocent', *New York Post*, 23 November 2001.

28 Editorial, 'Two fronts, one holy war', *New York Post*, 1 April 2002.

29 Editorial, 'The Pentagon's surrender lobby', *New York Post*, 29 May 2002.

30 Editorial, 'On borrowed time', *New York Post*, 18 June 2002.

31 Editorial, 'War with no Armey?', *New York Post*, 12 August 2002; Editorial, 'What rush to war?', *New York Post*, 17 August 2002.

32 Joe Strupp, 'The son also rises', *Mediaweek*, 16 December 2002.

33 Scott Collins, *Crazy Like a Fox: the inside story of how Fox News beat CNN*, Portfolio, New York, 2004, pp. 212–13.

34 *PM*, radio program, ABC Radio National, Sydney, 26 October 2004.

35 The study, carried out by the author, focused on these programs over the first fortnights of November 2002, January 2003 and March 2003.

36 Steven Kull, Clay Ramsay and Evan Lewis, 'Misperceptions, the media and the Iraq war', *Political Science Quarterly*, vol. 118, no. 4, 2003–04, pp. 569–98.

37 Editorial, *Sun*, 15 February 2002.

38 Editorial, *Sun*, 6 March, 30 July, 31 August & 4 September 2002.

39 Greg Sheridan, 'While the world dallies, Iraq busily arms', *Australian*, 15 August 2002; Greg Sheridan, 'In power we trust', *Australian*, 20 July 2002; Greg Sheridan, 'Kissinger's bow to Bush', *Australian*, 23 January 2003; Greg Sheridan, 'Iraqi diplomats expulsion a show of intelligence', *Australian*, 10 March 2003.

40 Katy Weitz, 'Why I quit the *Sun*', *Guardian*, 31 March 2003.

41 Robert Manne, *Do Not Disturb: is the media failing Australia?*, Melbourne, Black Inc., 2005, p. 76.

42 Richard Littlejohn, 'Starbucks Strategists get it wrong again', *Sun*, 8 April 2003.

43 Liz Cox, 'The bias busters' ball', *Columbia Journalism Review*, vol. 42, no. 1, May–June 2003, p. 72.

44 Peter Ryan, 'News Corp stocks rise', *PM*, radio program, ABC Radio, Sydney, 7 April 2004.

45 Tim Rutten, 'Former producer blows whistle on Fox News', *Oakland Tribune*, 2 November 2003.

46 Charlie Reina, 'The Fox News memo: Ex-Fox News staffer on the memo', Poynter Online, St Petersburg, FL, 31 October 2003. Available at <www.pssht.com/fauxarticles/foxnews_bias>.

47 The memos can be found at '33 internal Fox editorial memos reviewed by *MMFA* reveal Fox News Channel's inner workings', Media Matters, Washington, DC, 14 July 2004, <http://mediamatters.org/research/200407140002>. Other memos already mentioned can be found in Alexandra Kitty, *Outfoxed: Rupert Murdoch's war on journalism*, Disinformation, New York, 2005, pp. 76–7.

48 'Fox News internal memo', *Huffington Post*, posted 14 November 2006, <www.huffingtonpost.com/2006/11/14/fox-news-internal-memo-be_n_34128.html>.

49 *PM*, radio program, ABC Radio National, Sydney, 7 April 2004.

50 Dana Milbank, 'Bush hails Al Quaeda arrest in Iraq', *Washington Post*, 27 January 2004.

51 Michael Isikoff and Mark Hosenball, 'Case decidedly not closed', *Newsweek*, 19 November 2003.

52 Jim Lobe, 'Leak of secret memo by neo-cons widely criticized', *Inter Press Service*, 20 November 2003.

53 Daniel Benjamin, 'The case of the misunderstood memo', *Slate*, 9 December 2003, <www.slate.com/id/2092180>.

54 Stephen F. Hayes, *The Connection: how al Qaeda's collaboration with Saddam Hussein has endangered America*, HarperCollins, New York, 2004, pp. xvi–xvii, 185.

55 Editorial, 'The build-a-war workshop', *New York Times*, 10 February 2007.

56 Agence France Presse, 'Murdoch says US death toll in Iraq "minute"', 6 November 2006.

57 Figures taken from the Iraq Body Count website, <www.iraqbodycount.org>.

CHAPTER 9 FALSE DAWN ON CLIMATE CHANGE

1 Rupert Murdoch, 'Carbon plan the world can copy', edited speech, *Gold Coast Bulletin*, 10 May 2007.

2 John Cassidy, 'Murdoch's game', *New Yorker*, 16 October 2006.

3 Robin Hicks, 'Sustainability: green-sky thinking', *Campaign*, 14 July 2006.

4 Tim Blair, 'Winds of change', *Bulletin*, 16 August 2006.

5 Editorial, 'Well saved', *Sun*, 11 September 2006.

6 'Rupert Murdoch's speech on carbon neutrality', *Australian*, 3 November 2007.

7 Rupert Murdoch, 'Duty to the future', *New York Post*, 10 May 2007; see also Murdoch, 'Carbon plan world can copy'.

8 'Koch brothers: bioboxes', Associated Press, 28 March 1998. Charles Koch said that reading a book on free market economics in 1962 was a pivotal intellectual experience for him. To describe its management

practices, Koch Industries uses terms drawn from free market philosophy such as 'comparative advantage', 'creative destruction' and 'spontaneous order' (Patti Bond, 'The George-Pacific-Koch deal', *Atlanta Journal-Constitution*, 20 November 2005).

9 Neil Hickey, 'Is Fox News fair?', *Columbia Journalism Review*, 1 March 1998.

10 Patrick J. Michaels, *Sound and Fury: the science and politics of global warming*, Cato Institute, Washington, DC, 1992, inside front cover.

11 Patrick J. Michaels and Robert C. Balling, *The Satanic Gases: clearing the air about global warming*, (2000); Patrick J. Michaels, *Meltdown: the predictable distortion of global warming by scientists, politicians, and the media* (2004).

12 Sharon Begley, 'The truth about denial', *Newsweek*, 13 August 2007.

13 Paul Thacker, 'At Fox News, a pundit for hire', *New Republic*, 26 January 2006.

14 'Experts with a price on their heads', *Guardian*, 7 May 1998.

15 George Monbiot, *Heat: how to stop the planet burning*, Allen Lane, Camberwell, 2006, p. 35.

16 'Unresolved problem: Cato fellow questions global warming', *The O'Reilly Factor*, television program, Fox News, New York, 7 February 2007.

17 'What's the reality of global warming?', *Hannity & Colmes*, television program, Fox News, New York, 7 February 2007.

18 For a wider study of this phenomenon, see Maxwell T. Boykoff and Jules M. Boykoff, 'Balance as bias: global warming and the US prestige press', *Global Environmental Change*, vol. 14, no. 2, 2004, pp. 125–36.

19 George Monbiot, *Heat*, p. 14.

20 'Unresolved problem: President Bush, global warming and pollution control', *The O'Reilly Factor*, television program, Fox News, New York, 4 April 2001; O'Reilly, unlike Hannity, agrees that the world is warming.

21 'Interview with Myron Ebell, Deb Callahan', *Hannity & Colmes*, television program, Fox News, New York, 25 May 2004.

22 'Interview with Fred Singer, Dennis Avery', *Hannity & Colmes*, television program, Fox News, New York, 30 January 2007.

23 Editorial, 'The gray lady's all wet', *New York Post*, 30 August 2000.

24 Editorial, *New York Post*, 7 April 2001, 20 January 2002, 20 January 2003.

25 Steve Dunleavy, 'Eurotrash starting to reek of spoiled whine', *New York Post*, 18 June 2001. Lindzen's activity is outlined in Ross Gelbspan, *Boiling Point*, Basic Books, New York, 2005.

26 Editorial, 'New York's greenhouse gasbags', *New York Post*, 2 August 2004.

27 Kyle Smith, 'Gore's hot air', *New York Post*, 24 May 2006; Editorial, 'Weather willies', *New York Post*, 8 July 2006; Editorial, 'Gore the guzzler', *New York Post*, 1 March 2007.

28 Editorial, 'Carr right to kick start a power debate', *Australian*, 4 June 2005.

29 Editorial, 'Climate change facts', *Australian*, 14 January 2006.

30 Alan Oxley, 'Change the climate on emissions', *Australian*, 5 April 2005.

31 Christopher Pearson, 'Hotheads warned, cool it', *Australian*, 18 November 2006.

32 Jeremy Clarkson, 'Tony's gas tax makes me fume', *Sun*, 25 February 2000.

33 Jeremy Clarkson, 'Big cat is ready to make a meal out of rover', *Sun*, 10 November 2000.

34 Richard Littlejohn, 'Why I hate *The Weakest Link*', *Sun*, 17 April 2001.

35 Editorial, *New York Post*, 31 January & 3 March 2009.

36 'Are obese people causing global warming?', *Hannity & Colmes*, television program, Fox News, New York, 26 May 2008.

37 'Overweight people destroying the earth', *The O'Reilly Factor*, television program, Fox News, New York, 22 April 2009.

38 Editorial, 'Economic suicide', *New York Post*, 4 December 2009.

39 Editorial, 'Obama's jobs cap', *New York Post*, 8 December 2009.

40 Charles Hurt, 'It's a hot plot', *New York Post*, 14 December 2009.

41 Guy Adams, 'Leaked memos cast doubt on Fox News claim of neutrality', *Sunday Tribune*, 19 December 2010; Ben Dimiero, 'Foxleaks: Fox boss ordered staff to cast doubt on climate science', Media Matters, Washington, DC, 15 December 2010, <http://mediamatters.org/blog/201012150004>.

42 'Presidents polls falling', *Hannity*, television program, Fox News, New York, 24 November 2009.

43 'East Coast hit by blizzard', *Hannity*, television program, Fox News, New York, 10 February 2010.

44 'Book dispels arguments for global warming', *Hannity*, television program, Fox News, New York, 22 April 2010.

45 Amanada Griscom Little, 'The greening of Fox', Salon.com, 17 May 2007, <www.salon.com/news/feature/2007/05/17/murdoch>.

46 'Who do you trust?', *Glenn Beck*, television program, Fox News, New York, 6 January 2011.

47 Editorial, 'More heat than light', *Australian*, 18 April 2009.

48 Robert Manne, 'Cheerleading for zealotry not in public interest', *Australian*, 25 April 2009.

49 Editorial, 'Too much hot air in climate change row', *Australian*, 28 April 2009.

50 'Editor of the Australian wins coveted award', press release, Australian Petroleum Production and Exploration Association Ltd, Canberra, 1 June 2009.

51 'At last some cool heads on global warming', *Australian*, 28 January 2010.

52 Graham Readfern, 'Why our leading climatologist won't talk to the Australian any more', The Green Blog, 6 January 2009, <http://blogs.news.com.au/couriermail/greenblog/index.php/couriermail/2009/01/P15>.

53 'How low can you go?', *Weekend Australian Magazine*, 19–20 December 2009.

54 Rupert Murdoch, 'A memo to employees of News Corporation from chairman and CEO Rupert Murdoch', Global Energy Initiative, News Corporation, New York, March 2011.

55 Editorial, 'The true climate threat', *New York Post*, 28 January 2011; Editorial, 'Climate refugees, not found', *Wall Street Journal*, 21 April 2011.

56 Kevin Knobloch, 'NewsCorp's environmental hypocrisy', Union of Concerned Scientists, Cambridge, MA, 8 March 2011, <www.ucsusa.org/news/commentary/newscorps-environmental-hypocrisy-0509.html>.

EPILOGUE

1 Interview with Rupert Murdoch in *Dynasties: The Murdochs*, on ABC TV (Australia) broadcast, July 2002.

2 Ibid.

3 This was later resolved so that Wendi Deng's children would receive equal dividends but would not ultimately be given equal votes in the family trust.

4 Jeremy W. Peters, 'In rift between Murdochs, heir becomes less apparent', *New York Times*, 19 October 2011.

5 Rupert Murdoch, in *Dynasties: The Murdochs*.

6 Michael Wolff, *The Man Who Owns the News: Inside the secret world of Rupert Murdoch*, Knopf (Random House), Sydney, 2008, p. 364.

7 Neil Chenoweth, *Virtual Murdoch: Reality wars on the Information Superhighway*, Vintage, London, 2002, p. xi.

8 Transcript of speech at the Andrew Olle Media Awards, Sydney, October 2002.

9 Richard Kelly Heft with Emiliya Mychasuk, 'Child's play', *Sydney Morning Herald*, 30 December 1995.

10 Jane Martinson, 'Gosh I'm going to be in trouble', *Guardian*, 22 March 2010.

11 James Murdoch, MacTaggart Lecture, Edinburgh International Television Festival, 28 August 2009.

12 James Murdoch, 'Your compass in a changing world', speech to the Marketing Society, 24 April 2008.

13 Alastair Campbell and Richard Stott (eds), *The Blair Years: Extracts from the Alastair Campbell diaries*, Hutchison, London, 2007, p. 603.

14 Lucy Siegle, 'This much I know: James Murdoch', *Observer*, 7 June 2009.

15 David Wilkerson, 'Cable networks flying high', *Dow Jones News Service*, 17 August 2010; Neil Shoebridge, 'Post-Avatar, the bet's on cable', *Australian Financial Review*, 6 August 2010.

INDEX

Compiled by Sue Carlton

20th Century Fox 17, 130, 209

ABC (Australian Broadcasting
  Corporation) 32, 189
Aboriginal Australians 45, 52–3
Abu Ghraib 189
Accuracy In Media 64, 71
Adams, Joey 65
adversarial journalism 31, 58–9
affirmative action 23, 133, 134–5, 140, 175
Agnew, Spiro 71
AIDS (Acquired Immune Deficiency
  Syndrome) 78–9, 134, 140
  scepticism/denialism 35, 107–10, 142
Ailes, Roger
  as Fox News chief 9, 14–15, 17, 138–9,
    142–4, 146, 147–8, 218–19
  as Republican political strategist 142–3
Akerman, Piers 196
Allan, Col 1, 182
Amanpour, Christine 28
American Enterprise Institute 92, 134,
  139, 142, 167, 177
American Petroleum Institute 198, 205
Armey, Dick 183
Ashmead-Bartlett, Ellis 42
Aspen conferences 24–5, 121, 127–8, 129,
  139
Auletta, Ken 1, 12, 25–6
Australia 38, 40, 53–4
  Gallipoli myth 41–2
  relations with US 57–8

Australian 18, 19
  on climate change issue 196, 201–2,
    206–7
  Deamer's sacking 53
  founding 46–7
  free market economics 31
  journalists' revolt 55–6
  liberal line in 1970s 52–3
  stockmen's strike 52–3
  support for Iraq war 186, 188
  support for McEwen 48–9
Australian Labor Party 24, 41–2, 46, 54
  see also Whitlam
Avatar 209
Aznar, José María 18

Baker, Gerard 22
balanced journalism 139, 141, 147, 184–6,
  208
  Fox News 8, 138, 144, 147, 184,
    199–200
Barnes, Fred 145, 173, 176, 177
Barnett, Steve 21
BBC (British Broadcasting Corporation)
  21, 32, 87, 90, 109, 218, 219
  market competition 124–5, 153
Beck, Glenn 16, 196, 206
Beecher, Eric 28
Bellow, Adam 22
Benjamin, Medea 185
Berkowitz, Herb 141

Bernstein, Carl 58
Blair, Tony
  attendance at News Corporation
    conferences 20, 25, 150, 158–60
  climate change issue 194
  cross-media ownership rules 5, 160
  giving evidence to Leveson Inquiry 5
  on Murdoch 34
  Prodi affair 163, 164
  relationship with Murdoch 5, 150–1,
    157–8, 162, 163–71
  support from *Sun* 5, 19, 158, 161–2
Blitzer, Wolf 13
Bolt, Andrew 195–6
Bolton, John 178
book-publishing 22
Boston Herald 65, 74, 75, 82
Bozell, Brent 137–8, 141, 187
Bradlee, Ben 32, 71, 72
Breindel, Eric 80, 81, 133, 135, 145, 197–8
British Briefing 100–3
British Labour Party 5, 20, 23, 24, 43, 158
  negative campaigns against 99, 152–4
  see also New Labour
Broadside Books 22
Brock, David 136
Brodsky, Adam 173
Brooks, Rebekah 6–7
Brown, Gordon 6, 25, 150–1, 171, 218
Brown, Tina 93
BSkyB 7, 18, 123, 158, 195, 212, 219
Buchanan, Patrick 74, 129–30, 136, 137
Buckley, William 136, 177
Burnett, David 140, 141
Bush, George H.W. 8, 83, 130, 138, 176
Bush, George W. 13, 190–1, 192
  influence of neo-conservatives 75
  rejection of Kyoto protocol 201, 203
  support from News Corporation 9, 138,
    170, 173, 186, 189–90
Bush, Jeb 179
Businessmen for a Change in
    Government 54

Calero, Adolfo 102
Calwell, Arthur 46
Cameron, David 5–7, 218
Campaign for Nuclear Disarmament
    (CND) 90, 103

Campbell, Alastair 149–50, 158–61,
    163–4, 167, 219
Carter, Jimmy 65–6
Castro, Fidel 46
Cato Institute 30, 197–8
Cavuto, Neil 16
Centre for Independent Studies 31
Chao, Steve 128, 129, 139
Charen, Mona 134
Cheney, Dick 25, 127, 179, 191, 192
Cheney, Lynne 25, 127
Chicago Sun-Times 74, 77
Chifley, Ben 43
China 21
Christie, Chris 10
Church, Charlotte 2
CIA 23, 76, 103, 104, 183, 193
Clarkson, Jeremy 196, 203
climate change 25, 194–211
  balanced journalism 147
  Pebble Beach conference 25, 194–5
  scepticism/denial 8, 30, 195–6,
    197–203, 204–7
Climategate 204, 208
Clinton, Bill 22, 23, 135, 138, 179, 219
  electoral success 129, 130, 152, 175
  health care plan 176
  sanctions against Iraq 178
Clinton Global Initiative 203
Clinton, Hillary 23
CNN (Cable News Network) 13, 127,
    139, 143–4, 146, 147, 184
Coalition for Peace through Security 103
Cohn, Roy 65
cold war 62, 93–4, 97–8, 129, 217
Collins (publisher) 79–80
Colmes, Alan 146
Committee for a Free Britain 99–100
companies, stability of leadership 212, 214
Copenhagen climate change conference
    205
Coughlan, Michael 207
Coulson, Andy 6
Crier, Catherine 145
cross-media ownership rules 123, 156,
    157, 158, 160, 164–5
  sale of *New York Post* 82
Crossman, Richard 44
Crozier, Brian 103–4

culture wars 129–38, 183
Cuomo, Mario 132
Cuozzo, Steve 73–4, 79, 81

Daily (iPad newspaper) 20
Daily Mirror (Sydney) 46, 54
Daily Telegraph (Sydney) 54, 55, 196
Davy, Richard 94, 98
Deamer, Adrian 48, 52–3
Deng, Wendi (Murdoch's third wife) 2, 214
Deng Xiaoping 21
détente 63, 72, 94, 96–7, 98, 103
Devine, Frank 196
Dickenson, Tim 9
Distillers Company 24
Dole, Robert 178
Douglas-Home, Charles 85, 94–5, 96, 98
Dover, Bruce 28
Duesberg, Peter 107, 108
Dunleavy, Steve 69, 79, 196, 201
Dunn, Anita 16
Dunn, Martin 28
Dunstan, Don 46

economic liberalism 113, 122
Economist 26–7
education, free market competition 36–7, 100, 118
El Salvador 67, 73
endangered species 142, 195
Eric Breindel Journalism Prize 81
The Establishment vs. The People (Viguerie) 125
European Economic Community (EEC) 114
Euroscepticism 166–7
Evans, Harry 89–90, 91–4, 96, 106
ExxonMobil 30, 197, 198

Fairfax Media 32
Falklands crisis 91, 125
Feith memo 191–3
Ferraro, Geraldine 8, 68–70
Fisher, Andrew 42
Foot, Michael 159
Forum World Features 103
Foster, Vince 135

Fox Broadcasting network 17, 128, 139, 141
Fox News 138–48
    climate change issue 8, 196, 198–200, 204, 205–6, 209
    creation 8, 131, 138–40
    designed to challenge liberal media 139–40
    as 'fair and balanced' 8, 138, 144, 147, 184, 199–200
    hostility to Obama 14, 15–17, 19, 26, 66, 138
    inter-media agenda-setting by 27–8, 70
    political influence of 9–10, 13–14
    politicisation of 141–2, 188–9
    support for invasion of Iraq 138, 172–3, 181, 184–6, 188–90, 192
    support for Tea Party 15–16
    viewers' false beliefs about Iraq 185–6
'Fox News effect' 28–9
Frank, Thomas 125
Fraser, Malcolm 56
free market economics 30, 36–7, 57–61, 72, 114
    market populism 113, 125–6
Freedom House 64
Freud, Matthew 16–17, 218
Friedman, Milton 72, 75, 92, 118
Frost, David 50
Frum, David 10, 174
Fumento, Michael 107

Gaber, Ivor 21
Gallipoli myth 41–2
gay rights 76, 77–8, 133, 134
Geelong Grammar 38, 43
Giles, Frank 29, 67, 89–91
Gingrich, Newt 10, 177, 195
Goldsmith, Sir James 63, 104
Gorbachev, Mikhail 79–81, 98–9, 101
Gore, Al 25, 194, 195, 196, 200, 201, 219, 220
Gorton, John 49
Gould, Bryan 100
Grant, Hugh 2
Green, David 122
Grenada invasion 67–8, 73, 95–6
Gulf War (1990–91) 130, 139
Gumbel, Bryant 142

Guthrie, Bruce 29

Hamill, Pete 132
Hamilton, Sir Ian 42
Hannity & Colmes 184–5, 200, 204
Hannity, Sean 14, 16, 146, 185, 187, 196, 199, 200, 205–6
HarperCollins 18, 21, 22, 81, 104, 105, 137, 192
Harris, Ralph (Lord Harris of High Cross) 30–1, 99, 123
Hart, David 99–103, 104
Hayek, Friedrich 122
Hayes, Stephen 191–2
health care reform 16, 23, 26, 176
Herald group (Australia) 39, 44
Herald Sun 18, 195
Heritage Foundation 15, 75, 103, 141
Heseltine, Michael 86, 105
Hinton, Les 140–1, 158, 165
Hirschfeld, Abe 131–2
HIV (human immunodeficiency virus) 35, 107–9
see also AIDS
Hodgkinson, Neville 109
Hollings, Ernest 82
Hollywood vs. America (Medved) 129, 136–7
Holt, Harold 48
Hoover Institution 30, 134
Howard government 201, 202
Howard, John 22, 173
Howard, Michael 25, 170
Howe, Sir Geoffrey 68, 77, 97–8
Huckabee, Mike 10
Hufschmid, Kathryn (James Murdoch's wife) 6, 220
Hughes, Billy 42
Hume, Brit 144–5, 146
Hussey, Marmaduke 87

An Inconvenient Truth (film-Al Gore) 25, 194, 201, 220
Institute of Economic Affairs (IEA) 30, 121–3
Institute of Public Affairs 30
intellectual elite 115–16, 120, 126
inter-media agenda-setting 27–8, 70

Intergovernmental Panel on Climate Change 200, 207
International Freedom Research Foundation 101
Iraq
  human rights record 181
  invasion of (2003) 9, 13, 32, 138, 169–70, 172–93, 210
  links with al-Qaeda 9, 180, 185, 186, 190–3, 210
  weapons of mass destruction 9, 181, 186, 190, 210
Irvine, Reed 141
Israel 76, 113, 182, 183, 219

Jay, Robert 5
Jowell, Tessa 165

Kalikow, Peter 131
Keating, Paul 5
Keeler, Christine 50
Kemp, Jack 62, 66
Kennedy, Ted 82, 140
Kent, Bruce 103
Kerry, John 13, 190
Keynes, John Maynard 30
Khalilzad, Zalmay 178
Kiernan, Thomas 58, 68
Kinnock, Neil 19, 100, 149–50, 152, 153, 154, 158
Kirkpatrick, Jeane 30, 76, 136
Kirtzman, Andrew 145
Klein, Joel 18, 36
Kluge, John 63
Knightley, Phillip 40–1
Knobloch, Kevin 209
Koch, Ed 66, 78
Kramer, Hilton 81, 137
Kristol, Bill 8, 15, 23, 175–7, 178–80, 185
Kristol, Irving 81, 119, 127, 129
Kyoto protocol 201, 202, 203

Lamb, Larry 60
Lever, Harold 93
Lever, Rod 47–8
Leveson Inquiry 1–2, 4–5, 7
  see also phone hacking scandal
Libby, 'Scooter' 179
liberal elites 33–6, 61, 71, 115–16, 208

Lindzen, Richard 196, 201, 203
Littlejohn, Richard 187, 196, 203
London Economic Summit (1984) 113
Long, Gerald 90
Losing Ground (Murray) 119
Lowry, Rich 204
Luce Award 15

McCain, John 9, 15, 195
McConnell, Scott 178, 180
McEwen, John ('Black Jack') 47, 48
MacKenzie, Kelvin 155
McMahon, William 48–9
Maitre, Joachim 63
Major, John 105, 112, 152, 155–7, 158
    giving evidence to Leveson Inquiry 4–5
    media policy 156, 157, 160, 164
Manhattan Institute 31, 134
Manne, Robert 206
Marcos, Ferdinand 77
Media Research Centre 71, 137
Mediaset television network 163
Medved, Michael 129, 134, 136–7
Menadue, John 38, 49, 56–7
Meyer, Christopher 174
Meyer, Cord 73
Meyer, Herbert 101
Michaels, Patrick 195–6, 198, 199, 203
Milloy, Steven 198–9
miners' strike (1972) 52
miners' strike (1984–85) 100, 112
Mitchell, Chris 207
monetarism 92–3
Monopolies and Mergers Commission
    85–6, 160
    see also cross-media ownership rules
Montgomery, David 2
Moody, John 144, 188–90
Moore, John 119
Murdoch, Anna (Murdoch's second wife)
    175, 214, 216
Murdoch, Elisabeth (Murdoch's daughter)
    4, 17, 214, 215, 218–19, 220
Murdoch, Elisabeth (Murdoch's
    mother-*née* Greene) 39, 213
Murdoch, James (Murdoch's son) 6–7, 17,
    214–15, 219
    climate change issue 23, 195, 207, 219–20
    phone hacking scandal 212, 219

Murdoch, Sir Keith (Murdoch's father)
    38, 39, 40–2, 44
Murdoch, Lachlan (Murdoch's son) 17,
    84, 132, 214–15, 216, 220
    as publisher of *New York Post* 181–4,
    217–18
    resignation 215, 219
Murdoch, Rupert
  attitudes and opinions
    anti-establishment views 34, 45, 72,
        111, 132, 208
    attitude to Soviet Union 79–80, 93–4
    attitude to trade unions 59–60, 86
    Australian nationalism 43, 53–4
    calls for privatised broadcasting 123–5
    climate change issue 194, 196–8,
        203–4, 207–11
    contempt for 'liberal media' 31–5,
        58–9, 70–7, 131, 142
    free market conservatism 57–61, 81
    hostility to Europe 117, 155, 166–9
    passion for political ideas 29–31, 48
    political beliefs/ideology 3–4, 18–23,
        29–30, 37, 43, 46, 47, 111
    promotion of neo-conservatism
        174–5, 176–7, 179–80
    pursuit of profits 18, 19–21, 30, 131,
        132
    support for Iraq campaign 9, 26, 37,
        169–70, 172, 173–4, 180, 181,
        190–1, 193, 210
    welfare state 106, 120–1
  as media owner
    backing winners 20, 151–2
    buying *Times* and *Sunday Times* 85
    editorial control 29, 67, 84, 89–94,
        105
    establishing hereditary dynasty 212,
        214–16
    expanding media assets in Australia
        46, 54
    giving evidence at Leveson Inquiry
        4–5, 7
    global expansion of media assets
        49–50
    inherits Adelaide *News* 44–5
    interviewed by Frost 50
    purchase of *New York Post* 65
    surviving hacking scandal 12, 212–13

personal life
education 43–4
family background 38–43
personality 47–8, 149
religion 41
views on retirement 216
as political insider and activist
funding right-wing groups 99–104
hostility to Major 155–7
influence on British foreign policy
165–70
opposition to Whitlam 55–7
political donations 23–4, 54, 63–4
political influence 4–12, 19, 21, 23,
25–9, 62, 70, 85, 104
relationship with Blair 20, 150–1,
157–70
relationship with Chinese leadership
21
relationship with Reagan 7–8, 62,
63–8, 71, 72, 82–3
relationship with Thatcher 60, 68,
85–9
support for Australian Labour Party
53–5
visit to Cuba 46
Murray, Charles 119–22

National Health Service (NHS) 100, 114,
115
Nature 109
Neil, Andrew
anti-establishment views 114, 115–17
at Fox News 141–2
attitude to Europe 117–18
critic of the 'intellectual elite' 115–16,
120, 126
critic of welfare state 119–21
as editor of *Sunday Times* 6, 105, 110–15
market populism 125–6
on media ownership laws 165
on Murdoch's control 29
neo-conservatives 8, 89, 125–6, 174–5, 179
attitude to Iraq war 180, 182–3, 186
fear of Soviet Union 79, 93–4, 98–9
views on welfare 119, 126
writers at *New York Post* 81, 82
see also Kristol, Irving; Podhoretz,
Norman; *Weekly Standard*

Netanyahu, Benjamin 183
New Atlantic Initiative 167
New Labour 117, 150, 160, 166, 168
New York magazine 10
New York Post 65–6, 72–8, 130–8
campaign against Ferraro 8, 69–70
climate change issue 200–1, 204–5, 209
health care reforms 16
on HIV/AIDS crisis 78–9
hostility to Clinton 135–6
Lachlan Murdoch as publisher 181–4,
217–18
Murdoch as 'editor-in-chief' 133, 181–2
neo-conservative columnists 81, 82
opinion pages 74, 133–4
opposition to Reagan/Gorbachev arms
talks 79–81
purchase (1976) 7–8, 19
sale and repurchase (1988 and 1993)
82, 130, 131–2
support for Bush 9
support for Grenada invasion 67
support for Iraq invasion 173, 181–4,
186, 217
support for Reagan 66, 68
targeting of liberal celebrities 74
'Times Watch' column 137
New York Times 32, 33, 62, 73, 119, 132–3,
137, 183, 193
Newman, Paul 73–4
News (Adelaide) 44
News Corporation 17–20
AIDS scepticism/denial 108, 110
carbon neutrality 195, 196, 203, 206,
208–9, 211, 220
climate change issue 196–7
climate change denial 197–203,
207–8, 211
corporate culture 2, 3–4, 215–16
editors' 'anticipatory compliance' 28–9,
84, 92
generational transition 212–20
global assets 17–18, 19–20
global support for invasion of Iraq 173,
181, 186–90
impact of phone hacking scandal 11,
212–13, 214–15
involvement with think tanks 30–2
on Iraq/al Qaeda link 180, 192

political nature of 24–5
profits from cable networks 220
subsidising loss-making newspapers 19, 27
News International
alliance with IEA 123
cross-media ownership rules 156, 157, 160, 164–5
funds Crozier's Sherwood Press 104
news media: agenda-setting role 27–8, 70, 147, 155
News of the World 2, 155–6, 161
closure 1, 7
Keeler's memoirs 50
Murdoch's purchase 49, 59
Newton, Maxwell 49, 74–5
Nicaraguan Contras 64, 76, 102
Nicholson, Joe 79
Nixon, Richard 24, 34, 57–9, 65, 71, 96
North, Oliver 184
nuclear weapons 62–3, 79, 80, 90, 94, 99, 113
see also Iraq, weapons of mass destruction

Obama, Barack 9, 14–17, 19, 66, 138, 204–5
false reports about 14
health care plans 26
meeting with Murdoch 14–15
support from Elizabeth Murdoch 218
Obama, Michelle 14
O'Donnell, Frank 140
Olin Foundation 64
O'Reilly, Bill 145, 185, 199, 200, 204
O'Reilly Factor 184, 185, 199
O'Sullivan, John 25, 75, 105, 129
Owen, David 25, 114
Oxford Labour Club 43
Oxley, Alan 202

Palin, Sarah 9, 10, 15, 22
Palme, Olaf 57
Patten, Chris 21
Pearson, Christopher 196, 202
Pebble Beach conference 25, 194–6
Perle, Richard 98, 174, 185
Perot, Ross 130
Perry, Rick 10

Peyronnin, Joe 144
Philippines 76–7, 183
phone hacking scandal 1–3, 7, 11, 12, 15, 212–13, 214
see also Leveson Inquiry
Pianim, Elkin 218
Playford, Sir Thomas 45
Plimer, Ian 206
Podhoretz, John 176–7
Podhoretz, Norman 24, 73, 75–7, 80, 81
political correctness 34–6, 61, 107, 132, 141–2, 201, 209–11
popular culture
sex and violence 128–9, 130, 136, 137
see also culture wars
populism 34, 40–1, 61, 74, 125, 132, 219
Powell, Colin 177
Press Complaints Commission 156
Price, Lance 5, 149, 151, 164
printing industry
technological revolution 59
see also Wapping printing works
Private Eye 50
Prodi, Romano 163
Profumo, John 50
'Project Democracy' 64
Project for a New American Century 179
Project for a Republican Future 23, 175, 176, 177
Puttnam, David 164–5

al Qaeda 9, 180, 185, 186, 190–3, 210
Quadrant 23
Quayle, Dan 23, 175–6

Rabinowitz, Dorothy 72–3, 74, 80
Rather, Dan 72
Ravitch, Diane 37
Rawkus Records 215, 219
Reagan, Nancy 10, 69
Reagan, Ronald
attitude to Soviet Union 62–3, 64, 67–8, 72, 79–80, 93–4
Grenada invasion 67–8, 95–6
New York Post's endorsement 66, 68
'Project Democracy' 64
rejection of détente 63, 72, 96–7, 103
relationship with Murdoch 7–8, 62, 63–8, 71, 72, 82–3

on role of media 72
talks with Gorbachev 80
Reagan administration
growing opposition to 62–3
rift with Thatcher government 68, 95
'Star Wars' initiative 63, 97
support for Nicaraguan Contras 64, 76
Reaganism 8, 30, 32, 60–1
confrontation with Soviet Union 93
family values 77
impact on Murdoch 66
supply-side economics 72, 74
Reid, John 171
Reina, Charles 189
Republican Governors Association 23
'Republican Revolution' 131, 134, 176
Rice, Condoleezza 25
Rivett, Rohan 44–6
Robertson, Pat 41, 83, 130
Robinowitz, Joe 140–1
Robinson, Peter 139
Rollins, Ed 69
Romney, Mitt 11
Ronald Reagan Presidential Foundation 8, 82
Rothwell, Anna 75
Rothwell, Bruce 75
Rumsfeld, Donald 30, 178, 181, 183

Saddam Hussein 8, 174, 178, 179, 180–2, 185, 186, 187, 190–1, 210
Santorum, Rick 10–11
satellite television 4, 123, 124–5, 156, 160
see also BSkyB
Scaife group 64
Scaife, Richard (Dick) 103, 104
Schwarzenegger, Arnold 25, 194
Searby, Richard 84
Shalala, Donna 121
Shawcross, William 18, 39
Sheridan, Greg 186
Sherwood Press 104
Shine 215
Shinker, William 22
Sikorski, Radek 167
Sikorsky 86
Snow, Tony 141
Sound and Fury (Michaels) 198
South Africa 51, 76–7

Soviet Union 62–3, 64, 67–8, 72, 79–80, 93–4
collapse of 117, 129
Sowell, Thomas 136
Star TV network 21, 219
'Star Wars' initiative 63, 97–8
Stelzer, Irwin C. 110, 112, 119, 123, 128, 136, 161, 168, 174, 176
Straw, Jack 152
'Stuart case' 45
Sullivan, Andrew 177
Sulzberger, Arthur 33
Sun
agenda-setting role 155
anti-establishment views 51
anti-Labour negative campaigning 99, 152–4
attacking Major government 155
climate change denial 196, 202–3
coverage of celebrities 2
hostility to Kinnock 19, 152–4
Murdoch's purchase 50–1, 59
political stance in 1970s 51–2, 60
role in Labour's 1992 defeat 152–5
role in Labour's 1997 win 5, 161–2
support for Cameron's Conservatives 6
support for invasion of Iraq 186–7
Sunday Telegraph (Australia) 54
Sunday Times
AIDS scepticism/denialism 35, 107–10
alliance with Institute of Economic Affairs (IEA) 121–2
attacking the 'establishment' 115–17
conflicts with Thatcher 112
Insight team 112–15
investigative journalism 106, 113
Murdoch's editorial interference 89–94, 105
populist challenge to the 'intellectual elites' 115–16
rejection of integration with Europe 117–18
serialises Hollywood vs. America 137
tax-cutting 116–17
under Neil's editorship 110–26
warns of emerging underclass 119–21

Tea Party 9, 15–16
Thatcher, Margaret

blocks Monopolies Commission
  inquiries 85–6
memoirs 105
Murdoch's attack on 68
resignation 105
rift with Reagan administration 68, 95
support from Murdoch 60, 85–9
support for new plant at Wapping 87
Wyatt as Murdoch's intermediary 4,
  84–8, 105
Thatcherism 30, 89, 100, 111, 112, 125
think tanks 15, 30–2, 92, 134
  see also American Enterprise Institute;
    Cato Institute; Heritage Foundation;
    Institute of Economic Affairs
Thomas, Clarence 140
Thompson, E.P. 90
Times
  annual losses 19
  Crozier as columnist 103
  distrust of Gorbachev 98–9
  Hart as columnist 99–103
  Monopolies Commission inquiry 85
  Murdoch's editorial interference 67
  neo-conservative influence 77, 89, 96,
    98–9
  pro-Americanism 86, 95–9
  strikes 59
tobacco industry 114, 198, 199–200
Tobin, James 93
Turner, Ted 127, 139, 144
Tutu, Archbishop Desmond 76–7
Twitter 10

underclass 119–21
US Chamber of Commerce 23

Van Susteren, Greta 16
Veljanovski, Dr Cento 123
Vietnam war 46, 51, 53, 57, 72, 73, 126
Viguerie, Richard 125

Wall Street Journal 11–12, 17, 22, 32–3, 36,
  98, 143, 154, 208–9
  health care reforms 16
Wapping printing works 86–7, 112
Ward, Russel 40
Washington Post 32, 58, 71, 119, 141, 143,
  179
Watergate scandal 31, 58, 71
Wattenberg, Ben 136
Wave Hill strike 52
Weekly Standard 130–1, 177–9
  as agenda setter within the Right 180
  creation 8, 130, 177
  on Iraq/al Qaeda link 191
  support for Iraq invasion 23, 178, 180,
    188
  support for Palin 15
Weitz, Katy 186–7
welfare state 30, 106, 119–21, 122
  welfare dependency 119
Westland helicopters 86
White Australia policy 46
Whitlam, Gough 49, 53–8
Wick, Charles 63–5
Wick, Mary Jane 65
Wilson, Charles 77, 102
Wilson, Harold 51–2
Winthrop, Diana 140
Wireless Generation 36–7
Wolff, Michael 15, 216
Wolfowitz, Paul 178, 179
Wood, Roger 70
Woodruff, Judy 13
Woodward, Bob 58
World Briefing 101
Worsthorne, Peregrine 111–12
WTTG 140–1
Wyatt, Woodrow 4, 84–8, 105, 150

Yelland, David 29, 84
Young, Hugo 67, 90, 116